# TENNYSON

## POET AND PROPHET

Swinburne: The Portrait of a Poet
William Morris: His Life, Work and Friends
Samuel Butler: The Incarnate Bachelor
The Life of Laurence Oliphant
Christopher Marlowe
Richard Coeur de Lion
The Letters of William Morris to His Family and Friends
The Complete Poems of John Skelton

Alfred Tennyson in 1869, photographed by Julia Margaret Cameron

PHILIP HENDERSON

# TENNYSON
# POET AND PROPHET

ROUTLEDGE & KEGAN PAUL
LONDON AND HENLEY

*First published in 1978
by Routledge & Kegan Paul Ltd
39 Store Street,
London WC1E 7DD and
Broadway House,
Newtown Road,
Henley-on-Thames,
Oxon RG9 1EN
Set in 11 on 12 pt Old Style
and printed in Great Britain by
Ebenezer Baylis and Son, Ltd
The Trinity Press, Worcester, and London*

*British Library Cataloguing in Publication Data*

*Henderson, Philip*

*Tennyson.*
1. *Tennyson, Alfred,* Baron Tennyson—*Biography*
2. *Poets, English—19th century—Biography*
    *821'8        PR5581*

*ISBN 0 7100 8776 4*

*To my wife*
*Belinda*
*with love*

# CONTENTS

# ILLUSTRATIONS

A*

# PREFACE AND ACKNOWLEDGMENTS

Anyone undertaking to write another life of Tennyson must be deeply indebted not only to that monument of piety, *Alfred Lord Tennyson: A Memoir,* compiled by his son, together with his privately printed *Materials for a Life of A. T.,* but also to Sir Charles Tennyson's definitive biography of 1949 (new edition 1968), which for the first time explored the family background of Tennyson's youth, dominated as it was by the tragic figure of his brilliant and unstable father. Since then, this already very full account has been expanded in *The Tennysons: Background to Genius* by Sir Charles Tennyson and Mrs Hope Dyson (1974), which traces the history of each member of that 'extraordinary brood' and deals in detail with the quarrels between the two branches of the family, the wealthy Tennysons of Bayons Manor, Tealby, and the 'deprived' Tennysons of Somersby Rectory. Equally illuminating is Professor Christopher Ricks's brilliant *Tennyson* of 1972 and his indispensable edition of the *Poems* (1969). Important studies have appeared in the USA, notably Jerome H. Buckley's *Tennyson: The Growth of a Poet* (1960) and especially R. W. Rader's *Tennyson's 'Maud': The Biographical Genesis* (1963), which broke new ground in tracing the biographical background of that poem and of several others, while Joanna Richardson in her *The Pre-Eminent Victorian* of 1962 collected within convenient compass material which built up a living portrait of the man as seen by his contemporaries. Harold Nicolson's delightful *Tennyson: Aspects of his Life, Character and Poetry* of 1923 was a crucial turning point in Tennyson studies at a time when the poet's reputation had reached its lowest ebb, and when the reaction against the Victorian age found expression in the witty writings of Lytton Strachey and in Osbert Sitwell's quip 'Lawn Tennyson'.

But we are now far enough removed from the Victorians to see their age as one of the greatest periods in English history and Tennyson, its greatest poet, as the victim of a time of change in many ways as radical as our own. The most sensitive of the Victorians, too, felt the ground slipping from under their feet, menaced by giant forces, destructive of religion and the social fabric. It is these destructive forces that can be felt behind *In Memoriam, Maud* and *Locksley Hall Sixty Years After*. 'You must not be surprised at anything that comes to pass in the next fifty years,' said Tennyson towards the end of his life. 'All ages are ages of transition, but this is an awful moment of transition.' It was not without reason that to his own age Tennyson appeared as prophet, seer and enchanter, a nineteenth-century Merlin. It is because he thought deeply and persistently about the problems posed by science and sought to reconcile science and religion, that he inspired a love and veneration such as has been accorded to perhaps no other English poet, except Shakespeare. At the same time, with the publication of each of his more important works, he had to face often surprisingly bitter criticism, and it was not until comparatively late in life that he established his ascendancy. Even then he was not altogether free from damaging attacks. The extraordinary originality and violence of such a work as *Maud* produced an equally violent reaction, while *In Memoriam*, with its extreme idealisation of his love for Arthur Hallam, laid him open to moral reproof. At last, however, his critics fell silent in face of his enormous popularity with the public. Tennyson is one of the very few English poets to have made a large income from poetry, alone rivalling Byron. And this again is to the credit of the Victorian public, who read and enjoyed long poems to a far greater extent than we do today, when of course, there is no work of comparable stature to enjoy.

The present book makes no other claim than to be a personal interpretation, the record of the rediscovery of a great poet whose work has once again taken its rightful and pre-eminent place in our literature. For such a book, the accumulated biographical material is almost too extensive. Others, Sir Charles Tennyson, Professor Christopher Ricks and, most recently, Professor C. Y. Lang and Dr E. R. Shannon, in their forthcoming edition of the Tennyson letters, have examined the multitudinous manuscripts, thick as autumn leaves in Vallombrosa, at the Tennyson Research Centre, Lincoln. There seemed to me no point in duplicating their labours. Nevertheless, I wish to thank both Sir Charles and Hallam Tennyson for their benevolent interest, as well as Mr Laurence Elvin, Librarian of the Tennyson Research Centre, for his help in selecting many of the illustrations and for supplying me with the family tree.

Among many people who have helped me in the research and writing of this book, I would particularly like to thank Sir Charles Tennyson, Mr Richard Ormond, Mr Timothy Klein, Mr Laurence Elvin, Librarian of Lincolnshire Local History and Tennyson Collections, Mrs George Yates of Aldworth House, and my typist

Mrs Joan Haybittle. I should like to thank Brian Southam for suggesting that I should write this book and for his help in obtaining for me an Arts Council grant. I also wish to thank my editor, Stephen Brook, for his unfailingly helpful comments and my son, John Henderson, who has been particularly kind in the final stages of this book.

Quotations from Tennyson's poems are taken from the principal earlier texts, collated with *The Poems of Tennyson* edited by Christopher Ricks, London, 1969.

Every effort has been made to communicate with all copyright holders. The author and the publishers are grateful for permission to quote from the following copyright material. Sir Charles Tennyson, *Alfred Tennyson* (2nd edition, 1968) and Christopher Ricks, *Tennyson* (1972), both published by Macmillan & Co.; Professors Herbert M. Schueller and Robert L. Peters, *The Letters of John Addington Symonds* (vol. 1, 1967); Rutgers University Library and *Victorian Studies* for Edmund Gosse's 'Candid Snapshots'; Joanna Richardson, *The Pre-Eminent Victorian* (Jonathan Cape, 1962); and the British Library Department of Manuscripts for Making available to me Edmund Gosse's account of his visit to Aldworth, MS. Ashley 4536, and his description of Tennyson's funeral in Westminster Abbey, MS. Ashley 4538. I am grateful to Vivian Noakes for permission to quote from *Edward Lear* (1968) and have also drawn on *Edward Lear* by Angus Davidson (1938).

Illustrations from the Tennyson Research Centre, Lincoln, are published by permission of Lord Tennyson and the Lincolnshire Library Service. Other illustrations are reproduced by permission of the National Portrait Gallery, London; the National Monuments Record, London; and the British Library, London.

# CHRONOLOGY

1809    Born at Somersby (6 August), fourth son of the Rev. George Clayton Tennyson and of Elizabeth Tennyson (née Fytche).

1815    At Louth Grammar School, with his elder brothers Frederick (b. 1807) and Charles (b. 1808).

1820    Leaves Louth to be educated privately by his father.

1824    Breakdown of his father's health.

1827    (November) Enters Trinity College, Cambridge.

1828    Arthur Hallam (b. 1811) enters Trinity.

1829    Elected a member of the 'Apostles' (May); wins Chancellor's Gold Medal with his poem *Timbuctoo* (June); Hallam meets Tennyson's sister Emily at Somersby.

1830    (June) *Poems, Chiefly Lyrical*; visits Pyrenees with Hallam (July-September).

1831    (March) Death of the Rev. George Tennyson. Leaves Cambridge without taking a degree.

1832    Review of *Poems, Chiefly Lyrical* by 'Christopher North' (John Wilson) in *Blackwood's Magazine* (May); visits the Rhine country with Hallam (July); *Poems*, 1833 (December).

1833    Hallam engaged to Emily Tennyson; J. W. Croker attacks *Poems*, 1833, in *Quarterly Review* (April); death of Arthur Hallam in Vienna (September).

1834    Falls in love with Rosa Baring, but is disillusioned in her by 1835-6.

1836    Falls in love with Emily Sellwood at the marriage of his brother Charles to Emily's sister Louisa (May).

1837    Tennysons move from Somersby to High Beech, Epping (May).

1838    Engagement to Emily Sellwood.

1840    Engagement broken off; Tennysons move to Tunbridge Wells; ill-health sets in; invests his money in Dr Allen's wood-carving scheme, Pyroglyphs.

1842    *Poems* in 2 volumes (May).

1843 Dr Allen's Pyroglyphs collapses; Tennyson at a hydropathic hospital near Cheltenham.

1845 Accepts Civil List Pension of £200 a year.

1846 Visits Switzerland with Moxon, his publisher.

1847 *The Princess* (December).

1848 Visits Ireland and Cornwall, with a view to composing an Arthurian epic.

1850 *In Memoriam* published anonymously (May); marries Emily Sellwood (June); appointed Poet Laureate (November).

1851 Visits Italy with Emily (July to October).

1852 Birth of Hallam Tennyson (August); 'Ode on the Death of the Duke of Wellington' (November).

1853 Moves to Farringford, Isle of Wight (November), which he buys in 1856.

1854 Birth of Lionel (March).

1855 Hon. D.C.L. at Oxford (June); *Maud* (July).

1859 *Idylls of the King*: 'Enid', 'Vivien', 'Elaine' and 'Guinevere' (July).

1861 Visits Pyrenees with his family (June); death of Albert, the Prince Consort (December).

1862 Dedication of *Idylls of the King* to Prince Albert; first audience with the Queen at Osborne (April).

1864 *Enoch Arden* (August).

1865 Refuses a baronetcy; death of his mother (February).

1868 Foundation stone of Aldworth laid.

1869 Joins Metaphysical Society; *Holy Grail and Other Poems* (dated 1870).

1872 'Gareth and Lynette' (October); Imperial Library edition of the *Works* (1872–3) with Epilogue 'To the Queen', which completes *Idylls of the King*, except for 'Balin and Balan' (written 1874).

1873 Once more refuses offer of baronetcy.

1875 *Queen Mary*.

1876 *Harold*; *Queen Mary* produced by Irving.

1879 Death of his brother Charles Tennyson Turner (April).

1880 *Ballads and Other Poems*.

1881 *The Cup* produced by Irving with Ellen Terry (July).

1883 Visits Denmark with Gladstone (September).

1884 Hallam marries Audrey Boyle (June); *Becket* published (December).

1885 *Tiresias and Other Poems*.

1886 Death of Lionel on voyage home from India (April); *Locksley Hall Sixty Years After* (December).

1888 Severe rheumatic illness.

1889   *Demeter and Other Poems* (December).
1892   *The Foresters* produced in New York by Mary Anderson (March), after its refusal by Irving, who agrees to produce *Becket*.
Last illness and death at Aldworth (6 October).
Publication of *The Death of Œnone, Akbar's Dream and Other Poems*.

# FAMILY

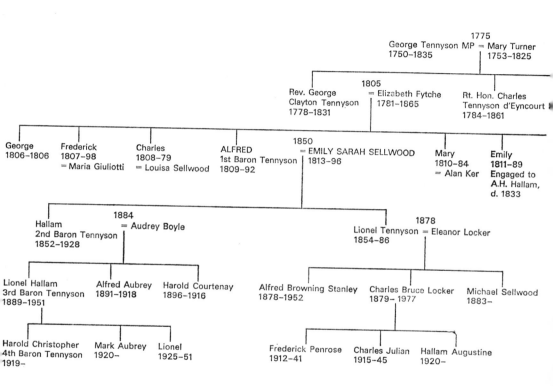

1775
George Tennyson MP = Mary Turner
1750–1835 | 1753–1825

1805
Rev. George = Elizabeth Fytche       Rt. Hon. Charles
Clayton Tennyson | 1781–1865          Tennyson d'Eyncourt
1778–1831                              1784–1861

George          Frederick        Charles          ALFRED                    1850                        Mary          Emily
1806–1806       1807–98          1808–79          1st Baron Tennyson    = EMILY SARAH SELLWOOD        1810–84       1811–89
                = Maria Giuliotti = Louisa Sellwood 1809–92                 1813–96                   = Alan Ker    Engaged to
                                                                                                                   A.H. Hallam,
                                                                                                                   d. 1833

Hallam                1884                                                1878
2nd Baron Tennyson    = Audrey Boyle                    Lionel Tennyson = Eleanor Locker
1852–1928                                               1854–86

Lionel Hallam        Alfred Aubrey    Harold Courtenay      Alfred Browning Stanley    Charles Bruce Locker    Michael Sellwood
3rd Baron Tennyson   1891–1918        1896–1916             1878–1952                  1879– 1977              1883–
1889–1951

Harold Christopher   Mark Aubrey   Lionel              Frederick Penrose   Charles Julian   Hallam Augustine
4th Baron Tennyson   1920–         1925–51             1912–41             1915–45          1920–
1919–

# TREE

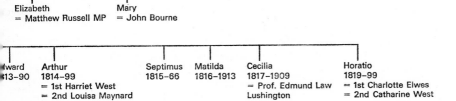

Elizabeth
= Matthew Russell MP

Mary
= John Bourne

|ward
13–90

Arthur
1814–99
= 1st Harriet West
= 2nd Louisa Maynard

Septimus
1815–66

Matilda
1816–1913

Cecilia
1817–1909
= Prof. Edmund Law
Lushington

Horatio
1819–99
= 1st Charlotte Elwes
= 2nd Catharine West

# I

Somersby lies in a remote wooded valley of the Lincolnshire wolds, some twenty-three miles from Lincoln. It is approached by the same steep winding lanes as in Tennyson's time. A weather-worn notice-board outside the small white house informs us that this is Tennyson's birth-place and that it is strictly private.

One's first thought is that it is a ridiculously small house for so large a family, at one time numbering, with servants, twenty-three. Opposite, on the other side of the road, stands the gloomy little church on its knoll, among tall elms and dark yews.

Here Alfred Tennyson would come as a boy to fling himself down among the graves to weep. At such times, he tells us, he longed to die. And yet he loved the place, as he loved his brilliant, frustrated father, who suffered all his life from having been passed over by his own father as the rightful head of the family in favour of his younger brother Charles and compelled to take Orders, for which he felt no vocation. It was Charles who inherited the bulk of his father's estate, became a Member of Parliament, and, claiming Norman blood, changed his name to Tennyson d'Eyncourt and built the great castellated manor of Bayons at Tealby. But Bayons, with its towers, its long curtain wall, its moat and portcullis and its acres of parkland, had long stood in ruin before it was demolished in the 1950s and its stone sold for building.

The Tennyson d'Eyncourt memorials may still be seen in Tealby church, with their little crowned lions supporting little emblazoned shields. Nevertheless, it is Alfred, the nephew whom Charles called a 'hobbledehoy', whose statue by G. F. Watts now stands in the precincts of Lincoln Cathedral, a great rugged cloaked figure, accompanied by his wolf-hound, looking down at the flower in his hand. It is he who became Lord Tennyson and Poet Laureate and the chief spokesman of his age. But it was Dr Tennyson, the poet's father, who recognised in his son, even when a boy, the future great poet, and it was to his father's library and his father's tuition in the classics that Alfred was indebted for the most valuable part of his education.

So that while Dr Tennyson could find no other outlet for his scholarship, apart from the obligatory sermons delivered for the most part to small congregations of illiterate farm labourers, it nevertheless found its justification in moulding the minds of his precocious and talented sons.

Sir Charles Tennyson, in his life of his grandfather, tells us that there seems to be 'little justification in fact' for Charles's pride in the d'Eyncourt ancestry. On the contrary, the Tennysons 'seem to have been a race of small yeomen, which can be traced from the fourteenth century onward in the narrow strip of country just north of the Humber, between Hull to the west and Partington to the east.'[1] Late in the eighteenth century, George Tennyson, Alfred's grandfather, acquired property near Market Rasen in Lincolnshire, where his father, Michael, practised as a surgeon, and had the good fortune to marry the Clayton heiress. George became a lawyer of considerable ability and managed to acquire a good deal of property one way and another. He made it his lifelong aim to ensure that the name of Tennyson should be worthily upheld. Quite early in the life of his eldest son, he decided that he was not fitted by temperament for this role, evidently finding him, with his 'excessive sensibility and intolerance of discipline', difficult to deal with. Thus we learn that at St John's College, Cambridge, George was frequently in trouble for idleness and insubordination. On one occasion he fired a pistol through the windows of Trinity, but fortunately escaped detection. He took a very good place in the College examinations and might have done as well in the tripos had he been willing to apply himself to mathematics, 'to excel in which', he wrote to his father, 'would require such continual application and exertion as would neither suit my health, time, nor inclination.'[2] The result was that he only took a pass degree in the spring of 1801. In the same year he was ordained deacon. By the autumn he was travelling in Russia, where the Emperor Paul had lately been assassinated. The ostensible motive of this visit was the coronation of Czar Alexander in Moscow, where Lord St Helens, an old St John's man, was representing England. But the date of the coronation was unexpectedly advanced and so George missed it, and nothing further was heard of him for three months. When he did return the story he had to tell was so wild as to suggest that his father's suspicions of his mental stability were only too well-founded. As later related by Alfred, it seems that soon after his arrival in Moscow, at a dinner party given by Lord St Helens, he leant across the Russian sitting next to him and said to his host: 'It is perfectly well known in England who murdered the Emperor Paul – it was Count So-and-So', a remark which produced a dead silence at the dinner table. After dinner St Helens, according to George, called him aside and said: 'Ride for your life from this city: the man across whom you were speaking to me was the Count So-and-So whom you accused of murdering the Emperor Paul.' Whereupon George took horse and rode through Russia till he came to the Crimea, where he fell ill and lay for a long time delirious, with no other attendance than that of the wild country people, who would dance round his bed with magical incantations. Once in every three months on English courier passed through the village where he lay, and as he passed blew a horn. It all depended on George's hearing this horn whether he could escape from Russia, for he had no money. In his delirium he would perpetually start up, thinking he had heard the horn. At last the courier came, the horn was blown, George heard it and arranged with the man to take him; and after many adventures he managed to reach England.[3]

George returned to England early in February 1802, but there is no independent witness to the truth of his story, which may have been invented either to account for his long absence or to create a romantic legend for his children. And this interpretation is suggested by other equally wild accounts of his travels on the Continent later in life, when his mental instability was still further advanced. At any rate, there being nothing else for it, he was duly ordained priest on 19 December and two days later inducted Rector of Benniworth. He seems to have settled in Louth, however, where he became engaged to Elizabeth Fytche, daughter of the rector of that parish and niece of a Bishop of Lincoln. At the same time his friend Mr Burton of Lincoln managed to secure for him the livings of Somersby and Bag Enderby, and on the strength of this he married Elizabeth in August 1805. They did not move to Somersby until 1808, for considerable repairs needed to be carried out at the rectory, where nurseries, bedrooms and outside offices had to be added.

By 1808 all was finished and George settled down 'reluctantly and rather defiantly' as Rector of Somersby and Bag Enderby, 'not a very exhilarating prospect for a young man of imagination with rather more than the average young man's desire for enjoyment.' The combined population of both parishes was under a hundred; there were no shops nearer than Spilsby, seven miles to the south-east; and the people of the surrounding wold and marsh were 'rough to the point of barbarism'. Their independent spirit is typified by the Rector's coachman, who, when reprimanded for not cleaning the harness, carried it into the drawing-room, flung it to the ground and shouted to the master: 'Clean it thyself, then!' And the cook was heard to exclaim of her master and mistress: 'If you raaked out Hell with a smaall tooth-coamb you wean't find their likes!'[4] Neither of these could be called Wordsworthian rustics, ennobled by living in

[3]

close proximity to Nature, though their language was certainly 'plain and emphatic' enough. Alfred remembered the coachman as half-mad and usually drunk.

Both Dr Tennyson and his bride were strikingly handsome. Elizabeth Fytche was one of the acknowledged beauties of the county; her husband, with his dark, Byronic good looks, six foot two in height, was always welcome at the Spilsby Sessions (in 1813 he took the degree of Doctor of Civil Law at Cambridge) for his wit and the brilliance of his conversation. His poetry was Byronic, too, and not at all the sort of thing one would expect from a country clergyman. At Somersby, during the early years of his married life, Dr Tennyson continued to build up a fine library, collecting sixteenth- and seventeenth-century folio editions of the classics, many of which he had obtained at the sale in 1806 of the library of Bennet Langton of Langton Hall, the friend of Dr Johnson. It is characteristic of him that when Alfred went back to school at Louth at the age of eight, he gave him a second edition of *Paradise Lost*. Dr Tennyson was also an accomplished player on the harp, and deeply interested in architecture and painting. Small wonder if such a man felt his talents wasted in an obscure Lincolnshire parish, even though some of the best minor Victorian poetry emerged from country vicarages.

At first the doctor's stipend from his various livings amounted to about £700 a year, plus an allowance from his father of £140 a year. His Benniworth flock, which alone brought him £500 a year, was too far away for him to carry out his pastoral duties on his own and he employed a curate at £35 a year, though the Somersby and Bag Enderby livings were only worth about £180 together. In 1815 his father secured him the vicarage of St Mary and St James at Grimsby. Even though he had to pay a curate £120 a year, this meant that his income rose to about £1,000 a year, adequate, one would have thought, for the needs of a country clergyman in those days. At any rate, it enabled the doctor to keep a carriage and pair, a groom and a valet.

Elizabeth Tennyson, however, bore twelve children in the first fourteen years of their marriage: George, who died in infancy in 1806; Frederick born in 1807; Charles in 1808; Alfred on 6 August 1809; Mary in 1810; Emily in 1811; Edward in 1813; Arthur in 1814; Septimus in 1815; Matilda in 1816; Cecilia in 1817; Horatio in 1819. The small rectory soon became rather crowded, and Alfred remembers sleeping seven to a room. Several domestics had also to be accommodated. Alfred, who did not marry until he was forty, was by no means so philoprogenitive. Possibly the example of his father, as well as the delicate, valetudinarian condition of his already middle-aged wife, acted as a deterrent. But it is not surprising that Elizabeth Tennyson should have declined into an invalid condition, latterly

[4]

spending much of her time lying on the drawing-room sofa, like many another Victorian lady. 'One of the most innocent and tender-hearted ladies I ever saw,' Edward FitzGerald wrote of her. The country boys, it is said, used to beat their dogs beneath her window, knowing that she would give them money to desist. To Alfred she was 'one of the most angelick natures on God's earth, always doing good by a sort of intuition'. When he married, his wife Emily was equally angelic, a replica, almost, of his mother. He worshipped both of them.

But as time went on, the doctor became increasingly gloomy. Doubtless the size of his family and the decline in his wife's health had something to do with it, for there could not have been very much peace in the little rectory for a man of his studious habits. At any rate, he had the reputation in the village of being 'amazing sharp' with his children. In a letter of 1819 he writes that he has eight children down simultaneously with measles, one desperately ill, 'and the worst of all is that Elizabeth has exerted herself so much in going up and down our abominable steep staircase in attending upon them, that I fear she is confined to the sofa and I much fear a miscarriage.'

Meanwhile Dr Tennyson could only contrast his own lot with that of his younger brother Charles, his father's favourite, with his rich wife, a house in Park Street, Westminster, and an affectionate welcome whenever he chose to visit Bayons Manor. Indeed the glaring discrepancy between his father's treatment of Charles and himself, when, after all, he was the rightful heir and should have had first consideration, but had only unkindness and brutal rebuffs, weighed increasingly on the doctor's mind as his health declined.

From the age of seven Alfred attended the Grammar School at Louth, presided over by a sadistic clergyman, the Rev. Dr Waite. In later life he recalled that he 'often could not hold his knife and fork for days after one of the headmaster's canings'. One poor boy was so brutally beaten by this reverend gentleman that he had to stay in bed for six weeks. Even during class Dr Waite could not resist 'touching up' the boys with his stick, as he patrolled the room, while the luckless boy who was 'construing' was exposed to his blows for every mistake. But in those days this kind of treatment was either taken for granted or treated as a joke. Alfred 'remembered to his dying day sitting on the stone steps on a cold winter's morning and crying bitterly after a big lad had brutally cuffed him on the head because he was a new boy'. He was bitterly homesick and would stand crying in a corner of the playing field, until one day another lout punched him in the stomach, saying that that would give him something to cry for. With the example of the headmaster, it is hardly surprising if the boys followed suit. Even in later life, when visiting Louth, Alfred would never go down the street where his old school stood. It was an immense relief when he was taken away to be coached by his father.

But by 1820 Dr Tennyson was at breaking point. 'With the sentiments you yet entertain and have entertained for more than twenty years, I cannot wonder you told Mr. Bourne you had not a spark of affection for me,' he wrote to his father on 14 August:[5]

> The rude and unprecedented manner in which you first addressed me at Hainton, after a long absence, on your return from York (I quote your own words, *'Now, you great awkward booby, are you here'*) holding me up to utter derision before Mr. Heneage, his sons and Sir Robert Ainslie, and your language and conduct in innumerable other instances, many of which have made a deep impression on my mind, sufficiently prove the truth of your own assertion. You have long injured me by your suspicions. I cannot avoid them for the fault is not mine. God judge between you and me. You make and have always made a false estimate of me in every respect. You look and have always looked upon me with a jaundiced eye, and *deeply and experimentally* feeling this, I am sure that my visiting you would not contribute to your satisfaction and at the same time would materially injure my own health and comfort. Conscious also that I am thrown into a situation unworthy of my abilities and unbecoming either your fortune or my just pretensions, and resisted in every wish to promote my own interests or that of my family by removing to a more eligible situation, unaccountably kept in the dark with respect to their future prospects, with broken health and spirits, I find myself little disposed to encounter those unprovoked and sarcastic remarks, which though they may be outwardly borne, are inwardly resented, and prey upon the mind – the injustice, the inhumanity and the impropriety of which everyone can see but yourself, and which in your last visit were levelled against the father of a large family in the very presence of his children, and that father between forty and fifty years of age. I should not have proceeded thus far had you not by your unjust aspersions set fire to the mass which was already disposed to ignite. You may forget or pass off as a jest what penetrates and rankles in my heart; you may break what is already bent, but there is a tribunal before which you and I may speedily appear, more speedily perhaps than either of us desire or expect – there it will be seen whether you through life have treated me with that consideration and kindness which a son has a right to expect from a father, and

[6]

whether (as you have been accustomed to represent me to myself and others) I have been deficient in filial affection and obedience.

To this letter, which would have moved any normal father, Old George replied in October that it was 'unkind and unjustifiable. I have ever been your affectionate father.' He added that he was making a will under which the doctor's younger children would receive between them £20,000. But it was too late; the damage already done was irreparable and Old George had, as his son expressed it so graphically, 'set fire to the mass which was already disposed to ignite' and 'broken what was already bent'. Dr Tennyson succumbed to drink and outbursts of fury and violence. Somersby became a hell.

It was precisely at this moment that Alfred and his brother Charles left school, aged eleven and twelve respectively, to be tutored by their father until they were ready for Cambridge in 1827. By 1822, however, the state of the doctor's health had become so alarming that he went to Cheltenham for a cure with his wife, on whom the strain of life at Somersby was beginning to tell no less alarmingly. As he wrote to his brother Charles in January 1824: 'We are three and twenty in family and sleep five or six in a room.'

Next month he wrote: 'You speak of going to Paris. How happy I should be to accompany you there. I am so netted in by the instruction of my family that I cannot. I think it would give me something like health of which I cannot boast at present. . . . But I feel my powers of mind sensibly declining, and the attacks to which I am subject must necessarily injure the intellect. I have had two in the last five days.'[6] Nevertheless, he adds that he has 'known some satisfaction in thinking that my boys will turn out to be clever men. Phoenix-like, I trust (though I don't think myself a Phoenix), they will spring from my ashes, in consequence of the exertions I have bestowed upon them.'[7] Dr Tennyson was particularly proud of Alfred and bound with his own hands the books into which he copied out his son's verses. There exists a quarto notebook belonging to this early period containing:

Vol. I 1820 The Poetry of Tennyson
Vol. II The Lyrical Poetry of Tennyson
Vol. III The Prose Writings of Tennyson

The book is in Latin, with Greek and English headings to poems in various metres: elegiacs, Sapphics and Alcaics. Alfred also composed an epic in six thousand lines in the style of Scott's *Marmion*. A few years later came the remarkable 'Armageddon' in the Miltonic manner and about the same time at least two blank verse plays, of which only *The Devil and the Lady*, in the manner of Ben Jonson, survives. A phoenix indeed!

In August 1825, at the age of sixteen, Alfred wrote to his uncle Charles: 'It is with great sorrow that I inform you that my poor father is not any better than before. He had another violent attack of the same nature yesterday. Indeed no one but those who are continually with him can conceive what he suffers, as he is never entirely free from this alarming illness. He is reduced to such a degree of weakness from these repeated attacks, that the slightest shock is sufficient to bring them on again. Perhaps if he could summon resolution enough to get out more, he would be relieved, but the lassitude which the fits leave incapacitates him from undergoing any exertion. He has already had two of these since my grandfather was here which is not much more than a week ago and sometimes previous to that had three each night successively.'[8]

It seems that the fits were epileptic and were followed by increasing eccentricity and absent-mindedness. At times the doctor even forgot his own name. By 1827 he was worse than ever and Alfred, finding the situation quite unbearable, went to stay with his grandfather at Bayons. Elizabeth Tennyson, writing to her father-in-law to thank him for having Alfred, says that they are unable to visit him because 'George will not allow any of the children to come with me, nor will he allow me to have the carriage unless I promise to remain from home for half a year, a condition which, of course, I cannot comply with as I dare not leave the children with him. . . . I cannot leave home for any length of time on account of poor George's violence which I fear increases. We had a terrible evening on Sunday.'[9]

Alfred and Charles now left for Cambridge and were admitted to Trinity in October, their Aunt Russell offering to contribute towards the expense. Frederick had gone up to Cambridge the year before; Septimus and Horatio were sent to school at Louth, and Edward was set to copy legal documents at Bayons, to prepare himself as a solicitor's clerk. Arthur was to be sent to sea, if possible. Meanwhile it was decided that their father should go to Paris with his brother Charles in the hope that a change of scene would prove restorative. His father's state of mind weighed heavily upon Alfred and reinforced the family tendency to melancholia, the 'black bloodedness of the Tennysons', which emerges in such early poems as 'Mariana', 'The Two Voices' and 'A spirit haunts the year's last hours', in which his verse has already achieved perfection:

The air is damp, and hushed, and close,
As a sick man's room when he taketh repose
    An hour before death;

[8]

My very heart faints and my whole soul grieves
At the moist rich smell of the rotting leaves,
    And the breath
    Of the fading edges of box beneath,
And the year's last rose.
  Heavily hangs the broad sunflower
    Over its grave i'the earth so chilly;
  Heavily hangs the hollyhock,
    Heavily hangs the tiger-lily.

But when Alfred, with Frederick and Charles, published their anonymous collection, *Poems by Two Brothers* in 1827, with Jackson of Louth, Alfred only contributed his most uninteresting and conventional work, pastiches of Gray, Byron, Moore and Scott, though rather more than half the book was by him. As Sir Charles Tennyson remarks: 'One can trace the subjects and the methods of almost all [the poems] to the Somersby library and very little to Alfred's experience.' He deliberately omitted his more original poems as being 'too much out of the common for the public taste'. Most of the pieces had been written between his fifteenth and seventeenth years.

When Dr Tennyson returned to Somersby after his holiday in France, it soon became clear that the improvement in his health was to be short-lived. The spasms in his chest recurred with renewed violence. 'Last night he suffered very much from the same cause,' Charles wrote to his grandfather. 'My father is lying for ease on the floor and it is now midnight.' As if this was not enough, the cook set fire to her dress and died from burns, though the doctor had tried to extinguish the flames with his bare hands. Charles wrote to Bayons: 'I write for my Father whose hand can scarcely pen a line at present it was burnt so terribly. He desires me to say that he cannot accept your kind invitation as the cook is in a dying state and he is obliged to superintend.' This tragedy did not improve the doctor's nervous condition especially as a malicious story was current in the village that he had given orders for a water-butt to be kept by the kitchen door so that the next cook who caught fire could jump into it without troubling the master.

And now the old resentment against his father and brother Charles, who was going from strength to strength in his political career and hobnobbing with the aristocracy, flared up again, and the unhappy man began writing angry letters once more to Bayons. He also feared that his sons were not making the best use of their time at Cambridge, which unfortunately appeared to be the case when Frederick was rusticated for three terms from Trinity for disobedience and impertinence. Evidently Frederick was no more respectful to his father than to the college authorities.

When Charles and Alfred also returned from Cambridge, they were sent to Bayons to be lectured by their grandfather, who afterwards wrote to his son Charles on 26 January 1829: 'Charles and Alfred left me on Friday. They did not act disrespectfully to me, but they are so untoward and disorderly and so unlike other people, I don't know what will become of them, or what can be done with, or about them. I tried to impress them with the feeling that they and Frederick were spending or wasting half their father's income and he had only half to maintain himself and his wife, and to educate 4 other boys and 4 girls and that unless the money expended for their education was to fit them for professions to get their livings, so that they might be out of the way for an expenditure on the education of their brothers and sisters and for putting their brothers in a way of getting their livings they, Frederick, Charles and Alfred, would be the ruin of them and act most unkindly and dishonourably. The three boys so far from having improved in manner or manners are worse since they went to Cambridge.'[10]

Charles and Alfred returned to the University at the end of the month. Dr Tennyson was left alone at Somersby with his wife, Frederick, and those children who were not at school, and he relapsed once more into his old drinking habits. A bitter antagonism towards Frederick was the result, and distressing scenes of violence ensued. On one occasion the doctor called in the constable to turn his son out of doors, threatening to kill him. In February, Elizabeth Tennyson wrote to Bayons that she could no longer live with her husband, with whom, she said, she had lived a miserable life for twenty years, and that her husband insulted her and the children with 'such degrading epithets . . . as a husband and a Father and above all a person of his sacred profession ought particularly to avoid. A short time since he had a large knife and a loaded gun in his room. The latter he took into the kitchen to try before he went to bed and was going to fire it off through the kitchen windows but was dissuaded. With the knife he said he would kill Frederick by stabbing him in the jugular vein and in the heart. . . . I shall take lodgings in Louth as soon as possible.'[11]

Today the doctor's condition would probably be diagnosed as acute manic depression, and sedatives, rest and other drugs would be prescribed and his condition brought under control. But that, even if it had been possible at that date, would not have solved his basic problems, ingrown through half a lifetime. Then all that could be prescribed was a change of scene, with the risk of the same pattern repeating itself on his return. And this, of course, is what occurred.

[10]

So, with the help of his father, his brother and Dr Rawnsley, leave of absence was obtained from the bishop and arrangements made for the service of the livings. But not surprisingly, the doctor could not make up his mind to any course of action. He went first to his father at Bayons then to his brother in London, where he could not face the necessary task of obtaining a passport and licence to travel. Eventually, however, in May he set off for Paris to stay with the Marthions, old friends of the family.

After a month the Marthions began to find the doctor's presence rather trying, so he set off on a tour of Switzerland. 'I have endeavoured to dissipate all mental feeling by violent exertion and the inspection of foreign manners and scenery,' he wrote to his father on 31 July. 'It will not do. I feel here as an isolated being, an outcast from England and my family. I am very uncertain of my movements and a mind ill at ease is generally so.

'P.S. I keep a journal and some of my observations on the manners and costume of the people where I have occasionally sojourned may perhaps amuse you on my return. I am very desirous of doing so but it will be of no avail as Mr. Fytche and Mary Ann Fytche have encouraged my family to act in open rebellion against me. Mr. Fytche may perhaps have some time or other rebellious children himself and he will then be able justly to appreciate his own infamous conduct toward me.'[12]

From this it would appear that the doctor had now transferred his resentment against his father and his brother to his wife's family, which he held responsible for the alienation of his own. He did not, of course, blame himself. From Switzerland he crossed into Italy. 'What business have you here without a passport?' demanded the Austrian official at the frontier. 'What business have you here at all?' replied the doctor magnificently, and he was allowed to pass.

Before he returned to England Dr Tennyson was to have several thrilling adventures, which have the hallucinatory quality of dreams. He related that at Rome during the carnival a man was actually stabbed in his arms. He was suspected of the crime, he said; the crowd turned on him and he only saved himself by protesting that he was an Englishman. Again, while crossing the Alps, he was nearly buried by an avalanche. His carriage was hurled over a precipice and, while the driver and the horses crashed to death thousands of feet below, he just managed to save himself by grasping hold of a pine tree.

He returned to Somersby, to his wife's distress, after staying with his brother in London, late in August 1830. 'It appears to me there is but little hope of any permanent tranquillity,' wrote Elizabeth Tennyson, 'I cannot but confess I have the greatest dread of what may happen.' For the doctor had scarcely landed in England before he sent off a furious letter abusing Frederick, who was fortunately on the Continent at the time. At Somersby there were at first only his wife, Charles and the younger children. He had not, since his return, been well enough to resume his pastoral duties, and had once more begun to drink heavily.

Alfred returned from Cambridge towards the end of September. Early next year it was evident that Dr Tennyson was dying. In February Alfred was summoned again. 'All shadow of hope with respect to my poor father's ultimate recovery has vanished,' he wrote to his Uncle Charles on 8 March. 'Yesterday he lost the use of one side. It is evident that he cannot last many hours longer. It is a great consolation to us, however, that he is free from all suffering and perfectly mild and tranquil, seeming not to interest himself in anything that passes. . . . We *must* lose him. May my end be as calm as his.'[13] The doctors diagnosed a slow typhus, and on 16 March 1831 Dr Tennyson died.

It would be a mistake to paint too black a picture of Alfred's childhood at Somersby. He loved both his parents, and his brothers and sisters; it was a deeply affectionate family, and after all it was during this formative period that all those influences of Nature came to him which were woven into the very fabric of his poetry and in which so much of his finest poetry had its origin. His observation of Nature in all her moods was both extensive and minute. Each year, before their father became ill, the family used to go for their summer holiday to Mablethorpe, where the full grandeur of the North Sea can be observed as nowhere else. As Tennyson was to write:[14]

Here often when a child I lay reclined:
    I took delight in this fair strand and free:
Here stood the infant Illion of my mind,
    And here the Grecian ships all seemed to be,
And here again I come and only find
    The drain-cut level of the marshy lea,
Gray sand-banks and pale sunsets, dreary wind,
    Dim shores, dense rains, and heavy-clouded sea.

Yet though perchance no tract of earth have more
    Unlikeness to the fair Ionian plain,
I love the place that I have loved before,
    I love the rolling cloud, the flying rain,
The brown sea lapsing back with sullen roar,
    To travel leagues before he comes again,
The misty desert of the houseless shore,
    The phantom-circle of the moaning main.

Tennyson owes more to the sea than any other English poet except Swinburne. 'The cottage to which the family resorted,' writes Hallam Tennyson in the *Memoir*, 'was close under the sea bank, the long low line of tussocked dunes. "I used to stand on this sand-built ridge," my father said, "and think that it was the spine-bone of the world." From the top of this the immense sweep of the marsh inland and the whole weird strangeness of the place greatly moved him. On the other side of the bank at low tide there is an immeasurable waste of sand and clay. . . . At night on the shore, when the tide is full, the sound is amazing. All around there is a low murmur of seething foam.' 'Nowhere,' wrote Drummond Rawnsley, 'are the waves in a storm higher than in the North Sea; nowhere have the breakers a more thunderous roar than on this Lincolnshire coast; and sometimes at half-tide the clap of the wave falling on the flat shore can be heard for miles.' Alfred used to wander along the shore alone, as he wandered through the lanes of Somersby, shouting lines of poetry as he composed them, sometimes all night. On one occasion, when he gave 'Good morning' in the early hours to a fisherman on Mablethorpe beach, the man muttered: 'Thou poor fool, thou doesn't know whether it be day or night.' 'To the country people [the Tennyson brothers] must have seemed strange beings wandering about wold and marsh at all hours of the day and night,' writes Sir Charles Tennyson, 'long-haired, down at heel, hatless and often coatless, their noses in books or absorbed in argument or declamation.'[15]

For all that, as the Rector's sons, they were a part of Lincolnshire society and attended dances at Horncastle Assembly Rooms and at the houses of their neighbours, the Edens and the Rawnsleys. It was to Rosa Baring and Sophy Rawnsley that Alfred addressed his early album verses, though to Rosa Baring of Harrington Hall his attachment went deeper. At one of these dances Alfred noticed with horror that his partner's white glove came away from his shoulder completely black, for a servant at the Rectory had cleaned his evening coat with the shoe-blacking brush.

Not only Frederick, Alfred and Charles, but nearly all the members of the family wrote poetry, the girls as well as the boys, and they provided their own amusement at home by writing and acting in their own plays. The Rectory was, in fact, a forcing house for poetry, however painful it may have become in other respects. But that, too, was fruitful for Alfred's later poetry, finally emerging in his most personal and original poem *Maud* with a nakedness and passion that horrified his contemporaries, who preferred the cooler and more artificial *Idylls of the King* and the religious speculation of *In Memoriam*, though there, too, the passion of his deepest love breaks out. When Byron died, Alfred, at the age of fourteen, 'felt as though

B                  [13]

the world had come to an end', and running to Hollywell Wood he threw himself on the ground and carved upon the sandstone the words: BYRON IS DEAD.

His son tells us that in later life Tennyson 'always spoke with affectionate remembrance of Somersby, of the woodbine that climbed into the bay window of his nursery, of the Gothic vaulted dining-room with stained-glass windows, as my Uncle Charles used to say making "butterfly souls" on the walls, of the beautiful stone chimney-piece carved by his father, of the pleasant little drawing-room which was lined with book-shelves, and furnished with yellow curtains, sofas and chairs, and looked out on to the lawn. This lawn was overshadowed one side by a walk under witch elms, and on the other by larch and sycamore trees. The ground is flat for a space to what in old days was a border of lilies and roses backed by hollyhocks and sunflowers . . . and then slopes down to a meadow, at the foot of which flows by "lawn and lea" the swift steep-banked brook, there were "brambly wildernesses" and "sweet forget-me-nots", and in which the "long mosses sway". The charm of this brook haunted him through life. . . .'

# 2

When Charles and Alfred went up to Cambridge in October 1827, Frederick had already made a name for himself there. His *Ode on the Pyramids* had been awarded the Browne Medal for Greek, and only his inadequacy in mathematics had prevented him from gaining a scholarship at Trinity. But he had little use for the recognised studies at the University and regularly absented himself from lectures and Chapel; and this behaviour, together with his insolent attitude towards the authorities, resulted in his rustication.

Alfred, too, was at first disappointed with Cambridge. 'I am sitting here,' he wrote to his Aunt Russell, 'owl-like and solitary in my rooms (nothing between me and the stars but a stratum of tiles). The hoof of the steed, the roll of the wheel, the shouts of drunken Gown and drunken Town come up from below with a sea-like murmur. . . . I know not how it is, but I feel isolated here in the midst of society. The country is so disgustingly level, the revelry of the place so monotonous, the studies of the University so uninteresting, so much matter of fact. None but dry-headed, calculating, angular little gentlemen can take much delight in them.'

The first time he and Charles went for dinner to the College, they could not face the noise, the lights and the lines of strange faces, and turned back to their lodgings in Rose Crescent. But Alfred's tall lanky figure, dark, almost Indian, complexion and leonine head could not fail to attract attention. FitzGerald saw him at Cambridge as 'a sort of Hyperion'. But he was still so shy, so countrified and careless in his dress that his cousin at Bayons called him 'the ploughman'. When a friend remarked on the dirtiness of his shirt, he is said to have replied: 'Yours wouldn't be half so clean, Heath, if you had worn it for a fortnight.' Clumsy and uncouth in manner, he spoke, as he continued to do all his life, with a broad Lincolnshire accent and invariably uttered, with embarrassing candour, what was in his mind. Yet, with all this, there was 'a sense of power and intense vitality about him' which could not fail to arouse curiosity. He must have stood out a mile among the more conventionally polished undergraduates, very much as Wordsworth must have done some years earlier. It is hardly surprising that W. H. Thompson, afterwards Master of Trinity, remarked, as he saw him standing shyly at the entrance to Hall, 'That man must be a poet.'

Little is known of Tennyson's time at Cambridge until the spring of 1829, when he met Arthur Hallam and joined the Apostles, a literary and debating society founded by the most talented of the undergraduates at Trinity. In the June of that year he won the Chancellor's Gold Medal for his remarkable poem 'Timbuctoo'. This poem, which has little to do with the set subject, is in Miltonic blank verse, when it was stipulated that it should be in heroic couplets. Charles Wordsworth wrote to his brother Christopher, who had won the medal in 1827: 'If such an exercise had been sent up at Oxford, the author would have had a better chance of being rusticated with a view of his passing a few months at a Lunatic Asylum, than of obtaining the prize. It is certainly a wonderful production: and if it had come with Lord Byron's name it would have been thought as fine as anything he ever wrote.' This is hardly an exaggeration. It is not surprising that Arthur Hallam should have written to Gladstone on 14 September: 'The splendid imaginative power that pervades it will be seen through all hindrances. I consider Tennyson as promising fair to be the greatest poet of our generation, perhaps of our century.' The 'hindrances' referred to the fact that the examiners had struck out the prefatory prose argument. Reviewing the poem in *The Athenaeum* of 22 July 1829, one of the Apostles, possibly Monckton Milnes, wrote: 'These productions have often been ingenious and elegant, but we have never before seen one of them which indicated really first-rate poetical genius, and which would have done honour to any man who ever wrote.' It was, Milnes added, certainly equal to most parts of Milton. But Tennyson, who does not seem to have taken the whole thing very seriously and had built the poem up out of his early blank-verse piece 'Armageddon', only entered the competition under pressure from his father. He called 'Timbuctoo' 'a wild and unmethodised performance' and was too shy to read it aloud in the Senate House, as was the custom, and arranged for Charles Merivale to read it for him.

His friends describe him at this time as having 'Johnsonian common sense' and as 'very genial, full of enjoyment, full of sensitiveness, full of humour, though with the passionate heart of a poet, and sometimes feeling the melancholy of life.' At times, Tennyson said that he passed through moods of 'misery unutterable'.

The most important event of Tennyson's Cambridge years was his meeting with Arthur Hallam, the son of Henry Hallam the historian. Arthur had been at Eton with Frederick and Gladstone; while there

[16]

he was judged the best poet of his time. After leaving Eton, he spent some months of 1827 in Italy, where he had embarked upon a study of Dante and become so fluent in Italian that he wrote poems in the language which won praise even from Italian scholars. He was also at this time perfecting himself in German and Spanish. Altogether Arthur Hallam was so intellectually precocious as to astonish his friends. Above all, he was a great admirer not only of Tennyson's poetry but of Tennyson himself, while Tennyson's love for Hallam became the greatest emotional experience of his life. Unfortunately Henry Hallam destroyed all Tennyson's letters to his son, while Tennyson's son destroyed all Hallam's letters to his father. Undoubtedly, both feared their emotional ardour might be open to misconstruction. But such highly-wrought emotional friendships, Elizabethan in their intensity, were not uncommon at that time at Cambridge. Hence Tennyson's lifelong attachment to Shakespeare's *Sonnets*. Such friendships were, of course, platonic and associated with reverence for 'the Good, the Beautiful and the True', as Hallam wrote somewhat dampingly to Monckton Milnes in July 1831: 'I am not aware, my dear Milnes, that in the lofty sense which you are accustomed to attach to the name of Friendship, we ever were or ever could be friends. What is more to the purpose, I never fancied that we could, nor intended to make you fancy it. That exalted sentiment I do not ridicule – God forbid – nor consider it merely ideal: I have experienced it and it thrills within me now – but not, pardon me, my dear Milnes, for speaking frankly – not for you. But the shades of sympathy are innumerable, and wretched indeed would be the condition of man, if sunshine never fell upon him save from the unclouded skies of tropical summer. Write a sonnet to me on the evening of 29th September. I will write one to you at the same time: between seven and eight, if possible.'[1] Hallam, the three Tennyson brothers, Milnes, Blakesley and James Spedding all wrote verses to each other.

But was Arthur Hallam really such a paragon? One thinks of him, of course, as the beloved spirit of *In Memoriam*. But to A. C. Benson he appeared otherwise. 'It is difficult,' writes Benson, 'to read the letters of Hallam without forming an impression unfavourable to Hallam. The letters appear, even with all due allowances, to be tinged with unhealthy precocity, and by what one should call priggishness, developed to a painful degree. . . . Still more disappointing is the portrait, by an inferior artist it is true, which hangs in the Election Chamber at Eton. It represents a rubicund, good-humoured, almost beery-looking young man, with a sly and sensual cast of the eye.'[2] But this should be contrasted with Fanny Kemble's description: 'There was a gentleness and purity almost virginal in his voice, manner and countenance, and the upper part of his face, his forehead and eyes, wore the angelic radiance that they still must wear in heaven.'[3] And just after Tennyson had won the Chancellor's Medal with 'Timbuctoo', a friend wrote: 'I received a letter this morning from Hallam. He is delighted that Tennyson is successful in the Timbuctoo business. He says that Tennyson borrowed the pervading idea from him, so that he is entitled to the honours of a Sancho Panza in the memorable victory gained in the year 1829 over the prosaicism and jingle-jangle of which Charles Wordsworth is the goodly impersonation.'

'It was not only fashionable but almost indispensable for every youth to be Byronic,' Milnes declared in an address to the Wordsworth Society in 1885. 'Of course, though at Cambridge we had not either the energy or perhaps the courage to be Corsairs or Laras, yet nevertheless we enjoyed the poetry and especially the later poetry of Lord Byron as something very cognate to our dispositions and tempers.' All the same, he added, he and his friends had felt the urgent need of some piety which would 'satisfy their higher aspirations and elevate their minds'. In Shelley and Keats, so lately dead and still unknown outside a small intellectual circle, they found their ideal antidote to Byronic cynicism and bravado. The Apostles printed at their own expense an edition of *Adonais*, from a copy brought back by Hallam from Pisa, and Keats was assiduously studied and admired. In fact, Milnes was to be Keats's first biographer. Wordsworth was also particularly admired for his moral elevation. 'He brings the mind to a sound and healthy tone,' Richard Trench wrote to Milnes in July 1828. To the Victorians going for a walk in the country became, under Wordsworth's influence, almost equivalent to going to church.

At this time Christopher Wordsworth, the poet's brother, was Master of Trinity, and was responsible for the pleasant neo-Gothic New Court built in the 1820s. Dr Wordsworth had left unchanged the Chapel system by which every undergraduate had to be in Chapel at seven o'clock in the morning. The day, which began with Chapel, continued with attendance at lectures from eight till ten, reading from ten till two, relaxation before dinner at three, then Vespers (Chapel again), tea and work from eight till midnight. Such, at least in theory, was the undergraduate's day. But the richer members of Trinity filled in the time with breakfast parties, with hams, fowls, pies, porter, champagne, coffee and tobacco, from ten till one; wine parties at which port, white wine and cherry brandy were consumed with fresh fruit and French plums, and later parties, beginning at seven in the evening. This set did not work, read Colburn's novels during lectures, and bothered little about preparing for degrees,

[18]

which were still to be obtained by means other than examinations, thus keeping alive the loose traditions of the eighteenth century in the midst of the increasingly earnest nineteenth-century University.[4] For such people Tennyson and the Apostles had only contempt.

At the regular meetings of the Apostles, Tennyson rarely joined in the general discussion, and sat in front of the fire smoking his clay pipe. But he would occasionally sum up the issue of the argument with a terse phrase, and although it was obligatory for each member to deliver at least one essay a term, Tennyson's only contribution was a paper on ghosts which he was too shy to read. Having failed to deliver his paper he had to resign, but was thereupon re-elected a 'honorary member extraordinary'. He was not too shy, however, to read his poetry. Otherwise such subjects were discussed as the Origin of Evil, the Derivation of Moral Sentiments, Prayer and the Personality of God, Have Shelley's Poems an Immoral Tendency?, Is an Intelligible First Cause Deducible from the Phenomena of the Universe? – to which Tennyson answered simply 'No!' Hallam Tennyson quotes a note to his father from Tennant, one of the Apostles, which has a pleasantly youthful undergraduate tone and is not as solemn as the subjects discussed might suggest: 'Last Saturday we had an Apostolic dinner, when we had the honour, among other things, of drinking your health. Edmund Lushington and I went away tolerably early; but most of them stayed till past two. John Heath volunteered a song; Kemble got into a passion about nothing but quickly jumped out again; Blakesley was afraid the Proctor might come in; and Thompson poured large quantities of salt upon Douglas Heath's head because he talked nonsense.' They also acted Shakespeare, and Hallam Tennyson recalls how his father and his Uncle Charles used to describe a performance of *Much Ado* in March 1830 in which Milnes took the part of Beatrice. 'When Beatrice sat down, her weight was such that she crashed through the couch, and sank to the floor, nothing to be seen but a heap of petticoats, much to the discomfiture of the players and the immeasurable laughter of the spectators. . . . My father, I may add, was famous in some parts of Shakespeare, especially Malvolio.' Tennyson was also famous for his declamation of ballads, such as 'Clerk Saunders', 'Helen of Kirkonnell' and 'Mary Margaret'. He would improvise verses by the score full of lyrical passion, and FitzGerald recalls 'that he used to repeat "Oriana" in a way not to be forgotten at Cambridge tables'. He also read Rabelais aloud so that his friends nearly tumbled off their chairs with laughter. He made light of the stercoracious qualities and used to say that 'the foulness was but a mask for the free-thinking'. Otherwise, he fenced and took long walks.

In June 1830 his *Poems, Chiefly Lyrical* was published; and Hallam reviewed the book next year in *The Englishman's Magazine*, where he made such extravagant claims for it that he brought down on the unfortunate poet's head the following year the ridicule of John Wilson ('Christopher North'), one of the most redoubtable critics of the day, in a blistering article in *Blackwood's Magazine* of May 1832. But Hallam was the first to demonstrate the peculiar qualities of Tennyson's poetry, through his close sympathy with the man himself:

> First, his luxuriance of imagination, and at the same time
> his control over it. Secondly, his power of embodying himself
> in ideal characters, or rather moods of character, with such
> accuracy of adjustment that the circumstances of the narrative
> seem to have a natural correspondence with the predominant
> feeling and, as it were, to be evolved from it by assimilative
> force. Thirdly, his vivid, picturesque delineation of objects, and
> the peculiar skill with which he holds all of them *fused*, to
> borrow a metaphor from Science, in a medium of strong
> emotion. Fourthly, the variety of his lyrical measures and the
> exquisite modulation of harmonious words and cadences to the
> swell and fall of the feeling expressed. Fifthly, the elevated
> habits of thought implied in these compositions, and importing
> a mellow soberness of tone, more impressive to our minds
> than if the author had drawn up a set of opinions in verse
> and sought to instruct the understanding rather than to
> communicate the love of beauty to the heart.

He called 'Recollections of the Arabian Nights', 'as majestic as Milton and sublime as Aeschylus'; of 'The Sea Fairies' he wrote: 'A stretch of lyrical power is here exhibited which we did not think the English language had possessed.' Of the keepsake verses to young ladies he said that they are 'like summaries of mighty dreams. . . . How original is the imagery and how delicate! How wonderful the new world thus created for us, the region between real and unreal!' But the very fact that he called Tennyson 'a poet of sensation' of the school of Shelley, Keats and Leigh Hunt was enough to give Wilson his cue. No less damaging in the eyes of Wilson was the fact that he was known, as far as he was known at all, as the poet of a coterie.

'*The Englishman's Magazine* ought not to have died,' Wilson began, 'for it threatened to be a very pleasant periodical. An Essay "on the genius of Alfred Tennyson" sent it to its grave. The super-human – nay, supernatural – pomposity of that one paper incapacitated the whole work for living one day longer in this unceremonious world. The solemnity with which the critic approached the object of his adoration, and the sanctity with which he laid his offerings on the shrine, were too much for our irreligious age. The Essay "on the genius of Alfred Tennyson" awoke a general guffaw, and it expired in convulsions. Yet the Essay was exceedingly well written – as well as if it had been "on the genius of Sir Isaac Newton". Therein lay the mistake. Sir Isaac discovered the law of gravitation; Alfred has but written some pretty verses and mankind were not prepared to set him among the stars. . . .

'At present he has small power over the common feelings and thoughts of men. His feebleness is distressing at all times when he makes an appeal to ordinary sympathies. And the reason is, that he fears to look such sympathies boldly in the face, – and will be metaphysical. What all the human race see and feel, he seems to think cannot be poetical; he is not aware of the transcendant and eternal grandeur of commonplace and all-time truths.' This was a shrewd hit and Tennyson certainly took it to heart in his *English Idyls*, as he did the strictures of all his critics, till he came to be known as the Poet of the People. 'The pervading character of the verses,' Wilson concluded, 'is a distinguished silliness and Alfred cuts a foolish figure.'[5]

It cannot be denied that there is a good deal of silliness in Tennyson's first book, and although Wilson made fun of it, he was not blind to the genuine achievements. He praises the 'Ode to Memory', 'Recollections of the Arabian Nights' and 'Mariana'; he even professes himself 'in love' with the 'airy fairy Lilians', with 'Claribel', 'Isobel' and 'Oriana', and credits Tennyson with 'a delicate perception of the purity of the female character and 'a fine ear for melody and harmony too – and rare and rich glimpses of imagination. He has *genius*.' But Tennyson was so irritated by this review that he unwisely published in his *Poems* of 1833 a squib against 'Christopher North':

You did late review my lays,
   Crusty Christopher;
You did mingle blame and praise,
   Rusty Christopher.
When I learnt from whom it came,
I forgave you all the blame,
   Musty Christopher;
I could *not* forgive the praise,
   Fusty Christopher.

It is usually maintained that what attracted Tennyson to Arthur Hallam was his confidence and the buoyancy of his spirits. But, as Christopher Ricks points out: 'Hallam was himself subject, frequently and fiercely, to the darkest feelings. His health, both physical and mental, was not strong. So some important threads in the relationship were dark ones.'[6] It had originally been his intention to contribute to *Poems, Chiefly Lyrical*, and that the publication should be a joint one, like Wordsworth's and Coleridge's *Lyrical Ballads*. But at this point Henry Hallam intervened. He disliked some of his son's poems, amatory and otherwise, and he objected to publication, whether independent or joint. In May 1829 Arthur Hallam had been severely ill as the result of an unhappy love affair and had been sent to the Continent to recover before returning to Cambridge in October. In the summer of 1829 he even confessed to Milnes his fears of going mad. 'In my fits of gloom I so often look death and insanity in the face, that the impulse to leave some trace of my existence on this bulk of atoms gathers strength with the warning that I must be brief.' And he went on to write of 'this incurable somnambulism we call Life'. Later, he wrote of himself: 'I am one of strong passions, irresolute purposes, vacillating opinions.' It would seem, therefore, that Hallam needed as much moral support from Tennyson as Tennyson is usually represented as seeking from him. In fact, as Ricks concludes: 'Tennyson's melancholia . . . found in Hallam the deepest reassurance, not of serenity but of similar suffering, doubts and morbidities which yet were not ignoble. Such morbidity could thus be seen as something other than a uniquely personal weakness or shame.'[7]

In December 1829, during Dr Tennyson's absence on the Continent, Hallam met Tennyson's sister Emily at Somersby and fell in love with her, which brought the two young men closer together than ever. Hallam was now almost one of the family.

Next year they set off together for the Pyrenees with funds for the Spanish insurgents who, under their leader General Torrijos, had raised the standard of revolt against the tyranny of Ferdinand VIII and his restoration of the Inquisition – the foxy-looking little man painted by Goya. The Apostles had, through John Sterling, become passionately involved in Spanish politics, like the young men of the 1930s who went to Spain to fight against the military rebellion of General Franco and his German and Italian Fascist allies, so gallantly and hopelessly. Tennyson and Hallam were not going to fight, but had they been arrested on the Spanish frontier they would probably have been shot. The venture was not, therefore, without danger. It is, nevertheless, the one 'progressive' political action of Tennyson's life.

After the destruction of the Constitution by Ferdinand in 1823, a number of Spanish Liberals had settled in London, but had been unable to maintain themselves for long, in spite of active English sympathisers. At last Torrijos determined to attempt a landing in

Spain with a small force in the hope of raising the country against the monarchy. At this point Sterling's cousin Robert Boyd, who had lately resigned from the Indian army and was on the look-out for adventure, met Torrijos and was persuaded to sink his capital in a small gunboat lying more or less derelict in the Thames, which he thereupon proceeded to repair and equip for the purpose of taking the insurgents to Spain, with help from many of Sterling's friends, including Trench, Kemble, Hallam and Tennyson. Unfortunately the Spanish government came to hear of the plan and protested to the Foreign Office, and at the last moment the ship was seized by the police. Sterling managed to escape and crossed the Channel in an open boat to St Valery with Torrijos, who then made his way to Gibraltar, where he met Boyd and the other insurgents. They were allowed to stay at Gibraltar till November 1831. But the rising in Spain against Ferdinand was followed by another protest to the British government for harbouring the rebels, and they were thereupon expelled from Gibraltar. They left in two small ships, were chased and driven ashore, and the whole party, 650 of them including Boyd, was summarily shot on the esplanade at Malaga. Tennyson's and Hallam's role had been confined to taking money and coded instructions from Torrijos to Ojeda at the Pont d'Espagne in the Pyrenees. An insurrection in the north was planned to coincide with Torrijos's landing in the south.

The two Englishmen were soon disillusioned when they met Ojeda, a ruffian whom they found desperately jealous of Torrijos and whose chief interest in the rebellion was, as he told them, to cut the throats of all the priests in Spain. Finding that the Englishmen were somewhat taken aback, Ojeda added: 'You know my good heart.' 'Yes, and what a black one it is,' Tennyson commented in a letter.[8] But if Tennyson was disillusioned by the Torrijos affair, he was enchanted with the wild valley of the Cauteretz, where he lingered on the way home, working on his 'Oenone'. The mountain scenery, with its streaks of snow, its pines and cataract, suggested to him the valleys of Greece, which he had not seen but which provide the background of this poem. On his way home in the diligence, he wrote 'Mariana in the South', between Narbonne and Perpignan. He seems to have found the whole experience exhilarating, though it was the wild mountain scenery which impressed him more than anything else. His early lines 'Written During the Convulsion in Spain' are nothing but rhetoric to encourage the others. The Torrijos affair cured him of any further outbursts of revolutionary fervour. Certainly, the longer he lived the more conservative he became, hymning the empire and the royal family in his laureate verses and condemning the Paris Commune as 'the red fool fury of the Seine'. When, in the 1880s, William

Allingham told him about William Morris's Socialism, he exclaimed:
'He's gone crazy!'

After Dr Tennyson's death in March 1831, Henry Hallam forbade
his son to visit Somersby or to see Emily again until he came of age
in February 1832, when, he hoped, Arthur would make a better
choice of a wife. For he did not look with much favour upon such an
impecunious and eccentric family as the Tennysons of Somersby.
When Alfred left Cambridge there seemed little likelihood of his
returning there to take a degree. 'I told him that it was a useless
expense unless he meant to go into the Church,' his Uncle Charles
wrote to Bayons. 'He said he would. I did not think he seemed much
to like it. The Tealby living was mentioned and understood to be
intended for him.' Was history to repeat itself? Was Alfred to be
forced into the Church against his inclinations, like his father? There
seemed to be no other opening, though as a matter of fact Alfred
was privately determined to follow no profession other than poetry.
But it was not clear how he hoped to live. Charles, however, felt a
genuine vocation for the Ministry, though some years later he
changed his name to Turner and became an opium addict; and
Edward, then eighteen, was already showing alarming signs of the
mental instability which was to result in his being confined to an
asylum for the rest of his life.

The whole family was now dependent on Old George. Dr Tennyson
had left debts of nearly £900, £170 to the wine merchants alone,
though there remained £600 in cash, and household furniture, books,
plate, &c., was valued at £1,235. It was then discovered that the
three elder boys had run up debts at the University: Frederick £330,
Charles £320 and Alfred £170. Negotiations for the settlement of these
liabilities dragged on miserably through the winter and summer of
1831. A complicated series of financial arrangements followed.
Elizabeth Tennyson was allowed £800 a year, from which was
deducted whatever her father-in-law spent on the maintenance and
training of the younger children, and the interest on the bonds
amounting to £1,426, which he had taken from Frederick, Charles
and Alfred, 'the total amount being calculated to cover the amounts
paid on behalf of all since Dr Tennyson's death.'[9] These humiliating
negotiations and the dependent situation of the family had a bad
effect on Alfred.

As soon as Arthur Hallam came of age in February 1832 – he was
at the time studying law in London – he wrote to his father declaring
his intention to visit Somersby, which he did soon after, spending
about five weeks there as Emily's accepted lover. During this time,
says Sir Charles, 'there was much making of music with her and
Mary, much reading of poetry in the Rectory drawing-room or on

the lawn sloping down to the meadow and the brook, much digging in the garden, . . . many walks with Alfred over the wolds and the marsh.' Once the two friends sat talking in the garden all night until dawn, 'when, thinking it too late to go to bed, they walked eastwards over the wolds to meet the sunrise.'[10]

Arthur Hallam wrote to his friend Brookfield about Emily: 'Every shadow of – not doubt, but uneasiness, or what else may be a truer name for the feeling that Alfred sometimes casts over my hopes – is destroyed in the full blaze of conscious delight with which I perceive that she loves me – and I – love her madly. . . . Now I feel above consequence, freed from destiny, at home with happiness.' But the happiness was not to last much longer. There were acrimonious and inconclusive negotiations between Henry Hallam and the Rev. Rawnsley, as Emily's guardian, and Uncle Charles about the marriage settlement. Henry Hallam wrote that he had originally hoped that Emily Tennyson would have broken off the engagement, seeing that his son was in no position to marry and that the most he could do now was to allow him £600 a year, adding that their comfort would largely depend on how much Mr George Tennyson could put up.

In July 1832 Alfred and Hallam went off for a tour of the Rhine, which did little to raise their spirits. At its commencement their boat was held up for a week in quarantine beside a dreary island in the Maas, where the cholera vessels were unloading corpses. 'Alfred is as sulky as possible,' Hallam wrote to Jack Kemble. 'He howls and growls sans intermission,' to which Alfred added a postscript: 'And good reason have I to be sulky, John, as plenty as blackberries: I am bug bitten, fly bitten, flea bitten, gnat bitten and hunger bitten. I have had no sleep for the past three nights and have serious thoughts of returning to England though it were in an open boat.'[11] At last they became so exasperated that they pulled down the Dutch colours from the mast and reversed them, and the skipper swore he would hang them both from the yard arm. Finally released, they went to Cologne and Bonn, climbed the Drachenfels and visited Nonnen-werth and Bingen, returning to England at the end of the month to be confronted with the inter-family bickering.

In December Hallam saw Alfred's next book through the press, the *Poems* of 1833. In April next year J. W. Croker, who had already savaged Keats, venomously attacked it in *The Quarterly Review* with heavy-handed sarcasm. The effect of this on Alfred was to produce a ten years' silence, as far as further publication was concerned. Some of the poems had already appeared in *Poems, Chiefly Lyrical*. But it was 'The Lady of Shalott' and 'The Lotos-Eaters' which aroused such malicious merriment in Mr Croker, who regarded them as

[25]

affected and obscure – the fate of all genuinely original work on its first appearance. But it should be remembered, of course, that we now read these poems in the often drastically revised forms which Tennyson prepared for later editions. 'Christopher North's' review of *Poems, Chiefly Lyrical* had been irritating enough, but it was at least good-humoured and gave some poems unqualified praise. Croker's review was mainly written in revenge for Tennyson's unlucky squib, which he quoted, against his friend 'Crusty Christopher'. Much of it seems to have been inspired by sheer bloody-mindedness. To have one's first book ridiculed was bad enough; to have one's second book damned outright was too much. Nor could Tennyson have been pleased to hear that his Uncle Charles thought *The Quarterly Review* 'scarcely too severe'. Samuel Rogers, however, publicly defended him as the most promising genius of the time; at Cambridge the Union Society held a debate on the motion 'Tennyson or Milton – which is the greatest poet?'; and the Apostles drank his health to resounding cheers.

Tennyson himself said later that he was nearer thirty than twenty before he became anything of an artist – which is certainly not so. But he was still capable of such embarrassing pieces as 'O Darling Room', which gave Croker his chance. Though he was bitterly hurt by Croker's attack, he still had the strength of mind to take his more serious criticism to heart. As FitzGerald wrote at the time: 'Tennyson has been making fresh poems which are finer, they say, than anything he has written, but I believe he is chiefly meditating on the purging and refining of what he has already done, and repents that he has published at all yet.'

Meanwhile, the spirit of the summer of 1833, which Tennyson spent at Somersby, with occasional visits from Hallam, is reflected in 'The Gardener's Daughter'. In this poem, commenced in 1832 and continued during 1833–4, when Tennyson was in love with Rosa Baring – the gardener's daughter is, in fact, called Rose – are many of his most luxuriantly Keatsian lines celebrating the English countryside in high summer.

> From the woods
> Came voices of the well-contented doves.
> The lark could scarce get out his notes for joy,
> But shook his song together as he neared
> His happy home, the ground. To left and right,
> The cuckoo told his name to all the hills;
> The mellow ouzel fluted in the elm;
> The redcap whistled, and the nightingale
> Sang loud, as though he were the bird of day.

But all the spirit of summer is concentrated in the figure of Rose herself:

> One arm aloft –
> Gowned in pure white, that fitted to the shape –
> Holding the bush, to fix it back, she stood,
> A single stream of all her soft brown hair
> Poured on one side: the shadow of the flowers
> Stole all the golden gloss, and wavering
> Lovingly lower, trembled on her waist –
> Ah, happy shade – and still went wavering down,
> But, ere it touched a foot, that might have danced
> The greensward into greener circles, dipt,
> And mixed with shadows of the common ground!
> But the full day dwelt on her brows, and sunned
> Her violet eyes, and all her Hebe bloom,
> And doubled his own warmth against her lips,
> And on the bounteous wave of such a breast
> As never pencil drew. Half light, half shade,
> She stood, a sight to make an old man young.

The last six lines are a condensation of the original, bolder version:

> An unforgotten vision! The clear heat
> Bathing the ripe anemones, that kissed
> Each other in her lips, deepened the blush
> Below her violet eyes and underneath
> Glowed on one polished shoulder, – basking warm
> Between the half-seen swell of maiden breasts,
> Moulded in smoothest curves. Half-light, half-shade . . .

One can understand Tennyson doing away with the awkward comparison of the girl's lips to anemones, but the substitution of 'such a breast/As never pencil drew' for 'the half-seen swell of maiden breasts' only weakens the effect. Tennyson probably judged the original version too indelicate for drawing-room taste, and the *English Idyls* were written deliberately to appeal to that taste, as were the pretty album verses to the various girls with whom he flirted: Margaret, Kate, Adeline, Lilian, Claribel. They have something in common with the little poems written by John Skelton in old age to the young girls who were weaving his garland of laurel:

> Merry Margaret,
>     As midsummer flower,
>
> Gentle as falcon
> Or hawk of the tower . . .

[27]

Or        My maiden Isabel,
            Reflaring rosabel.
        The fragrant camomel,
            The ruddy rosary,
        The sovereign rosemary,
        The pretty strawberry;
            The columbine, the nept,
        The jelofer well set,
        The proper violet . . .

Tennyson lacks Skelton's freshness, of course, being sentimentally
Victorian: for example, 'Lilian', written to Sophy Rawnsley:

        Airy, fairy Lilian,
            Flitting, fairy Lilian,
    When I ask her if she love me,
    Claps her tiny hands above me,
            Laughing all she can;
    She'll not tell me if she love me,
            Cruel little Lilian.

But while writing 'The Gardener's Daughter', as he later told
Browning, he 'felt his life to be in flower'. There can be little doubt
that the gardener's daughter is a portrait of the voluptuous Rosa
Baring of Harrington Hall, with her violet eyes, soft brown hair and
'Hebe bloom', with whom he fell in love.

[28]

# 3

The Hallams went abroad during the first week in August 1833 and reached Vienna at the end of the month. On 6 September Arthur wrote to Alfred and Emily enthusiastically about the picture galleries there. 'I longed for you: two rooms full of Venetian pictures only; such Giorgiones, Palmas, Bordones, Paul Veroneses! and oh Alfred, such Titians! by Heaven, that man could paint! I wish you could see his Danaë. Do you just write as perfect as Danaë!' On 15 September Arthur suddenly died of an apoplexy.

One evening, early that month, Mary and Matilda Tennyson had seen a tall figure. clothed in white, pass down the lane in front of the Rectory. They followed it until it passed through the hedge, where there was no gap, and disappeared. Matilda was so upset by this experience that she ran home and burst into tears. On 1 October, she went for a dancing lesson at Spilsby and collected a letter at the post office addressed to Alfred. It was from Arthur Hallam's uncle, Henry Elton:[1]

At the request of a most afflicted family, I write to you because they are unequal, from the abyss of grief into which they have fallen, to do it themselves.

Your friend, Sir, and my much loved nephew, Arthur Hallam, is no more – it has pleased God to remove him from this his first scene of Existence, to a better World, for which he was Created.

He died at Vienna on his return from Buda, by apoplexy – and I believe his Remains come by sea from Trieste.

Mr. Hallam arrived this Morning in 3 Princes Buildings.

May that Great Being, in whose hands are the Destinies of Man – and who has promised to comfort all that Mourn pour the Balm of Consolation on all the Families who are bowed down by this unexpected dispensation!

I have just seen Mr. Hallam, who begs I will tell you, that he will write himself as soon as his Heart will let him. Poor Arthur

had a slight attack of Ague – which he had often had – Ordered
his fire to be lighted and talked with as much cheerfulness as
usual – He suddenly became insensible and his Spirit departed
without Pain – The Physician endeavoured to get any Blood
from him – and on Examination it was the General Opinion that
he could not have lived long.

Matilda found Alfred sitting at a table in the Gothic dining-room;
she gave him the letter and went upstairs, and he broke the news to
Emily.

For Alfred, says Sir Charles Tennyson, 'a sudden and brutal stroke
had annihilated in a moment a love "passing the love of women".'
He did not know where to look for 'the Balm of Consolation', and
Emily became ill for many months. But, marvellously, the overwhelming shock of Hallam's death released in Alfred a spring of
poetry that now welled up from depths of his being that he had not
plumbed before. He wrote the first quatrains of what became *In
Memoriam*, and the 'Morte d'Arthur'; he wrote 'Ulysses', 'Tithon',
and began 'Tiresias'. 'Tithon', in its final form as 'Tithonus'
perfectly enshrines his grief:

> The woods decay, the woods decay and fall,
> The vapours weep their burthen to the ground,
> Man comes and tills the field and lies beneath,
> And after many a summer dies the swan.
> Me only cruel immortality
> Consumes! I wither slowly in thine arms,
> Here at the quiet limit of the world,
> A white-haired shadow roaming like a dream
> The ever-silent spaces of the East,
> Far-folded mists, and gleaming halls of morn.

It is remarkable that Tennyson was so soon to rise sufficiently
above this annihilating sorrow to produce such golden work; some
may agree with FitzGerald that he never surpassed it and that all
his finest poetry appeared in the two volumes of 1842, that is, before
his marriage and before he became the idolised Laureate. 'There is
more about myself in "Ulysses", which was written under the sense
of loss and that all had gone by,' Tennyson said later, 'but that still
life must be fought out to the end. It was more written with the
feeling of his loss upon me than many poems in *In Memoriam*.'[2]
'Tithonus', he said, was intended as a 'pendant to "Ulysses" and
"Tiresias".'

Tennyson did not allow himself to be conquered by his grief; he
did not remain moping at Somersby with the spectacle of his heart-

broken sister before him.[3] He went to London, met his friends and resumed the habits of ordinary life. He set himself a programme of study, which included history, chemistry, botany, electricity, animal physiology, mechanics and theology, with a different subject for each day of the week. Nevertheless, with Frederick about to leave permanently for Italy, Charles now an opium addict, Edward confined to an asylum and Septimus showing signs of going that way too, the responsibility for his family devolved mainly upon him. 'I think it my duty to inform you of Septimus' state of mind,' he wrote to his Uncle Charles on 15 January 1834. 'My grandfather talks of letting him stop at home two or three months longer – if this be acted upon I have very little doubt but that his mind will prove as deranged as Edward's although I trust that his intellect may yet be preserved by getting him out into some bustling, active line of life *remote from the scene of his early connections.* . . . At present his symptoms are not unlike those with which poor Edward's unhappy derangement began. He is subject to fits of the most gloomy despondency accompanied by tears – or rather he spends whole days in this manner, complaining that he is neglected by all his relations and blindly resigning himself to every morbid influence.' Accordingly, Septimus was apprenticed to a neighbouring doctor and his condition rapidly improved. Later, Rossetti used to tell of his first meeting with Septimus at Henry Hallam's, when he rose from the floor where he had been lying and announced: 'I am Septimus, the most morbid of the Tennysons.' One sometimes feels that the members of this remarkable family rather prided themselves on their melancholia and ill-health, on 'the black-bloodedness of the Tennysons'. As for Emily, Henry Hallam felt partly responsible for her desolation, since he had at first opposed her engagement to Arthur, and he now allowed her £300 a year and invited her to visit him at Molesey Park.

In July Alfred was in London to see Frederick off to Italy. He visited his friends at Cambridge and spent several days with the Heaths at Kitlands, near Dorking, exploring the wooded country round Leith Hill. He returned to Somersby at the end of August to meet his friend Tennant, who was also suffering from acute depression. He then arranged for his brother Horatio to go to the school that Tennant was opening at Blackheath. We also find him alone, 'communing with himself' at the cottage at Mablethorpe:

And here again I come and only find
    The drain-cut levels of the marshy lea –
Gray sandbanks, and pale sunsets, – dreary wind,
    Dim shores, dense rains, and heavy-clouded sea.

All Nature seemed to reflect his grief. Here he resumed work on the elegies of *In Memoriam*, 'The Two Voices', in which he reflects upon suicide, and 'Ulysses'. For as well as writing new poems, he was engaged throughout 1834 in a creative revision of his earlier work. The elegies of *In Memoriam* were now steadily accumulating, its earlier stanzas circulating among his friends, who tried to persuade him that it was time to publish once more. Nothing, however, would induce him to do so. Instead he wrote to 'Christopher North' apologising for his earlier squib about 'Crusty Christopher' and lamenting some of the poems which had aroused that critic's ridicule. This letter was provoked by a satire called *Criticism and Taste*, in which John Lake attacked Wilson for his *Blackwood*'s article on Tennyson, who now feared that it would stir up the crusty critic or his friend Croker to further ridicule of his poems. 'I could wish,' he wrote, 'that some of the poems broken on your critical wheel were deeper than ever plummet sounded. Written as they were before I had attained my nineteenth year they could not but contain as many faults as words, I never wish to see them or hear of them again – much less to find them dragged forward once more on your boards, if you should condescend to divide Mr. L. from his one idea by replying to him. Perhaps you should not use him too harshly – tho' his arrogance deserves reproof; a consideration of the real imbecility of his nature ought to blunt the weapon.' He concludes by hoping that now 'we have shaken hands', adding that he had 'enjoyed the tone of boisterous and picturesque humour' of Wilson's original *Blackwood*'s article, which we may doubt. But the critic did not reply to this letter.

Earlier, in 1833, James Spedding had written to Tennyson to say that J. S. Mill was contemplating writing an article on his poems in *The London Review*. He had replied: 'It is the last thing I wish for, and I would that you or some other who may be friends of Mill would hint as much to him. I do not wish to be dragged forward again in any shape before the reading public at present, particularly on the score of my old poems.' Nevertheless Mill's long, careful article in *The London Review* of July 1835 should have satisfied the apprehensive poet, particularly as Mill began by disposing of Croker's article in *The Quarterly* as 'contemptible', and by ranking 'The Lady of Shalott' with 'The Ancient Mariner' and 'Christabel'. But when Spedding invited Tennyson to Mirehouse in Cumberland in February 1834 to meet FitzGerald, he at first refused, feeling that he should not spend the money. But later, having sold the Chancellor's Gold Medal for £15, he wrote to accept.

April and May were spent in the Lake District, first at Mirehouse on Bassenthwaite, then at Ambleside, though that year Tennyson was unlucky in the weather and for many days it rained continuously.

But he read to his friends in the evenings many of the poems that were to appear in the 1842 volumes, intoning the 'Morte d'Arthur' as they rowed across Bassenthwaite and Windermere in a haunting voice that reminded his listeners of the wind in a pinewood. He also read a good deal of Wordsworth, whose best work he admired more than that of any poet since Milton. But he could not be persuaded to visit the old poet at Rydal Mount. Spedding was more than ever impressed by Alfred's nobility of spirit and the tenderness of his heart, but thought that he had not sufficient faith in his own powers. Afterwards, FitzGerald wrote: 'I will say no more than that the more I see of him the more cause have I to think him great. His little humours and grumpiness were so droll that I was always laughing. I must however say further that I felt what Charles Lamb describes, a sense of depression at times from the overshadowing of a so much more lofty intellect than my own. . . . I could not be mistaken in the universality of his mind.' One might set against this the foolish remarks of W. H. Auden, for whom Tennyson is 'the poet of the nursery' and 'the stupidest of the English poets'. In fact, Tennyson at this time was in the habit of representing himself as an old man, much as the youthful T. S. Eliot does in 'The Love Song of J. Alfred Prufrock' and 'Gerontion', with much the same effect of disillusion-ment and ennui. Tennyson spoke through the *personae* of Ulysses and Tithonus just as Eliot spoke through Prufrock and Gerontion, though Eliot's weariness and enervation was less a personal mood (though his health was bad at the time) than a reflection of the spiritual condition of the generation which had survived the long-drawn-out, pointless slaughter of the Great War. Again, the spectator behind *The Waste Land* is Tiresias, 'old man with wrinkled female breasts', who has 'foresuffered all', though Tennyson's imagery is far from the sordid aspects of city life which obsessed Eliot, the admirer of Baudelaire and the French Symbolists, when any sustained nobility of tone had become impossible. The spiritual condition of Tennyson's Ulysses is a more personal desolation, but he still feels that:

Some work of noble note, may yet be done,
Not unbecoming men that strove with Gods. . . .
               Come, my friends,
'Tis not too late to seek a newer world.
Push off, and sitting well in order smite
The sounding furrows; for my purpose holds
To sail beyond the sunset, and the baths
Of all the western stars, until I die.
It may be that the gulfs will wash us down:

[33]

It may be we shall touch the Happy Isles,
And see the great Achilles, whom we knew.
Though much is taken, much abides; and though
We are not now that strength which in old days
Moved earth and heaven; that which we are, we are;
One equal temper of heroic hearts,
Made weak by time and fate, but strong in will
To strive, to seek, to find, and not to yield.

Such was the spirit of the great Victorian poet, hardly the 'poet of the nursery'.

World-weariness is far more pronounced in 'The Lotos-Eaters', though this is perhaps the most beautiful poem Tennyson ever wrote. Eliot was right to call him 'a Virgil among the Shades, the saddest of all English poets' and 'the most instinctive rebel against the society in which he was the most perfect conformist'.[4] Yet Ulysses remains, as Goldwin Smith remarked in 1855, 'a hungry heart', roaming aimlessly to lands beyond the sunset, in the vain hope of seeing 'that great Achilles, whom we knew' – in other words, Arthur Hallam.

When Old George died in July 1835, Elizabeth Tennyson refused to attend his funeral, which caused further resentment at Bayons. Doubtless, she did not relish seeing her brother-in-law as the new squire. Under the will Alfred got a small property at Grasby, worth about £200 a year. An estate at Scarthoe, worth £15,000 to £20,000, was to be sold for the benefit of the seven younger brothers and sisters. The Grimsby property went to Frederick, charged with an annuity of £200 a year to his mother; £3,000 was left in trust for Edward. The old man had not done too badly by his elder son's family. The remainder of his father's estates were left to Charles, who now took the name of Tennyson d'Eyncourt and commenced to rebuild Bayons as a great neo-Gothic castle. 'Everywhere were to be seen badges and coats of arms of the d'Eyncourts, Lovels, Beaumonts, Marmions, Grays, Plantagenets, Lancasters, Bardolphs and others from whom Charles claimed descent,' writes Sir Charles Tennyson. 'Cottages were pulled down and roads sunk and diverted, to form a fine rolling park, which was populated with deer and horned sheep. A moat was made along the western front and the lake below stocked with curious aquatic birds. Stained glass, tapestry, armour and old pictures were purchased for the interior, and a special wallpaper for the state rooms was copied from one in the palace at Blois. Several portraits were commissioned of Edward III and other royal personages who figured in the new pedigree. As for the general plan, Charles had endeavoured to give the impression of an ancient manor house which had gradually evolved out of a feudal castle.'[5]

*Folie de grandeur*? Yes, but the effect must have been extremely fine and did credit to Charles's imagination and taste, however irritating it may have been to the Somersby Tennysons and the neighbours, one of whom, calling at Bayons, was told by the butler, so the story goes: 'The Right Honourable Gentleman is walking on the barbican.' Another story was soon in circulation, that Charles had called at a hotel at Harrogate for dinner and put his card at the head of the table, the place he claimed as a Privy Councillor. The story was repeated in *The Times* and the *Observer* and caused Charles much well-deserved embarrassment. His self-aggrandisement also seems to have affected his political career: preferment did not come and Charles's hopes gradually faded away. But he kept his seat in Parliament, which left him little leisure to live in the baronial style he had prepared for himself. Alfred's attitude appears in *Maud*, where he wrote contemptuously of his uncle's 'gewgaw castle':

New as his title, built last year,
There amid perky larches and pines
And over the sullen-purple moor
(Look at it) pricking a cockney ear.

But *Maud*, as R. W. Rader was the first to point out, was largely inspired by Tennyson's infatuation with Rosa Baring.[6] As can be seen from Laurence's portrait of him of about 1840 without his beard and moustache, he was strikingly handsome. Unfortunately his good looks did not compensate, in the eyes of the local gentry, for his lack of money, though he seems to have had enough to devote himself entirely to poetry. Rosa's grandfather had been Chairman of the East India Company and had died worth two million; her father, William Baring, had leased Lulworth Castle in Dorset, but was drowned while out boating. His widow then married in 1824 Arthur Eden, grandson of Sir Robert Eden, Comptroller of the Exchequer. The family lived at Harrington Hall, two miles from Somersby. Rosa was five years younger than Tennyson and in 1838 she married Robert Shafto. Her portrait now hangs at the Shafto home at Litworth Park, Durham. Tennyson seems to have fallen in love with Rosa in 1833, and next year wrote a birthday poem to her dated 23 September 1834. On 3 November there was a farewell party at Somersby for Rosa, who was leaving for London with her family. The Rev. John Rashdall's diary of 1833–5 recalls the event: 'Somersby till 4; with Barings &c; took leave of them. Rosa the prettiest and most elegant girl I ever was intimate with.' Rashdall, an old Cambridge friend of Tennyson's, was from 1833–4 curate of Orby, a hamlet ten miles from Somersby.

[35]

Tennyson was also much attracted by his other neighbour, Sophy Rawnsley, but the poems he wrote to her were light-hearted and suggest that his attachment was no more than mild and flirtatious. His feelings for Rosa, however, certainly went deeper, since her family's refusal of him in favour of a richer man left him with a permanent sense of grievance, which comes out in several of his longer poems: in *Locksley Hall, Edwin Morris, Aylmer's Field*, with its rage against 'filthy marriage-hindering Mammon', and most powerfully in *Maud*, where he writes, 'And the soul of the rose went into my blood'. These poems, as Rader points out, involve 'the love of a high-strung, idealistic young man, brooding and inclined to morbidity, for a young woman of wealth and position, and the frustration of that love, through the snobbish opposition of the girl's family.'

In *Edwin Morris* (1839), the lovers are discovered together embracing, on the terrace:

> She moved
> Like Proserpine in Enna, gathering flowers:
> Then low and sweet I whistled thrice; and she,
> She turned, we closed, we kissed, swore faith, I breathed
> In some new planet: a silent cousin stole
> Upon us and departed: 'Leave,' she cried,
> 'O leave me!' 'Never, dearest, never: here
> I brave the worst:' and while we stood like fools
> Embracing, all at once a score of pugs
> And poodles yelled within, and out they came,
> Trustees and Aunts and Uncles: 'What! with him!
> Go' (shrilled the cotton-spinning chorus); 'him!'
> I choked. Again they shriek'd the burthen – 'Him!'
> Again with hands of wild rejection 'Go! –
> Girl, get you in!' She went – and in one month
> They wedded her to sixty-thousand pounds,
> To lands in Kent and messuages in York,
> And slight Sir Robert with his watery smile
> And educated whisker.

A similar scene occurs in *Maud*. Are we to suppose that such scenes, with their sense of personal grievance, have no autobiographical basis? Tennyson said they had no such basis, but the same situation occurs too often in his poems for us to believe that.

Two sonnets to Rosa Baring record a lovers' quarrel at a ball, perhaps the ball mentioned by Rashdall on 3 November 1834. They have a deeper note than the poems to Sophy.

Sole rose of beauty, loveliness complete,
If those words were bitter or unjust,
Yet is thy gentle nature so discreet
That they will pass thee like an idle gust.
Henceforward, fancy shall not force distrust,
But all my blood in time to thine shall beat,
Henceforth I lay my pride within the dust
And my whole heart is vassal at thy feet.
Blow, summer rose, thy beauty makes me shamed
That I could blame thee! Heaven's dewdrop pure
Bathe, with my tears, thy maiden blossom sweet:
Blow, summer rose, nor fall; and, oh, be sure
That if I had not lov'd, I had not blamed;
For my whole heart is vassal at thy feet.

The second sonnet is more ardent and recalls Mercutio's invocation of Romeo by the beauties of Rosaline, without its bawdy touches, of course.

By all my grief for that which I did say,
By all the life of love that never dies,
By all that Paradise for which we pray
And all the Paradise that round thee lies,
By thoughts of thee that like the Heavens rise,
Star after star, within me, day by day,
And night by night, in musing on thine eyes
Which look me through when thou art far away,
By that madonna grace of parted hair
And dewy sister eyelids drooping chaste,
By each dear foot, so light on field, or floor,
By thy full form and slender moulded waist,
And that all perfect smile of thine, I swear
That these rash lips shall blame thee, Rose, no more.

Neverthless, he was to blame her, and bitterly. He seems to have grown disillusioned about her some time in 1835 and, finally, in 1836 he wrote the 'Three Sonnets to a Coquette':

The form, the form alone is eloquent!
A nobler yearning never broke her rest
Than but to dance and sing, be gaily drest,
And win all eyes with all accomplishment:
Yet in the whirling dances as we went,
My fancy made me for a moment blest
To find my heart so near the beauteous breast
That once had power to rob it of content.

[37]

A moment came the tenderness of tears,
The phantom of a wish that once could move,
A ghost of passion that no smiles restore –
For ah! the slight coquette, she cannot love,
And if you kissed her feet a thousand years,
She still would take the praise, and care no more.

Another sonnet, 'How thought you that this thing could captivate?'
concludes:

A hand displayed with many a little art;
    An eye that glances on her neighbour's dress;
        A foot too often shown for my regard;
An angel's form – a waiting-woman's heart;
    A perfect-featured face, expressionless,
        Insipid, as the Queen upon a card.

A sonnet written to Sophy Rawnsley, after a quarrel at a Spilsby
ball in 1836, is quite different in tone from the poems to Rosa Baring,
and bespeaks a constant affection rather than sexual involvement:

To thee, with whom my best affections dwell,
That I was harsh to thee, let no one know;
It were, O Heaven, a stranger tale to tell
Than if the vine had borne the bitter sloe:
Though I was harsh, my nature is not so:
A momentary cloud upon me fell:
My coldness was mistimed like summer-snow;
Cold words I spoke, yet loved thee warm and well.
Was I so harsh? Ah, dear, it could not be.
Seemed I so cold? What madness moved my blood
To make me thus belie my constant heart
That watch't with love thine earliest infancy,
Slow-ripening to the grace of womanhood,
Through every change that made thee what thou art.

*Locksley Hall*, written 1837–8, is altogether a more important
poem and seems to have had its origin in Tennyson's disillusionment
with Rosa Baring and was 'probably influenced by the talk in 1837
of her engagement and her marriage in October 1838.'[7] Rader points
out, too, that Rosa's was an arranged marriage.

Falser than all fancy fathoms, falser than all songs have sung,
Puppet to a father's threat, and servile to a shrewish tongue!

Is it well to wish thee happy? – having known me – to decline
On a range of lower feelings and a narrower heart than mine!

[38]

Yet it shall be: thou shalt lower to his level day by day,
What is fine within thee growing coarse to sympathise with clay.

As the husband is, the wife is: thou art mated with a clown,
And the grossness of his nature will have weight to drag thee down.

He will hold thee, when his passion shall have spent its novel force,
Something better than his dog, a little dearer than his horse. . . .

Better thou and I were lying, hidden from the heart's disgrace,
Rolled in one another's arms, and silent in a last embrace.

Cursèd be the social wants that sin against the strength of youth!
Cursèd be the social lies that warp us from the living truth!

Cursèd be the sickly forms that err from honest Nature's rule!
Cursèd be the gold that gilds the straitened forehead of the fool! . . .

Am I mad, that I should cherish that which bears but bitter fruit?
I will pluck it from my bosom, though my heart be at the root. . . .

Comfort? comfort scorned of devils! this is truth the poet sings,
That a sorrow's crown of sorrow is remembering happier things.

Drug thy memories, lest thou learn it, lest thy heart be put to
    proof,
In the dead unhappy night, and when the rain is on the roof.

Though *Locksley Hall* was not written until the family had left
Somersby and Tennyson was living at High Beech, Epping, and when
he had already met and fallen in love with his future wife, Emily
Sellwood, its strident bitterness is evidence of the hold that the
memory of Rosa still had upon him and how deep his passion for her
had been, for it is probable that she was as much attracted by
Tennyson as he was to her and that she had betrayed her nature, as
he said, by marrying for wealth. Hence his bitterness, even though a
very different kind of love had already dawned for him. That
Locksley Hall is Harrington Hall, Rosa's home, is clear from the
opening lines of the poem.

'Tis the place, and all around it, as of old, the curlews call,
Dreary gleams about the moorland flying over Locksley Hall;

Locksley Hall, that in the distance overlooks the sandy tracts,
And the hollow ocean-ridges roaring into cataracts. . . .

Here about the beach I wandered, nourishing a youth sublime
With the fairy tales of science, and the long result of Time.

*Locksley Hall* contains much else besides Tennyson's youthful love affair. In it he turns hopefully to the world of action, to 'the fairy tales of science', to visions of the future with

> . . . the nations' airy navies grappling in the central blue;

> Far along the world-wide whisper of the south-wind rushing warm,
> With the standards of the peoples plunging through the thunder-
> storm;

> Till the war-drum throbbed no longer, and the battle-flags were
> furled
> In the Parliament of man, the Federation of the world.

> There the common sense of most shall hold a fretful realm in awe,
> And the kindly earth shall slumber, lapt in universal law.

> So I triumphed ere my passion sweeping through me left me dry,
> Left me with the palsied heart, and left me with the jaundiced
> eye. . . .

> Yet I doubt not through the ages one increasing purpose runs,
> And the thoughts of men are widened with the process of the suns.

> What is that to him that reaps not harvest of his youthful joys,
> Though the deep heart of existence beat for ever like a boy's? . . .

> Hark, my merry comrades call me, sounding on the bugle-horn,
> They to whom my foolish passion were a target for their scorn:

> Shall it not be scorn to me to harp on such a mouldered string?
> I am shamed through all my nature to have loved so slight a thing.

It is clear that much of the anger and bitterness of the poem derives from the image of 'him that reaps not harvest of his youthful joys' – in love.

*Locksley Hall*, as Christopher Ricks remarks, 'was Tennyson's first attempt to face as a poet some of the most painful of his experiences. It was also the first of his poems to manifest a stridency.'[8] It was also his first attempt to disentangle himself from these experiences by taking a wider view of history. But, as always when he turns from the lyrical elegaic tone which was natural to him, he becomes strident. The supreme example of this is that astonishing outburst of his old age, *Locksley Hall Sixty Years After*, in which the anger and bitterness of the first *Locksley Hall* are only intensified, an indication that the rancour arising from the frustration of this first love still lay working deep within him. Tennyson always maintained that Locksley Hall was 'an imaginary place' with 'an imaginary hero'. But in his dedication of the *Idylls of the King* to the

Prince Consort – that is, after his marriage to the angelic Emily Sellwood – he praised in the Prince 'the sublime repression of himself' and 'the white flower of a blameless life'. It is the effects of this very 'repression of himself' that one can see in the masterly drawing of the later Tennyson in 1884 by Frederick Sandys. In this context, T. S. Eliot, in his profoundly illuminating essay 'In Memoriam', already referred to, writes of 'emotion so deeply suppressed, even from himself, as to tend rather towards the blackest melancholia. . . . And it is emotion which, so far as my reading of the poems can discover, attained no ultimate clear purgation'[9]—as borne out by such a poem as 'Lucretius' (1868), with its all too evident terror of self-surrender to sex.

In May 1836 Alfred's brother Charles married Louisa Sellwood of Horncastle, whose bridesmaid was her sister Emily. Alfred, as Charles's best man, took Emily to the church, and fell in love with her as they stood together at the altar rails behind the bridal pair. Afterwards he wrote a sonnet on the occasion:

O Bridesmaid, ere the happy knot was tied,
Thine eyes so wept that they could hardly see;
Thy sister smiled and said, 'No tears for me!
A happy bridesmaid makes a happy bride.'
And then, the couple standing side by side,
Love lighted down between them full of glee,
And over his left shoulder laughed at thee,
'O happy bridesmaid, make a happy bride.'
And all at once a pleasant truth I learned,
For while the tender service made thee weep,
I loved thee for the tear thou couldst not hide,
And prest thy hand, and knew the press returned,
And thought, 'My life is sick of single sleep:
O happy bridesmaid, make a happy bride!'

Tennyson was 'sick of single sleep' and his avowal took the form of a discreet pressure of Emily's hand. But by her return of the pressure an understanding was established between them, though she had to wait fourteen years before the avowal led to marriage.

At that time Tennyson was twenty-seven, Emily twenty-three. It was by no means his first meeting with her, for the Tennyson and Sellwood families had been acquainted for some years. In fact, Emily wrote in her *Narrative for Her Sons* that the Tennysons were among her family's closest friends and that 'Dear Aunt Cecilia and Aunt Matilda often came to my father's house and we lent each other books, and the brothers also came to us sometimes. . . . The first time I was at Somersby as far as I remember, except for a

morning visit, was one night and day in 1830 when Arthur Hallam
was there. They were all fond of games such as capping verses. That
night we played "The Emperor of Morocco is Dead" and Arthur
Hallam was pleased with me because I went through the trying
story between my two big candles with so much gravity. Next
morning we some of us went to Hollywell [the wood behind
Somersby]. Arthur Hallam was walking with me when your father
made his appearance in a cloak, and sportively said, "Are you a
Dryad or a Naiad or what are you?" '

From the first, adds Emily, Tennyson had seemed to her a mysterious creature somehow lifted above other mortals, and she appeared
to him as a frail, evanescent, sylph-like thing. Emily had been
brought up 'strictly' by her Aunt Betsy, who, she says, would 'beat
stripes in her hand with a riding whip, for unfinished sewing prick
their fingers with a needle, for lessons undone stand them in a corner
with dunce caps on.' But her father was her 'idol' and after his
death she wrote that 'he deserved, if ever Father deserved it, to be
held in unapproachable sacredness by his children.'[10] When Emily
married Tennyson, she seems to have transferred to him the worship
she had earlier given to her father. Though Emily lacked the sensual
allure of Rosa Baring, she had qualities of mind and heart which
Tennyson valued far more. For him, as for most Victorians, there
was always something dangerous in physical attraction, as though
the highest type of woman was expected to be without it. It was only
a 'low' woman who aroused his more 'primitive' instincts. Hence the
proliferation of prostitutes and accommodation houses in Victorian
London. As Tennyson was to write in *In Memoriam*, CXVIII:

> Arise and fly
> The reeling Faun, the sensual feast;
> Move upward, working out the beast,
> And let the ape and tiger die.[11]

though, as he remarked to Mrs Bradley: 'God gives us Poets a good
share of the animal with better gifts and we have much to answer
for.' Indeed, the healthy animal side of his nature filled him with
shame and guilt. As Pallas proclaims in 'Œnone':

> Self-reverence, self-knowledge, self-control,
> These three alone lead life to sovereign power.

and he exalted

> passion pure in snowy bloom
> Through all the years of April blood.

The fact that Tennyson could break off his engagement to Emily

Sellwood in 1840 and neither see nor write to her for another ten years, does not, on the face of it, argue any great ardour. But there is no doubt that he did love her deeply. His main reason for breaking off their engagement was lack of money and the fact that he would not do anything except write poetry. This was our gain, but his loss. 'I only write what I feel,' he said, 'and will never write anything else.' Nor was he ready to publish again. Also he felt that Emily's family disapproved of him and that this caused her pain. He came to idealise her to such an extent that he convinced himself that he was unworthy of her. 'During my ten years' separation from your father,' Emily wrote to her sons, 'the doctor thought I was going into a consumption and the Lincolnshire climate was pronounced to be too cold for me; and we moved to London, to look for a home in the south of England.' Her father had forbidden her either to write to Tennyson or to receive letters from him; it says much for the subjection of Victorian women that she obeyed. Such a state of affairs seems quite monstrous today. All she admitted was that the ten years' parting 'may have been a mistake'. But 'Love and Duty', written in 1840, is full of the anguish of their parting:

Of love that never found its earthly close,
What sequel? Streaming eyes and breaking hearts?
Or all the same as if he had not been? . . .

       For how hard it seemed to me,
When eyes, love-languid through half tears would dwell
One earnest, earnest moment upon mine,
Then not to dare to see! when thy low voice,
Faltering, would break its syllables, to keep
My own full-tuned, – hold passion in a leash,
And not leap forth and fall about thy neck,
And on thy bosom (deep desired relief!)
Rain out the heavy mist of tears, that weighed
Upon my brain, my senses and my soul! . . .

Could Love part thus? was it not well to speak,
To have spoken once? It could not but be well.
The slow sweet hours that bring us all things good,
The slow sad hours that bring us all things ill,
And all good things from evil, brought the night
In which we sat together and alone,
And to the want, that hollowed all the heart,
Gave utterance by the yearning of an eye,
That burned upon its object through such tears
As flow but once a life.

[43]

> The trance gave way
> To those caresses, when a hundred times
> In that last kiss, which never was the last,
> Farewell, like endless welcome, lived and died . . . .
>
> Oh then like those, who clench their nerves to rush
> Upon their dissolution, we two rose,
> There – closing like an individual life –
> In one blind cry of passion and of pain,
> Like bitter accusation even to death,
> Caught up the whole of love and uttered it,
> And bade adieu for ever.

For ever? On one occasion during these weary years, Tennyson and Emily met by accident at the Lushingtons' Park House, near Maidstone. Emily left at once and Tennyson does not seem to have done anything to stop her. His mother offered to give him enough money to marry on, but they would not accept it, feeling that it would be unfair to those members of the family who were still unmarried. They met once more at Park House during these years, and Edmund Lushington, who had married Tennyson's sister Cecilia, offered to sell his carriage horses and give them the proceeds. But they would not accept that either. So the dreary separation continued.

# 4

The family finally left Somersby in melancholy mood in May 1837. They went to live at Beech Hill House, High Beech, Epping. Alfred took his farewell of the Rectory in some of the loveliest stanzas of *In Memoriam* (CI):

Unwatched, the garden bough shall sway,
  The tender blossom flutter down,
  Unloved, that beech will gather brown,
This maple burn itself away;

Unloved, the sun-flower, shining fair,
  Ray round with flames her disk of seed,
  And many a rose-carnation feed
With summer spice the humming air.

The move was organised by Alfred, who could be surprisingly practical on occasion. He also furnished the new house completely.

The night before they left Somersby he had a dream, recorded in section CIII of *In Memoriam*. He seems to be living in a hall, 'and maidens with me', singing 'of what is wise and good and graceful'. In the centre of the hall stands a statue to which they sing and which, though veiled, is known to him:

The shape of him I loved, and love
For ever.

A dove brings in 'a summons from the sea'. The maidens weep and wail when they realise he must go, and lead him down to a little boat moored at the side of the river below. They all get into the boat and as they glide down the river, the maidens become ever more splendid, while he himself grows in stature, too, as the maidens continue to sing 'Of that great race which is to be'. As they draw out to sea, they approach the shining sides of a great ship:

The man we loved was there on deck,
  But thrice as large as man he bent

c                                    [45]

To greet us. Up the side I went,
And fell in silence on his neck;

Whereat those maidens with one mind
  Bewailed their lot; I did them wrong:
  'We served thee here,' they said, 'so long,
And wilt thou leave us now behind?'

So rapt I was, they could not win
  An answer from my lips, but he
  Replying, 'Enter likewise ye
And go with us:' they entered in.

And while the wind began to sweep
  A music out of sheet and shroud,
  We steered her toward a crimson cloud
That landlike slept along the deep.

Tennyson said that the maidens were 'the Muses, poetry, the arts –
all that made life beautiful here, and which we hope will pass with us
beyond the grave.' He did not go on to explain, though it hardly
needs pointing out, that the veiled statue and the god-like form on
the ship were both Arthur Hallam, Hallam as Tennyson made him
in his poetry and Hallam as he longed to reunite with him after
death. It is also natural that the maidens should weep, seeing that
he was prepared to leave them for his beloved friend. As in most
dreams, the symbolism is clear enough, when once one knows the
emotional pattern which gives rise to it.

The same motif lies behind the anguished lines Tennyson had
written soon after Hallam's death, which became the germ of *Maud*:

Oh! that 'twere possible,
  After long grief and pain,
To find the arms of my true love
  Round me once again. . . .

Always I long to creep
  To some still cavern deep,
And to weep, and weep and weep
  My whole soul out to thee.

The house at High Beech was considerably more spacious than the
cramped quarters of the Rectory. It stood in a small park, and there
was a lake on which Alfred used to skate in winter, his blue cloak
blowing out behind him. Epping Forest was almost at the door, and
he would lead his mother in the little carriage drawn by a Shetland
pony through the glades and quiet lanes. But, Sir Charles Tennyson

[46]

tells us, Alfred 'never had much to say in favour of his new abode', finding the local society 'artificial, frozen, cold and lifeless'. However, its nearness to London meant that he could see more of his friends, and during the next three years he was to see much of FitzGerald, Spedding, Thackeray, Monckton Milnes, Gladstone and Rogers. He was now altogether in better spirits, though he complained of nervousness. 'How should he do otherwise,' commented Spedding, 'seeing that he smokes the strongest and most stinking tobacco out of a small blackened clay-pipe on an average nine hours every day?' He would sit up till two or three in the morning, reading out his new poems to his particular friends: 'very droll, very wayward,' said Fitz. 'A growler, but a man of genius,' said Thackeray. At other times, he would sit smoking by the fire while Thackeray worked, sometimes growling out a line of poetry, as it came into his mind, or some grim, comical story. He actually came to like London, the central roar of the Strand and Fleet Street, St Paul's, the Abbey, and particularly the Thames bridges. But he was sometimes filled with horror by the thought that all these seething human crowds would one day be lying horizontal stark and stiff in their coffins. As T. S. Eliot was to write after him:

A crowd flowed over London Bridge, so many,
I had not thought death had undone so many.

But for the most part, the crowds excited him and he enjoyed dining with friends at some old city tavern on his chop or steak, calling to the 'fat head waiter at the Cock, Go fetch a pint of port', and then lighting his clay pipe and disappearing into clouds of shag tobacco. He had rooms in Mornington Place, Camden Town. At High Beech they kept three maids and a footman, which does not sound like poverty. Nor does the house standing in its own park. In 1855 Alfred bought for his mother a charming house in Flask Walk, Hampstead, on the corner of New End Square, where she lived with Matilda, and his married sister Emily Jesse had the larger adjoining house, Rosemount, No. 75.

At Sterling's club, Tennyson met Carlyle, Forster, Landor and Macready. With Carlyle he became very friendly, the two men sharing an identity of outlook upon the basic things of life, both distrusting the new scientific outlook and basing themselves upon intuition and emotion, which Carlyle called 'the heat of inward evidence'. Nevertheless, he saw Tennyson as 'a life-guardsman spoilt by making poetry' and advised him to put his thoughts into prose. But he admired him enormously and has left the best descriptions of him we have. 'A fine, large-featured, dim-eyed, bronze-coloured, shaggy man is Alfred,' he wrote to his brother in September 1840, 'dusty, smoky, free and easy: who swims outwardly and inwardly with great composure in an articulate element as of tranquil chaos and tobacco smoke; great now and then when he does emerge; a most restful, brotherly, solid-hearted man.' And again, this time to Emerson: 'One of the finest-looking men in the world. A great shock of rough, dusty dark hair; bright, laughing, hazel eyes; massive aquiline face, most massive, yet most delicate; of sallow brown complexion, almost Indian looking, clothes cynically loose, free and easy, smokes infinite tobacco. His voice musical, metallic, fit for all laughter and piercing wail, and all that lie between: speech and speculation free and plenteous: I do not meet in these late decades such company over a pipe!'

Jane Welsh Carlyle describes an evening spent with Tennyson at Cheyne Row, Chelsea, in 1839.

I . . . had made up my mind for a nice long quiet evening of looking into the fire, when I heard a carriage drive up, and men's voices asking questions, and then the carriage was sent away! and the men proved to be Alfred Tennyson of all people and his friend Mr. Moxon. Alfred lives in the country and only comes to London rarely and for a few days so that I was overwhelmed with the sense of Carlyle's misfortune in having missed the man he likes best. . . . Alfred is dreadfully embarrassed with women alone – for he entertains at one and the same moment a feeling of almost adoration of them and an ineffable contempt! adoration I suppose for what they *might* be contempt for what they *are*! The only chance of my getting any right good of him was to make him forget my womanness – so I did just as Carlyle would have done, had he been there: got out *pipes* and *tobacco* and *brandy and water* – with a deluge of *tea* over and above. – The effect of these accessories was miraculous – he professed to be ashamed of polluting my room, 'felt,' he said, 'as if he were stealing cups and sacred vessels in the Temple' – but he smoked on all the same – for three mortal hours! – talking like an angel – only exactly as if he were talking with a clever man – which – being a thing I am not used to – men always adapting their conversation to what they take to be a woman's taste – strained me to a terrible pitch of intellectuality.

We can hardly doubt that, on his side, Tennyson was equally charmed by his enchanting hostess, shy of her as he doubtless was, unused to encountering such wit and fineness of response in a young woman, unless it were Emily Sellwood, whom he now seldom saw.

[48]

But even so, Emily's letters cannot be compared with Jane's, being far too effusively pious.

Sir Charles Tennyson has pointed out that 'the last date in the time sequence of *In Memoriam* is April 1838 – the April following the move from Somersby. The reference occurs in the two beautiful spring sections (CXV and CXVI) which open what Tennyson himself defined as the closing division of the poem, and lead straight to the serenely triumphant conclusion. . . . The mood in which the poem closes is strong evidence that he regarded it as having brought to an end the long period of depression following Arthur's death, and given him new hope and new purpose in life. I think that a good part of this last sequence of *In Memoriam* was probably written during the next two years.'[1] As Tennyson said: 'The poem begins with a funeral and ends with a marriage.' His letters to Emily Sellwood during these years 1838–40 were mostly destroyed by Hallam Tennyson at his father's request. But the fragments which he and Sir Charles Tennyson have printed give a good idea of Tennyson's state of mind at this time:

I murmured (like a hen in the sunshine) lines and half lines of some poem to thee, I know not what: but I could not think of thee, thou white dove, brooding in thy lonely chamber, without movements of the truest affection toward thee and an admiration of thee which no years can render less. God bless thee, sweetest, and God will bless thee for thou seemest to me such as pure eyes delight to dwell on. . . .
Thou didst make thyself wings of love and of faith and hast flown over the interval betwixt thee and me and hast settled in my bosom but how thou should'st have found thyself there, without wings, I know not.

Again, in December 1839:

I need thy assurances to make up the deficiencies in my own strength: thence most likely comes my preaching. If thy love for me is a strengthening influence to thyself, so shall mine for thee be to myself – if thy love makes thee discomforted, I pine in discomfort, and if thou dost, oh wherefore should I live? How should this dependence on thy state coexist with my flying from thee? ask not. Believe that it does. 'Tis true, I fly thee for my good, perhaps for thine, at any rate for thine if mine is thine. If thou knewest why I fly thee there is nothing thou wouldst more wish for than that I should fly thee. Sayest thou 'are we to meet no more?' I answer I know not the word

[49]

nor will know it. I neither know it nor believe it – the
immortality of man disdains and rejects it – the immortality
of man to which the cycles and the Aeons are as hours and as
days. Annihilate within yourself these two dreams of Space and
Time. To me often the far-off world seems nearer than the
present, for in the present is always something unreal and
indistinct, but the other seems a good solid planet, rolling
round its green hills and paradises to the harmony of more
steadfast laws. There steam up from about me mists of weakness,
or sin, or despondency, and roll between me and the far planet,
but it is still there.

If this meant that he and Emily would only meet at some future
time on some far planet, this letter must have been cold comfort to
her who wanted him in the here and now. But in September 1840 Mr
Sellwood forbade all further communication between Tennyson and
his daughter, so their engagement was thereupon broken off. By 1839
Charles's marriage to Louisa Sellwood had foundered, owing to his
addiction to opium, and it is understandable that Mr Sellwood should
have felt uneasy at the prospect of another of his daughters married
to a Tennyson. In his eyes, Alfred must have appeared a bohemian
of no settled occupation; and in the face of his opposition and Emily's
subservience to him there was little Alfred could do. But that he
should submit, loving her as he did, to neither seeing nor writing to
her for ten years is almost incredible. The result was that both he and
Emily became ill. In 1840 FitzGerald described Alfred as 'really ill
in a nervous way, what with hereditary tenderness of nerve and
having spoiled what strength he had by excessive smoking, &c . . .
poor fellow, he is quite magnanimous and noble natured, with no
meanness or vanity or affectation whatever, but very perverse
according to the nature of his illness.'

The Tennysons moved this year from High Beech to Tunbridge
Wells, for the sake of Elizabeth Tennyson's health; but Alfred did
not like this town of well-to-do invalids, and he became increasingly
restless and despondent. From Tunbridge Wells, however, he visited
the Lushingtons at Park House. He had not seen Edmund Lushington since Cambridge and their renewed acquaintance now developed
into a close friendship. Next year the family moved to Boxley, a
village two miles from Park House, where Alfred renewed his friendship with Harry and Franklin Lushington. There also he met Edward
Lear, who became a faithful friend and admirer. In October 1842
Edmund Lushington married Cecilia Tennyson, which brought the
two families closer together than ever.

While at High Beech, Tennyson had become involved with a Dr

Matthew Allen; he was much impressed by his sound and progressive theories on the treatment of mental illness. At Fairmead, near Epping Allen was at that time treating the poet John Clare, for whom he had tried to raise a small fund. It was his kindness to Clare which largely disposed Tennyson in his favour, and after his visit to Fairmead he is reported as saying that Allen's patients were 'the most agreeable and the most reasonable persons he had met with'. He may even have talked to Clare, who did not leave Fairmead until July 1841.

Gradually, Allen came to have a considerable influence over the Tennyson family; and he persuaded Alfred to sink his entire capital of £3,000 in a scheme for carving wood by machinery, which he said would bring 'artistic' furniture within the range of the masses. To further this, on the face of it, appalling scheme, Alfred sold his lands at Grasby, left to him by his grandfather, and added to this a legacy of £500. He also persuaded Edmund Lushington to contribute to the scheme. Carlyle described Allen as 'a speculative, hopeful, earnest-frothy man'; subsequent events proved this estimate only too true, however sound Allen may have been in his medical practice, for his wood-carving scheme failed and Alfred lost his money. He was only just in time to prevent his mother from investing her entire capital in Allen's 'Pyroglyphs', and he forced Allen to release her from the bond which she had already signed by threatening to expose him. Not that Allen was initially dishonest; he believed implicity in his project. It was his agent who turned out to be a rogue and made off with nearly all the funds. Allen then seems to have lost his head and continued to induce still more people to invest in his already bankrupt company. He now turned to Frederick, the most well-to-do member of the Tennyson family, writing to him in November 1841: 'Yesterday it was the decided opinion of the Bankers and Solicitors that in 12 months your share will be worth £10,000 and that in another five years it ought to give you that yearly.' But Frederick found some difficulty in raising money on his property at Grimsby and so was not caught.

The loss was particularly hard for Alfred, since a successful speculation would have gone far towards removing Mr Sellwood's main objection to him as a shiftless bohemian poet. Fortunately, however, Edmund Lushington had insured Dr Allen's life in Alfred's favour; so when he died a broken man in June 1845, Alfred recovered most of his capital.

An insistent demand for the publication of his poems now came not only from his English friends, but also from Charles Stearns Wheeler, tutor in Greek at Harvard and the friend of Emerson and Lowell, who was anxious to edit them for Little & Brown, threatening, as Tennyson wrote that if 'I will not publish in England, they will do it for me in the land of free men.' Early in 1841 he wrote to FitzGerald: 'You bore me about my book, so does a letter just received from America. *Damn*! I may curse, knowing what they will bring forth. But I don't care.' His reply to Wheeler of 22 February, however, showed that he did care.

> I am rejoiced that I have made myself friends on the other side of the Atlantic, and feel what a high privilege it is for a writer to be born into a language common to two great peoples: and so believe me not insensible, or if that seem to savour too much of the coldness of mere courtesy, believe me deeply sensible of the honour my American friends have done me even in making a request to which I feel it impossible to accede as they perhaps might wish. I am conscious of many things so exceedingly crude in those two volumes that it would certainly be productive of no slight annoyance to me, to see them republished as they stand at present, either here or in America, but I will tell you what I will do, for when I was wavering before, your letter decided me. I have corrected copies of most that was worth correction in those two volumes and I will in the course of a few months republish them in England with several new poems and transmit copies to Little & Brown and also to yourself (if you will accept one) and you can then of course do as you choose with them.

Tennyson spent the rest of the year revising his poems. By early 1842 he was at Mablethorpe again, getting his poems ready for the printer. On the way back he visited the Rawnsleys at Halton, where he met Catherine Franklin again, after five years. 'He looked very much like the old man of the sea,' she wrote afterwards, 'as if seaweed might cling to him, unkempt and unbrushed and altogether forlorn as to the outer man.' In London again he called on Fitz-Gerald, who carried him off to Moxon to complete arrangements for the publication of his poems. These were written in a large ledger-like volume ('a butcher's book', Fitz called it) the margins of whose pages had been stripped off for pipe lights 'taking care,' he told Fitz, 'not to damage the manuscript!' The pages were now carefully torn from the book and sent to Moxon. But Tennyson was depressed when the proofs began to arrive, and wished he had never agreed to publication. 'Poor Tennyson has got home some of his proof sheets,' wrote FitzGerald, 'and now that his verses are in hard print thinks them detestable. There is much I had always told him of – his great fault of being too full and complicated – which he now sees, or fancies he sees, and wishes he had never been persuaded to print. But with all his faults he will publish such a volume as has not been published since the time of Keats: and which once published will never be suffered to die.' All the same, Fitz objected to a good deal in the Juvenilia. 'It is a pity he did not publish the new volume separately. The other will drag it down. And why reprint the Merman, the Mermaid, and those everlasting Eleanores, Isabels – which always were, and are and must be, a nuisance. . . . Every woman thinks herself the original of one of the stupid Gallery of Beauties.'

But when the two volumes appeared in May 1842, they established Tennyson as the foremost poet of the generation after Keats, Shelley and Byron. 'Don't abuse my book,' he wrote to Fitz. 'You can't hate it worse than I do, but it does me no good to hear it abused; if it is bad you and others are to blame who continually urged me to publish. Not for my sake but for yours did I consent to submit my papers to the herd, damn 'em, and all reproach comes too late. If you had known how much I have gone through since I saw you, you would pardon my ungracious silence in return for so many kind letters.'

Of the two volumes of *Poems*, 1842, the first contained a selection of his earlier poems, drastically revised; the second volume consisted of new work. 'Morte d'Arthur', 'Lancelot and Guinevere' and 'Sir Galahad' were evidence of his early preoccupation with the Arthurian legends. The volumes also contained 'Love and Duty' and the *English Idyls* and *Eclogues*: 'The Gardener's Daughter', 'Audley Court', 'Dora', 'Edward Gray', and *Locksley Hall*. There was also the revised 'Lotus-Eaters', 'Œnone', and 'The Lady of Shalott', 'Ulysses', 'St Simeon Stylites', and 'Break, Break, Break', which he wrote in a Lincolnshire lane at five o'clock in the morning.

Apart from Spedding's review in the *Edinburgh* of April 1843, the critics showed no sense of Tennyson's achievement, and contented themselves with repeating all the old charges of 'Christopher North' and Croker: affectation, obscurity, shallowness, charges which seem inexplicable today. Spedding concluded his article with the remark that 'Powers are displayed in these two volumes adequate to the production of very great work.' The editor of the *Edinburgh*, before publishing the article, struck out the word 'very'. There were, too, the devoted admirers at Cambridge, and Carlyle wrote: 'Truly, it is long since in any English book, poetry or prose, I have felt the pulse of a real man's heart as I do in this same – a right valiant, true, fighting, victorious heart; strong as a lion's, yet gentle, loving and full of music.' FitzGerald always maintained that these two volumes of 1842 contained Tennyson's finest work and that his subsequent poems lacked 'the old champagne flavour' and were evolved by a highly efficient poetical machine. But, as this remark was prompted by *In Memoriam*, which, to say the least, contains much of Tennyson's

c*                            [53]

greatest poetry, one can only say that it exhibits a curiously myopic critical sense.

Wordsworth particularly admired 'Dora'. 'Mr. Tennyson,' he said, 'I have been endeavouring all my life to write a pastoral like your "Dora" and have not succeeded.' But 'Dora' now appears as a sentimental, milk-and-water piece. Unfortunately it is of such poems that many people think when the name of Tennyson is mentioned. They seldom think of 'The Kraken', that primeval monster rising from the nightmare depths of the unconscious, where

> above him swell
> Huge sponges of millennial growth and height:
> And far away into the sickly light,
> From many a wondrous grot and secret cell
> Unnumbered and enormous polypi
> Winnow with giant arms the slumbering green.

Neither do they think of 'Anacaona', which has the rhythm of the rumba:

> A dark Indian maiden,
>     Warbling in the bloomed liana,
> Stepping lightly flower-laden,
>     By the crimson-eyed anana,
> Wantoning in the orange groves
>     Naked, and dark-limbed and gay,
> Bathing in the slumbrous coves,
> In the cocoa-shadowed coves,
>     Of sunbright Xaraguay,
> Who was so happy as Anacaona,
>     The beauty of Espagnola,
>     The golden flower of Hayti? . . .

> Naked, without fear, moving
>     To her Areyto's mellow ditty,
> Waving a palm branch, wondering, loving,
>     Carolling 'Happy, happy Hayti!'
> She gave the white men welcome all,
>     With her damsels by the bay;
> For they were fair-faced and tall,
> They were more fair-faced and tall,
>     Than the men of Xaraguay,
> And they smiled on Anacaona,
>     The beauty of Espagnola,
>     The golden flower of Hayti!

Following her wild carol
　　She led them down the pleasant places,
For they were kingly in apparel,
　　Loftily stepping with fair faces.
But never more upon the shore
　　Dancing at the break of day,
In the deep wood no more, –
By the deep sea no more, –
　　No more in Xaraguay
Wandered happy Anacaona,
　　The beauty of Espagnola,
　　The golden flower of Hayti!

For the fair-faced men were the Spaniards, and they killed Anacaona, enslaved the people of Hayti, put irons upon them and drove them into pens and beat them. 'Anacaona' was written in 1830 and belongs to the Cambridge period. Hallam Tennyson tells us: 'My father liked this poem, but did not publish it because the natural history and the rhymes did not satisfy him.' He returned to the theme of colonisation in 'Columbus' in 1879, basing his poem on Washington Irving's *Life of Columbus* (1828), which he had also used for 'Anacaona'. Columbus was sent back to Spain in chains, which he preserved and hung in his chamber 'as relics and memorials of the reward of my services'. This poem, too, shows an unusual side of Tennyson, the poet of British imperialism and the defender of Governor Eyre of Jamaica.

And seeing what a door for scoundrel scum
I opened to the West, through which the lust,
Villany, violence, avarice, of your Spain
Poured in on all those happy naked isles –
Their kindly native princes slain or slaved,
Their wives and children Spanish concubines,
Their innocent hospitalities quenched in blood,
Some dead of hunger, some beneath the scourge,
Some over-laboured, some by their own hands, –
Yea, the dear mothers, crazing Nature, kill
Their babies at the breast for hate of Spain –
Ah God, the harmless people whom we found
In Hispaniola's island-Paradise!
Who took us for the very Gods from Heaven,
And we have sent them very fiends from Hell;
And I myself, myself not blameless, I
Could sometimes wish I had never led the way.

[55]

Only the ghost of our great Catholic Queen
Smiles on me, saying 'Be thou comforted!
This creedless people will be brought to Christ
And own the holy governance of Rome.'

One wonders how far Tennyson intended to be ironical.

In his *English Idyls*, 'Dora', *Edwin Morris* and 'Audley Court', Tennyson was following the prescription of Wordsworth's Preface to *Lyrical Ballads* by drawing incidents from low, or rather commonplace, life related in the ordinary language of men. It was these poems which first made him popular, until the touching tale of *Enoch Arden* beat all records by its popularity. A more erotic side of his nature finds expression in 'Mariana' and 'Mariana in the South', through the agony of crucified sex, though there must have been many Marianas among unmarried Victorian women. 'She has a lovely face,' murmurs Sir Lancelot, too late, as he looks down at the dead Lady of Shalott, who had been so bold as to leave her loom to look out of her window as he rode past. But it was the reflection in her mirror of the 'two young lovers lately wed' that caused the Lady to cry out in anguish 'I am half-sick of shadows'. Just as in the early poems of Tennyson there is this cry of crucified sex, so in the later poems there is the ever-recurring fear of sex, the fear that comes out most clearly in 'Lucretius', who had spurned Aphrodite for the 'Passionless bride, divine Tranquillity'. But Aphrodite has her revenge upon him in dreams of Dionysian abandon, when his wife puts an aphrodisiac in his drink:

The mountain quickens into Nymph and Faun;
And here an Oread – how the sun delights
To glance and shift about her slippery sides,
And rosy knees and supple roundedness,
And budded bosom-peaks – who this way runs
Before the rest – A satyr, a satyr, see,
Follows; but him I proved impossible;
Twy-natured is no nature: yet he draws
Nearer and nearer, and I scan him now
Beastlier than any phantom of his kind
That ever butted his rough brother-brute
For lust or lusty blood or provender:
I hate, abhor, spit, sicken at him: and she
Loathes him as well; such a precipitate heel,
Fledged as it were with Mercury's ankle-wing,
Whirls her to me: but will she fling herself,
Shameless upon me? Catch her, goat-foot; nay,
Hide, hide them, million myrtled wilderness,

And cavern-shadowing laurels, hide! do I wish –
What?-that the bush were leafless? or to whelm
All of them in one massacre?

The final humiliation is that Lucretius, despite the echo of *Lycidas*, recognises in himself the instincts of a *voyeur*. Having lost tranquillity and self-respect, he kills himself. The editor of *Macmillan's Magazine*, where 'Lucretius' first appeared in May 1868, cut the lines about the Oread, thinking them indecent. Tennyson wrote to him: 'With respect to the Oread please yourself, but send the full passage to America. They are not so squeamish as we are. . . . My wife is copying "Lucretius". . . . *She* says she does not think it will shock people.' But while reading it to her, he chuckled: 'What a mess little Swinburne would have made of it!'

# 5

Jane Carlyle, in a letter to her husband, gives a glimpse of Tennyson in 1843 at some private theatricals organised by Dickens and Forster.

> Passing through a dim passage, I came on a tall man leant against the wall, with his head touching the ceiling like a caryatid, to all appearances asleep, or resolutely trying it under the most unfavourable circumstances. 'Alfred Tennyson!' I exclaimed in joyful surprise. 'Well,' said he, taking the hand I held out to him, and forgetting to let it go again. 'I did not know you were in town.' said I. 'I should like to know who you are,' said he. 'I know that I know you, but I cannot tell your name,' and I had actually to name myself to him. Then he woke up in good earnest, and said he had been meaning to come to Chelsea. 'But Carlyle is in Scotland,' I told him, with due humility. 'So I heard from Spedding already, but I asked Spedding would he go with me to see Mrs. Carlyle, and he said he would.' I told him, if he really meant to come, he had better not wait for backing, under the present circumstance, and then pursued my way to Macready's box.

The next evening Tennyson duly called at Cheyne Row, much to Jane's delight, but 'Craik prosed and John babbled for his entertainment; and I, whom he had come to see, got scarcely any speech with him.'

Tennyson gives the impression at this time of listlessly drifting about London. In fact, the years 1840–5 were in many ways the most wretched in his life. He was separated from Emily; he had lost his money; he felt more nervously ill than ever, and he could not write. Although he reported in September 1842 that his *Poems* had caused a sensation, that does not seem to have raised his spirits. Indeed, so severe was his hypochondria that his friends despaired of his life. 'I have', he wrote, 'drunk one of those most bitter draughts out of the cup of life, which go near to make men hate the world they move in.' His brother Arthur had, like his father, now succumbed to drink and voluntarily placed himself in the Crichton, 'an institution nobly endowed for the insane and others who like to place themselves there in order to conquer an evil propensity', as his mother wrote to her brother-in-law Charles Tennyson d'Eyncourt. He had also run into debt. Horatio had returned from Tasmania, having failed to make a success of his venture there. There had been talk of his going to Demerara to seek his fortune, but he had since abandoned all ideas of a professional career. Septimus was unable to settle to any employment and had gone to Italy with Frederick, where Arthur joined them.

In December 1843, FitzGerald reported of Alfred that he had never seen him so hopeless. 'It is very kind of you to think of such a poor forlorn body as myself,' Alfred wrote to him next year. 'The perpetual panic and horror of the last two years had steeped my nerves in poison: now I am left a beggar but I am or shall be shortly somewhat better off in nerves. I am in an Hydropathy Establishment near Cheltenham (the only one in England conducted on pure Priessnitzan principles). I have had four crisises. . . . Much poison has come out of me. . . . I have been here already upwards of two months: of all the uncomfortable ways of living sure an hydropathical is the worst: no reading by candlelight, no going near a fire, no tea, no coffee, perpetual wet sheet and cold bath and alternation from hot to cold: however I have much faith in it.

'My dear Fitz, my nerves were so bad six weeks ago that I could not have written this and to have to write a letter on that accursed business [Dr Allen's Pyroglyphs] threw me into a kind of convulsion. I went through Hell. . . . I am such a poor devil now I am afraid I very rarely see you. No more trips to London and living in lodgings, hard penury and battle with my lot.' He began to think that perhaps he should leave England altogether and join his brothers at Fiesole, where they could live on eight shillings a day. But he stayed on at Cheltenham with his mother and his sisters. In July he went to Wales and 'walked up Snowdon three times'. Park House became his headquarters in the late summer and autumn, and he went to London several times to visit Carlyle, who, says FitzGerald, 'opened his Valhalla to him and kept a pipe for him in one of the nitches in the garden wall at Cheyne Row'. By January 1845 he had, as we have seen, recovered the greater part of the capital he had sunk in Dr Allen's Pyroglyphs, thanks to Edmund Lushington's foresight, and FitzGerald could report: 'Last night he came in looking much better, but a valetudinarian almost: – not in the effeminate way; but yet in as bad a man's way. Alas, for it, that great thoughts are to be lapped in such weakness.'

Even by July 1845, Tennyson does not seem to have improved very much in spirits. He was once more smoking heavily and drinking his daily bottle of port. When the Irish poet Aubrey de Vere visited him, he seemed much out of spirits and said that he 'could no longer bear to be knocked about the world, and that he must marry and find love and peace or die. He was very angry about a very favourable review of him. Said he could not stand the chattering and conceit of clever men, or the worry of society or the meanness of tuft-hunters, or the trouble of poverty, or the labour of place, or the preying of the heart upon itself. He complained much about growing old, and said he cared nothing for fame, and that his life was thrown away for want of a competence and retirement. Said that no one had been so much harassed by anxiety and trouble as himself.'

Yet Tennyson was still only thirty-six and in the prime of life, and his friends were working for him. 'It has struck me as a distinctly necessary Act of Legislation, that Alfred should have a pension of £150 a year,' Carlyle wrote to Milnes. 'They have £1,200 every year to give away. A hundred and fifty to Alfred, I say; *he* is worth that sum to England! It should be done and must.' Earlier this year, too, Henry Hallam had written to Sir Robert Peel pointing out that Tennyson 'is considered by many as the very first among the younger class of living poets. He is at least a man of a fertile and thoughtful mind, and few would hesitate to ascribe to him the high praise of genius.' Henry Hallam concluded by saying that this opinion of Tennyson was shared by Samuel Rogers, Henry Taylor and Monckton Milnes. Peel, after reading some of Tennyson's poems, said that he had 'formed *a very high estimate of his powers*'. Gladstone then wrote to Peel and, after citing Rogers's high praise, remarked: 'Still it appears established that, though a fine and even a great poet, he can hardly become a popular, and is much more likely to be a starving one.' In September 1845 Peel recommended to the Queen that a pension of £200 a year should be granted to Tennyson for life.

This, however, did not solve his main problem. If the original £3,000 had not been judged enough for him to marry Emily Sellwood on, £200 a year would certainly not satisfy Mr Sellwood. 'Lady Harriet told me,' wrote sprightly Jane Carlyle, 'that he wanted to marry, "must have a woman to live beside – would prefer *a lady*, but cannot afford one; and so must marry a maid-servant." Mrs. Henry Taylor said she was about to write him on behalf of their housemaid, who was quite a superior character in her way.' So Tennyson's predicament had become common gossip in Victorian drawing-rooms and a subject for Jane Carlyle's slightly malicious wit. Even his pension aroused resentment in some quarters, as he feared it would. One of his principal enemies was Edward Bulwer-Lytton, a friend of his Uncle Charles Tennyson d'Eyncourt. Lytton was a supporter of the old actor and playwright James Sheridan Knowles and was very angry that he had been passed over in favour of Tennyson, who was without either a wife or children. He therefore introduced into the second part of his satire *The New Timon* a spiteful attack upon him.

> Not mine, not mine (O Muse forbid!) the boon
> Of borrowed notes, the mock-bird's modish tune,
> The jingling medley of purloin'd conceits,
> Outbabying Wordsworth, and outglittering Keats,
> Where all the airs of patchwork-pastoral chime
> To drowsy ears in Tennysonian rhyme! . . .

> Let school–Miss Alfred vent her chaste delight
> On 'darling little rooms, so warm and bright!'
> Chaunt 'I'm aweary' in infectious strain,
> And catch her 'blue fly singing i' the pane!'
> Tho' praised by Critics, though adored by Blues,
> Tho' Peel with pudding plump the puling Muse,
> Tho' Theban taste the Saxon's purse controls,
> And pensions Tennyson, while it starves a Knowles,
> Rather, be thou, my poor Pierian Maid,
> Decent at least in Hayley's weeds arrayed,
> Than patch with frippery every tinsel line
> And flaunt, admired, the Rag-Fair of the Nine.

And Lytton followed this up by printing the unfortunate little poem 'O Darling Room' in a note.

For his part, Tennyson had always felt contempt for Bulwer-Lytton, whom he had described in 1837 as one 'who, big as he is, sits to all posterity astride upon the nipple of Literary Dandyism and "takes her milk for gall". . . . Moreover, he stated in a note that I belonged to a very rich family. The younger son, his friend, who had inherited was rich enough, but the older branch was shut out in the cold, and at the time I had nothing.' Forthwith he wrote 'The New Timon and the Poets', signed 'Alcibiades', which Forster sent to *Punch* (26 February 1846):

> We knew him, out of Shakespeare's art,
>     And those fine curses which he spoke;
> The old Timon, with his noble heart,
>     That, strongly loathing, greatly broke.

> So died the Old: here comes the New:
>     Regard him: a familiar face:

I *thought* we knew him: What, it's you
 The padded man – that wears the stays –

Who killed the girls and thrilled the boys
 With dandy pathos when you wrote,
A lion, you, that made a noise
 And shook a mane *en papillotes* . . .

*You* talk of tinsel! Why, we see
 The old mask of rouge upon your cheeks.
*You* prate of nature! You are he
 That split his life about the cliques.

A Timon you! Nay, nay, for shame:
 It looks too arrogant a jest –
The fierce old man – to take *his* name,
 You bandbox. Off, and let him rest.

As soon as this appeared, Tennyson regretted it and sent *Punch* some lines which appeared on 7 March as 'Afterthoughts':

Too harsh! I loathe it and retract,
 Yet see, sir, spite of spite is born,
And men turn vermin in the fact
 Of paying aught of scorn with scorn.

Ah God! the petty fools of rhyme
 That shriek and sweat in pigmy wars
Before the stony face of Time,
 And looked at by the silent stars:

Who hate each other for a song,
 And do their little best to bite,
And pinch their breathren in the throng,
 And scratch the very dead for spite:

And strain to make an inch of room
 For their sweet selves, and cannot hear
The sullen Lethe rolling doom
 On them and theirs and all things here. . . .

The public reaction to this literary squabble was entirely in Tennyson's favour and made Lytton look very small and mean. A few years earlier, the reverse would have been the case.

'Alfred looks haggard, dire and languid,' wrote Carlyle in exasperation, 'they *have* got him however to go and *draw* his Pension; that is reckoned a great achievement on the part of his friends! Surely no man has a right to be so lazy in this world; and none that is so lazy will ever make much way in it, I think.' There is no doubt that Tennyson was all too sorry for himself. But for all his complaining and hypochondria, he was at work on his next long poem, *The Princess*.

In August he visited Switzerland with Moxon, but he complains about that, too. Of the mountains he said: 'I couldn't take them in, I suppose, crags I could.' Even the Swiss people aroused his contempt – 'no words can describe their lowness in the scale of men, gain-greedy, goitred, miserable-looking poor devils' – a mingling of contempt and pity, which, as Ricks observes, 'could slide easily into a mingling of self-contempt and self-pity'. At Lucerne they called on Dickens, who had invited Tennyson to share his house with him. On the way home, Tennyson said to his companion: 'Moxon, you have made me very unhappy by something you said to me at Lucerne.' Apparently Moxon had tactlessly remarked: 'Why Tennyson, you will be bald as Spedding before long.' Immediately on his return to England, Tennyson is said to have undergone the treatment of a Mrs Porter, who, Brookfield reports, 'rubs his head and pulls out dead hairs at 10/- an hour. But really, his hair is such an integral part of his appearance it would be a great pity if he should lose it.' Indeed, a bald Tennyson does not suit one's picture of the future leonine Laureate at all.

The pattern of Tennyson's life at this time was still what Darley called 'a kind of genteel vagrancy'. Next year, 1847, he took another water-cure, this time at Dr Gulley's Umbersale Hall, near Birmingham. 'They tell me not to read, not to think: but they might as well tell me not to live,' he complained. The small boys of the village used to follow the patients through the lanes, calling out: 'Shiver and shake! shiver and shake!', and suiting the action to the word, which Tennyson found very hard to bear. Afterwards, he returned to Mablethorpe to put the finishing touches to *The Princess: A Medley*.

This strange poem was published in November without the marvellous lyrics, which were not added until the third edition. FitzGerald thought it 'a wretched waste of power at a time of life when a man ought to be doing his best, and I almost feel hopeless about Alfred now'. Carlyle described it as 'very gorgeous, fervid, luxuriant, but indolent, somnolent, almost imbecile'. Tennyson's intention was to deal with the question of the higher education of women, but at the same time he robs the poem of all contemporary relevance, indeed of seriousness, by giving his University a quasi-fairy tale setting:

Something made to suit with time and place,
A Gothic ruin and a Grecian house,

A talk of college and of ladies' rights,
A feudal knight in silken masquerade.

It is a tale told by different friends to each other during a picnic at the summer fête held by the Mechanics' Institute in the grounds of what is clearly the Lushingtons' Park House. The University is presided over by the formidable Princess Ida and guarded from male intrusion by armed Amazons. However, neither the fortified walls nor 'the eight mighty daughters of the plough' are proof against the promptings of maternal instinct and love when the two young men, disguised as women, invade the University and attend its lectures among the 'sweet girl graduates', where they

> Sat along the forms, like morning doves
> That sun their milky bosoms on the thatch.

Echoing *Love's Labour's Lost*, the whole scheme, based upon chastity and dedication to learning, thereupon collapses.

Among those who tell the tale, the girls 'wished for something real: true heroic, true sublime', but the poet justifiably objects 'Which yet with such a framework scarce could be':

> Then rose a little feud betwixt the two,
> Betwixt the mockers and the realists:
> And I, betwixt them both, to please them both,
> I moved in a strange diagonal,
> And maybe neither pleased myself nor them.

There is evidence, however, that Tennyson was much interested in the subject of women's rights; his friend F. D. Maurice was a pioneer in women's education. But, perhaps fearing ridicule, the only way he could treat the subject was by adopting a defensive tone of burlesque and steering a diagonal course between two contradictory positions. It was a subject that occupied many people in the mid-nineteenth century. Queen's College, London, was founded in 1848, a year after *The Princess* appeared, Girton in 1869, and Mill's *The Subjection of Women* appeared in the same year. The bantering, patronising tone of the poem is set in the Prologue:

> And one said smiling 'Pretty were the sight
> If our old halls could change their sex, and flaunt
> With prudes for proctors, dowagers for deans,
> And sweet girl-graduates in their golden hair.
> I think they should not wear our rusty gowns,
> But move as rich as Emperor-moths . . . yet I fear,
> If there were many Lilias in the brood,

[64]

However deep you might embower the nest,
Some boy would spy it.'
　　　　At this upon the Sward
She tapt her tiny silken-sandaled foot:
'That's your light way: but I would make it death
For any male thing but to peep at us.'
　Petulant she spoke, and at herself she laughed;
A rosebud set with little wilful thorns,
And sweet as English air could make her, she.

'If women were to play such freaks,' Tennyson wrote to the Canadian editor S. E. Dawson, 'the burlesque and the tragic might go hand in hand.'

It is in the more sober part of the poem that his considered attitude to women and marriage is to be found, where he writes:

　　　　Either sex alone
Is half itself, and in true marriage lies
Nor equal, nor unequal: each fulfils
Defect in each, and always thought in thought,
Purpose in purpose, will in will, they grow,
The single pure and perfect animal,
The two-celled heart beating, with one full stroke,
Life.

It is here that one feels the influence of Emily Sellwood, with whom Tennyson had earlier discussed his poem. But he tended to idealise women, his mother in particular, and this comes out in the Prince's description of his own mother, who is presented as the ideal woman:

Not learned, save in gracious household ways,
Not perfect, nay but full of tender wants,
No angel; but a dearer being, all dipt
In angel instincts, breathing Paradise
Interpreter between the Gods and men.

The Victorian social scene is confined to the Prologue and the Conclusion, which presents a view of society ruled over by an enlightened and unselfish landed gentry. Throughout one marvels at the range and flexibility of Tennyson's verse, which can take in almost any material, from the idyllic to the prosaic, from the modern inventions of the Prologue to geology and the fantasies of Victorian medievalism. *The Princess*, with its strange eclecticism, was perfectly attuned to its age; hence its enormous success with the reading public. Sheer skill in versification could scarcely go further.

The poem ends with a picture of a peaceful, prosperous rural England seen from the lawns of Park House:

[65]

> We climbed
> The slope to Vivian-place, and turning saw
> The happy valleys, half in light, and half
> Far-shadowing from the west, a land at peace;
> Gray halls alone among their massive groves;
> Trim hamlets; here and there a rustic tower
> Half-lost in belts of hop and breadths of wheat;
> The shimmering glimpses of a stream; the seas;
> A red sail, or a white; and far beyond,
> Imagined more than seen, the skirts of France.
> 'Look there, a garden!' said my college friend,
> The Tory member's elder son, 'and there!
> God bless the narrow sea, which keeps her off,
> And keeps our Britain, whole within herself,
> A nation yet, the rulers and the ruled –
> Some sense of duty, something of a faith, –
> Some reverence for the laws ourselves have made,
> Some potent force to change them when we will,
> Some civic manhood firm against the crowd –
> But yonder, whiff! there comes a sudden heat,
> The gravest citizen seems to lose his head,
> The king is scared, the soldier will not fight,
> The little boys begin to shoot and stab,
> A kingdom topples over with a shriek
> Like an old woman, and down rolls the world
> In mock heroics stranger than our own;
> Revolts, republics, revolutions, most
> No graver than a schoolboys' barring out;
> Too comic for the solemn things they are,
> Too solemn for the comic touches in them,
> Like our wild Princess with as wise a dream
> As some of theirs. . . .'
>
> 'Have patience,' I replied, 'ourselves are full
> Of social wrong; and maybe wildest dreams
> Are but the needful preludes of the truth. . . .
> This fine old world of ours is but a child
> Yet in the go-cart. Patience! Give it time
> To learn its limbs: there is a hand that guides.'

A comfortable doctrine which, perhaps, only a Victorian Englishman could enunciate. Finally, there is the reassuring portrait of Sir Walter Vivian himself, the ideal country squire:

> No little lily-handed Baronet he,
> A great broad-shouldered genial Englishman,

A lord of fat prize-oxen and of sheep,
A raiser of huge melons and of pine,
A patron of some thirty charities,
A pamphleteer on guano and on grain,
A quarter-sessions chairman, abler none;
Fair-haired and redder than a windy morn;
Now shaking hands with him, now him, of those
That stood the nearest – now addressed to speech –
Who spoke few words and pithy, such as closed
Welcome, farewell, and welcome for the year
To follow. . . .
            Why should not these great Sirs
Give up their parks some dozen times a year
To let the people breathe?

It is not surprising that the Victorians enjoyed *The Princess*, whatever the critics might say. Reviewing the poem in *Frazer's Magazine* for September 1850, Charles Kingsley wrote that Tennyson 'makes of his "Medley" a mirror of the nineteenth century, possessed of its own new art and science, its own temptations and aspirations, and yet grounded on, and continually striving to reproduce, the forms and experiences of all past time.' It was not till his old age, in *Locksley Hall Sixty Years After*, that Tennyson rejected all idea of progress and hope for the human race. His prophetic soul foresaw the twentieth century. Christopher Ricks, in the best discussion of the poem, pertinently remarks that *The Princess* is 'a skilful evasion of all the questions that tormented Tennyson – touched on half-seriously, half-flippantly, and finally tranquillised.'[1]

When revising the poem for its fourth edition in 1857, Tennyson made the Prince subject to 'weird seizures', such as he was subject to himself in his mystical moments:

On a sudden in the midst of men and day,
And while I walked and talked as heretofore,
I seemed to move among a world of ghosts,
And feel myself the shadow of a dream.

Sir Charles Tennyson suggests that these seizures 'symbolised the effect upon Tennyson's mind of his separation from Emily and of his long-deferred union with her. Looking back on his life during those years of loneliness he felt that he had indeed been like one living in a world of illusion remote from reality.'[2] This may well be so. Nevertheless Tennyson's 'weird seizures' did not cease with his marriage, and he regarded them as mystical states of mind in which the material reality became illusion. It is true, however, that when the

Prince is sure that his love for Ida is returned his seizures cease. But what of Ida? She finds that love is the higher wisdom to be learned in lowly service in hospital rather than at the University, while nursing the Prince of his wound sustained in the tournament. She, in fact, declines from the emancipated almost-Shavian young woman of the earlier sections of the poem into the 'sweet humility' of the ministering angel of Victorian sentiment.[3]

A third edition of *The Princess* appeared in 1850, with considerable revisions and the addition of the lyrics, which, according to Tennyson, 'are the best interpreters of the poem'. These lyrics are sung by the ladies at intervals during the telling of the tale:

Between the rougher voices of the men
Like linnets in the pauses of the wind,

For the fifth edition Tennyson enlarged the Prologue, with its gratifying picture of Victorian security. But perhaps the best comment on *The Princess* is Gilbert and Sullivan's *Princess Ida*. And now, with the growing sales of *The Princess* and the *Poems* of 1842, Tennyson began to make an income from his poetry at last.

'I could go to Italy,' Tennyson wrote to Fitz early in 1848, 'if I could find anybody to go with me, which I can't, so I suppose I shan't go, which makes me hate myself and all the world.' He was being lionised in London, 'bedined *usque ad nauseam*', he said. The Irish poet Aubrey de Vere 'found him quite fevered with a succession of dinner parties'. He talked of escaping to Devon and Cornwall, for he had heard that there were larger waves at Bude than anywhere else in the British Isles. Also the possibility of a long poem on the Arthurian legends was beginning to stir ever more in his mind. But Aubrey persuaded him to come to Ireland first, where the waves were greater even than in Cornwall and the cliffs 'rose to a height beside which Beachy Head would look insignificant'. So Tennyson set off to Curragh in County Limerick.

'Alfred Tennyson is very restive,' wrote Aubrey de Vere, 'and I hope I shall make the visit pleasant to him. I wonder why he came, and whether he is fond of me. I fear not much so. Yesterday when I looked up at dinner and saw him sitting between my sister-in-law and her sister, in this remote land, strange to him, I felt all at once such an affection for him as made his noble face look very dim and misty. He has indeed a most noble countenance, so full of power, passion and intellect – so strong, dark and impressive. He is as simple as a child and not less interesting for his infirmities. He is all in favour of marriage and indeed will not be right till he has someone to love him exclusively. He is to breakfast alone, and sits alone half the day, musing and writing poetry.'

[68]

Aubrey de Vere sounds like a perfect host and evidently understood his difficult guest well enough. In the evening there was music, Mozart and Beethoven, played by Aubrey's eldest brother, and Tennyson would read aloud. Once, after finishing one of the sorrowful tales of his favourite Crabbe, he looked round reproachfully and said: 'I don't see any of you weeping.' They acted *The Day Dream* as a charade, a beautiful girl whom Tennyson used to call 'that stately maid' taking the part of the Sleeping Beauty and the poet himself that of the Prince, who breaks the spell of her slumber. Another evening there was a dance, which he denounced as 'a stupid thing', when a lady who was accustomed to speak her mind scolded him sharply: 'How would the world get on,' she asked, 'if others went about it growling at its amusements in a voice as deep as a lion's? I request that you will go upstairs, put on an evening coat and ask my daughter Sophia to dance.' He did so and was the gayest of the gay for several hours, turning out to be, moreover, an excellent dancer. One evening, a young girl who sat next to him at dinner spoke of a certain marriage as 'a very *penniless* one'. Tennyson rummaged in his pocket, extracted a penny and slapped it down loudly close to her plate, saying: 'There, I give you that, for that is the God you worship!' The girl was a little frightened, but more amused; they made friends and he promised to send her a pocket Milton. He was as true as his word, and some months later she received from England a Milton beautifully bound.[4]

With Aubrey de Vere, he climbed to the top of Knock Patrick. This was the time of the great potato famine and wholesale evictions, culminating in the Smith O'Brien insurrection. Tennyson witnessed much misery among the poor population in this 'most distressful country', which rightly blamed England for its plight. One day a Fenian crept up behind him as he climbed a mountain and, mistaking his swarthiness, whispered in his ear: 'Be you from France?' which, like the rest of Europe, was once more in revolutionary turmoil. Another time, in a small tavern, he found a young Irishman brandishing a sword and swearing that he would drive it up to the hilt in the body of any Englishman he encountered, so he would. Tennyson stepped forward and offered him his penknife, saying: 'I am an Englishman. There is my pen-knife and you know you will not so much as stick that into me.'

Years later, he said to William Allingham:[5]

'Ireland is a dreadful country. I heartily wish it was in the middle of the Atlantic.'
'Below the surface?' I asked.
'No, no, a thousand miles away from England. I like the

Irish – I admit their charm and their manners, but they are a fearful nuisance.'

Next month he returned to the subject.[6]

T. 'Couldn't they blow up that horrible island and carry it off in pieces a long way off?'
W.A. 'Why did the English go there?'
T. 'Why did the Normans come to England? The Normans came over here and seized the country, and in a hundred years, the English had forgotten all about it, and they were living together on good terms.' I demurred: Tennyson went on, raising his voice. 'The same Normans went to Ireland, and the Irish with their damned unreasonableness are raging and fuming to this hour. . . .'
W.A. 'But suppose all these to be bygones. You speak of a century, a short time in history – think what Ireland had to complain of only in the last century – the penal laws, and the deliberate destruction of their growing industry, by the English government.
T. 'That was brutal! Our ancestors *were* horrible brutes! And the Kelts are very charming and sweet. I love their Ossians and their Finns and so forth – but they are most damnably unreasonable.'

Back in London again, Tennyson met Emerson at dinner with Coventry Patmore. The American, though admiring his poetry, felt, until he met him, that he lacked power and substance and that he was only 'a perfect music-box for all manner of delicate tones and rhythms'. But face to face with the man himself in all his quiet rugged strength and lofty demeanour, he soon changed his mind. He felt, nevertheless, that 'he had the manner of one accustomed to be indulged and petted'. Brookfield, who was of the company, told Emerson that Alfred would go with him to France, if he wished it, but that he would 'find him heavy to carry'. Alfred, however, declined, remarking grimly that if he went he would certainly not come back alive. But if Emerson intended to visit Italy he would set off at once with him, for he had been waiting two years for some-one to go with him to that country.

On 5 May 1848, however, with the Arthurian legends in mind, he went to Cornwall. Arriving at Bude, he exclaimed to the girl who opened the door to him of the house where he was to lodge: 'Where is the sea? Show me the sea!' She opened the back door and, running out of it, he fell down six feet over a wall on to the shingle and injured his leg.

During his six weeks' convalescence, the doctor introduced him to many people, so that when he continued his journey he was able to stay with shopkeepers and farmers, instead of having to put up at hotels. Wherever he went, he found people who knew and loved his poems. At Morwenstow he met the poet Stephen Hawker, a man steeped in legends and medieval lore, who sometimes took the services at his church accompanied by nine cats. Hawker dressed somewhat unconventionally in a claret-coloured coat with long tails, a blue fisherman's jersey with a little red cross woven into it at the place where the soldier's spear had pierced the side of Jesus, knee-high wading boots and a flesh-coloured beaver hat without a brim, imitated from that said to be worn by the priests of the Orthodox Church. He was also addicted to practical jokes, and in his youth is said to have sat for several evenings naked on the rocks of the shore with an oilskin tail and a seaweed wig, impersonating a merman. Tennyson visited Hawker accompanied by his, Hawker's, brother-in-law, John Dinham, without giving his name. Hawker's first impression was of 'a tall swarthy man with an eye like a sword'. They talked of Cornwall and King Arthur and Hawker quoted from his visitor's *Morte d'Arthur*. Tennyson asked him how he could bear to live in such a lonely spot; for reply Hawker quoted *Locksley Hall*. 'Why, that man seems to be your favourite poet,' said Tennyson. 'Not mine only,' replied Hawker, 'but England's.' Tennyson then told him his name and at once all Hawker's reserve vanished and the two men wandered together about the shore, talking of Arthur and the Cornish legends. Hawker told him many stories of smugglers and wrecks on that wild coast, where the bodies of drowning men were dashed to pieces on the rocks and robbed by the savage wreckers, who would entice ships on to the rocks at night by their lanterns. He sometimes had to bury nine or ten drowned or murdered men at a time. After an evening meal, Tennyson left with his arms full of Arthurian books and manuscripts. 'His eyes', said Hawker later, 'seemed not only to shine but to glare.'

Stephen Hawker was himself no inconsiderable poet in his best work, 'The Quest of the Sangreal', written fifteen years later, which is actually more vigorous and more medieval in feeling than *Idylls of the King*, with its startling opening lines:

Ho! for the Sangrael! vanished vase of Heaven!
That held, like Christ's own heart, an hin of blood!
Ho! for the Sangrael! How the merry shout
Of reckless riders on the rushing steed
Smote the loose echo from the drowsy rock
Of grim Dundagel: throned along the sea.

Uprose they for the quest! the bounding men,
Of the siege perilous and the granite ring!
They gathered at the rock: yon ruddy tor, –
The stony depth where lurked the demon-god,
Till Christ, the mighty Master, drove him forth.

Tennyson's journal, or poetical notebook, of his Cornish tour can be left to speak for itself.

Sunday. Rainy and bad, went and sat in Tintagel ruins, cliff all black and red and yellow, weird-looking thing.

6th [June]. Slate quarries, one great pillar left standing; ship under the cliff loading; dived into a cavern all polished with the waves like dark marble with veins of pink and white. Followed up little stream falling through the worn slate, smoked a pipe at little inn, dined, walked once more to the old castle darkening in the gloom. . . .

7th. Camelford, Slaughter Bridge, clear brook among alders. Sought for King Arthur's Stone, found it at last by the rock under two or three sycamores, walked seaward, came down by the churchyard. Song from ship.

7th. Walked seaward. Large crimson clover; sea purple and green like a peacock's neck. 'By bays, the peacock's neck in hue.'

14th. Read part of *Oedipus Coloneus*.

19th. Finished reading *Fathom* [Smollett's *Ferdinand Count Fathom*?]. Set off for Polperro, ripple-mark, queer old narrow-streeted place, back at 9. Turf fires on the hills; jewel-fires in the waves from the oar, which Cornish people call 'bryming'.

July 1st. Museum. After dinner went to Perransabuloe. Coast looked gray and grand in the fading light. Went into cave, Rembrandt-like light thro' the opening.

6th. Went to Land's End by Logan Rock, leaden-backed mews wailing on the cliff, one with two young ones. Mist. Great yellow flare just before sunset. Funeral. Land's End and Life's End.

Miss Rundle, later Mrs Rundle-Charles, author of *The Schönberg-Cotta Family*, met Tennyson at her uncle's house Upland, four miles from Plymouth, when she was twenty. Her account of these meetings give a very good idea of his familiar conversation and general behaviour in society:[7]

he came into the drawing-room, and said to my mother, 'You
have a party,' which he did not seem to like. My father then
called me in to make tea for Mr. Tennyson in the dining-room,
and we had a quiet talk; a powerful, thoughtful face, kind
smile, hearty laugh, extremely near-sighted. He spoke of
travelling: Dresden, unsatisfactoriness of picture-gallery seeing;
the first time he was in Paris he 'went every day for a fortnight
to the Louvre, saw only one picture, "La Maîtresse de Titien", '
the second time looked only at 'Narcissus lying by a stream,
Echo in the distance and ferocious little Love'. Mr. Ruskin
set his own thought against the united admiration of
centuries, but he spoke of a 'splendid chapter on Clouds' in
*Modern Painters.*

Then he turned to Geology, Weald of Kent, Delta of a
great river flowing from as far as Newfoundland. 'Conceive,'
he said, 'what an era of the world that must have been,
great lizards, marshes, gigantic ferns!' Fancied, standing by a
railway at night, the engine must be like some great
Ichthyosaurus; . . . then spoke of Peach, the Cornish geologist
on the Preventive Service, maintaining a wife and seven
children on £100 a year, whilst we in one annual dinner,
champagne, turtle, &c., spend £25.

He spoke of the Italians as a great people (it was in 1848,
the year of revolutions) 'twice matured'. He had read a poem
of mine on Italy: said he felt 'great interest in the Italian
movement as in all great movements for freedom'; that perhaps
all looked equally disorderly as they arose; that the German
revolutions (of 1848) were miserable plagiarisms. We went
into the drawing-room and I played Mendelssohn. Mr.
Tennyson came and talked to me about Schiller. . . . Knew by
heart Goethe's Gedichte 'Summer breathings'. Felt the grand
intellectual power of *Faust*, but threw it aside in disgust at
first reading. . . . At supper he spoke of Goethe's *Tasso*:
he felt with Tasso, did not care for anything else in the play.
'Leonora, discreet, prudential young lady, could not of course
care for the poor poet – it would not have been the thing, it
would not have done.' He spoke of the snobbery of English
society.' It was getting late, so my aunt asked him to stay the
night, but he said he had breakfasted alone for a dozen
years. . . .

Next morning (Tuesday, July 25th) Mr. Tennyson came
again: he talked about lower organisms feeling less pain than
higher, but would not fish; could not comprehend the feeling
of animals with ganglia, little scattered knots of nerves and

no brain; spoke of wonderful variety of forms of life, instinct of plants, &c., told the story of a Brahmin destroying a microscope because it showed him animals killing each other in a drop of water; 'significant, as if we could destroy facts by refusing to see them'. . . . Then he spoke of my poems, said he liked some very much, especially some lines on the gentianella; then he kindly made one or two verbal criticisms in the one called 'The Poet's Daily Bread'. 'Have you printed?' he said. 'Do not publish too early, you cannot retract.' I ventured to thank him for his poems, in which we delighted. 'I thank you for yours,' he said graciously. We went into the kitchen garden, he talked of flowers and cabbages, picked gooseberries, he 'used as a boy to lie for hours under a gooseberry bush reading a novel, finishing his gooseberries and novel together'; he liked the kitchen garden, 'so wholesome'. 'I would rather stay with you bright girls than dine with Mr. W.,' he said. . . . Afterwards we drove him into Plymouth. 'You would not think me a shy man, but I am always shy with false or conventional people; people are sometimes affected from shyness, and *grow* simple.' Then we talked of Carlyle: 'You would like him for one day,' he said, 'but get tired of him, so vehement and destructive.' Then he said to me, 'Do you know the *Odyssey*? I like it better as a whole than the *Iliad*. I should have met you before; why didn't you write? I could teach you Greek in a month. . . . I will send you the *Odyssey*, I have two copies in my portmanteau: I will be grave when I next meet you; I vary.'

Tennyson spent the autumn at Malvern and Cheltenham, taking another water-cure. His nerves were still disordered. 'He has gone to a new doctor,' wrote FitzGerald in November, 'who gives him iron pills and altogether this really great man thinks more about his bowels and his nerves than about the laureate wreath he was born to inherit. Not but he meditates new poems; and now The Princess is done, he turns to King Arthur – a worthy subject indeed – and has consulted some histories of him, and spent some time visiting his traditionary haunts in Cornwall. But I believe the trumpet can wake Tennyson no longer to great deeds; I may mistake and prove myself an owl, which I hope may be the case. But how are we to expect heroic poems from a valetudinary? I have told him he should fly from England and go among savages.'

Frederick was now on a brief visit to London; and when he left for Italy Alfred joined him, but two days later he changed his mind and was back again in town, where he took rooms in Ebury Street. Otherwise we find him staying with his mother at Cheltenham, which he described as 'a polka, parson-worshipping place', though while he was there he became friendly with the poet Sydney Dobell. Coventry Patmore describes him spending an evening in London with a dozen friends: 'Not to be sure his equals, but as near his equals as could be found. All the evening he wouldn't utter a syllable, but sat silent with his pipe – at last he rose and left the room with the words "I'm going to Cheltenham, I have had a glut of them." ' In fact, he was often there, at Bellevue House, St James's Square, between 1846 and 1850, occupying a little room at the top of the house, with books and papers strewn all over the floor, the chairs and table. Here he entertained his friends, discussing religion with Boyd, afterwards Dean of Exeter; Foxton, author of *Popular Christianity*; Rashdall, Vicar of Malvern; Frederick Robertson, then Boyd's curate; and Dobson, Principal of Cheltenham College. Of Christianity he said, 'It is tugging at my heart.' One acquaintance, his son tells us, would keep assuring him that it was the greatest honour of his life to have met him, till Tennyson exclaimed: 'Don't talk damned nonsense!' He would also go for long walks in the country with Dr Ker's brother Alan.

In a letter to Aubrey de Vere of October 1849, Tennyson writes of his delight in Scotland, which he had visited that autumn. 'I have seen many fine things in Scotland, and many fine things did I miss seeing, rolled up as they were tenfold in Scotch mists. . . . I steamed from Oban to Skye, a splendid voyage, for the whole day, with the exception of three hours in the morning, was blue and sunny; and I think I saw more outlines of hills than ever I saw in my life; and exquisitely shaped are those Skye mountains. Loch Coruisk, said to be the wildest scene in the Highlands, I failed in seeing. After a fatiguing expedition over the roughest ground on a wet day we arrived on the banks of the loch, and made acquaintance with the extremest tiptoes of the hills, all else being thick in wool-white fog. Dunkeld is lovely, and I delighted in Inveraray, though there likewise I got drenched to the skin till my very hat wept tears of ink. I rejoiced in Killeen, but on the whole perhaps I enjoyed no day more than the one I spent at Kirk Alloway by the monument of poor Burns, and the orchards, and "banks and braes of bonny Doon". I made a pilgrimage thither out of love for the great peasant; they were gathering in the wheat and the spirit of the man mingled or seemed to mingle with all I saw.' 'I can't tell you how it was, Fitz,' he said later, 'but I fell into a passion of tears.'

At Millport, where several people had recently died of cholera, feeling a few pains in his stomach, Tennyson began to suspect that he might have become infected too. But his fears were groundless and, on the way back to London, he spent a few weeks in Lincolnshire, where he received a letter from Mrs Gaskell asking him to send a copy of his poems to an old Lancashire weaver, Samuel Bamford: 'the most hearty (and it's saying a good deal) admirer of Tennyson I know'. Bamford had been searching the second-hand bookshops as a new copy of the poems was beyond his means at fourteen or eighteen shillings, though he already knew most of them by heart. Tennyson told Forster that he regarded Bamford's admiration as the highest honour he had yet received, and replied to Mrs Gaskell that he would send him the poems as soon as he got back to London. Samuel Bamford was, according to Mrs Gaskell, 'a great, gaunt, stalwart Lancashire man, formerly hand-loom weaver, and author of *The Life of a Radical.*' He was nearly seventy and living 'in that state which is exactly decent poverty with his neat little apple-faced wife'.

Tennyson's letter from Mablethorpe to Forster concluded: 'I am here on this desolate sea-coast. My friends have fêted me in this country so long that I think it high time to move, but they will not let me go yet.'

# 6

The elegies to the memory of Arthur Hallam were now completed. Moxon, if not Tennyson himself, was anxious to publish them and offered an advance of £300, which Tennyson could hardly refuse. But they might have been lost altogether, for when he gave up his rooms at Mornington Place he left his manuscript book behind in the cupboard where he kept his provisions. 'I went up to my room yesterday to get my book of Elegies,' he wrote to Coventry Patmore from Bonchurch, Isle of Wight, on 28 February 1850, 'you know what I mean, a long Butcher ledger-like book. I was going to read one or two to an artist here: I could not find it. I have some obscure remembrance of having lent it to you. If so, all is well. If not, will you go to my old chambers and institute a vigorous inquiry? I was coming up today on purpose to look after it, but as the weather is so furious I have yielded to the wishes of my friend here to stop till tomorrow.'

When he called, Mrs Lloyd told Patmore that the room had already been let to someone else and that he could not come in. No such book as he described had been left behind. But Patmore insisted on looking himself, forced his way into the house, and finally found the butcher's book at the back of the cupboard as Tennyson had described.

The manuscript recovered, Tennyson had a few copies privately printed and distributed to his friends. *Fragments of an Elegy* contained ten sections less than the first edition of *In Memoriam A.H.H.*, which was published anonymously in May 1850. Tennyson had intended calling it *The Way of a Soul*, and it was Emily Sellwood who made the brilliant suggestion of *In Memoriam*. Indeed, it was this collection of poems which finally dispelled her doubts about Tennyson's religious beliefs, in her view the principal bar to their marriage. Tennyson had sent a copy to Drummond Rawnsley, now Vicar of Shiplake, near Henley, and it was Catherine Rawnsley who sent Drummond's copy to Emily, with Tennyson's leave. 'Do you really think I should write a line with the Elegies, that is in a separate note, to say I have returned them?' Emily wrote timidly to Catherine Rawnsley on 1 April. 'I am almost afraid, but since you say I am to do so I will, only I cannot say what I feel;' adding in a postscript: 'I thought I would write my note before the others came. Here it is, no beginning nor end, not a note at all, a sort of label: Katie told me the poems might be kept till Saturday. I hope I shall not have occasioned any inconvenience by keeping them to the limit of time, and if I have I must be forgiven, for I cannot willingly part from what is so precious. The thanks I would say for them and for the faith in me which has trusted them to me must be thought for me, I cannot write them. I have read the poems through and through and through and to me they were and they are even more and more a spirit monument grand and beautiful in whose presence I feel admiration and delight, not unmixed with awe. The happiest possible end to this labour of love! But think not its fruits shall so soon perish, for they are life in life, and they shall live, and as years go on be only the more fully known and loved and reverenced for what they are.

'So says a true seer. Can anyone guess the name of this seer? After such big words shall I put anything about my own little I? – that I am the happier for having seen these poems and that I hope I shall be the better too.'

Both Catherine Rawnsley and Charles Kingsley, a close friend of Drummond Rawnsley, who met Emily at Shiplake Rectory, persuaded her that there could now be no impediment to her marriage to Tennyson. Two months later, on 1 June, Emily Sellwood and Alfred Tennyson were married in Shiplake church. It is a curious thought that the night before her marriage Emily slept at Holmwood in Shiplake Row, the house that was soon to become the home of Admiral Swinburne and his family, Algernon Swinburne's periodic refuge from his hectic and disorderly life in London.

The arrangements for the marriage were so hurried that neither the wedding cake nor the wedding dresses were ready in time. It was as though, after both of them had waited so long for each other, there was not another moment to lose. Tennyson was now forty-one and Emily in her late thirties. Those present at the ceremony included Drummond Rawnsley, who married them, Catherine Rawnsley and her two small daughters, who acted as bridesmaids together with Jenny Elmhirst, Henry Sellwood (Emily's father), Charles Weld (the husband of Emily's sister Anne), Edmund and Cecilia Lushington and Greville Phillimore of Shiplake House. No other member of Tennyson's family was present, but Charles Tennyson Turner, his favourite brother, who was married to Emily's sister Louisa, wrote a letter of congratulation: 'Dear double sister and long-single brother, oh what a queer world it is! I hope however it has done a brace of amiable people some geniune good, whirligig as it is – this time at least. Well! The thing is to come off on the 13th, daddy says. Good wishes in crowds from me I despatch on dove's wing to you. I am going to keep pigeons, would they were carrier pigeons! then would I trouble them under their wings with missives of congratulation to arrive more swiftly than the railroad too! Coo! Coo! Coo!'

The 'queerness' in Charles's view was probably because Alfred had broken off his engagement to Emily ten years ago, and he himself had been separated from his wife Louisa owing to his addiction to opium, but was now reunited with her. Tennyson said 'it was the nicest wedding he had ever been at', and later that 'the peace of God came into my life before the altar when I married her'. After the ceremony bride and bridegroom drove to Pangbourne; and as they drove Tennyson made up a charming impromptu poem which he sent next day to Catherine Rawnsley with a brief note: 'Dear Kate, you managed it all very well yesterday. Many thanks, Yours ever, A.T. P.S. Dubbie's fees must be come at as he can best manage. The clerk and shifts are owing.'

### To the Vicar of Shiplake

Vicar of this pleasant spot
  Where it was my chance to marry,
Happy happy be your lot
  In the Vicarage by the quarry.
You were he that knit the knot!

Sweetly, smoothly flow your life.
  Never tithe unpaid perplex you,
Parish feud, or party strife,
  All things please you, nothing vex you,
To have given me such a wife!

Live and prosper! Day by day
  Watch your standard roses blowing,
And your three young things at play,
  And your triple terrace growing
Green and greener every May!

Sweetly flow your life with Kate's,
  Glancing off from all things evil,
Smooth as Thames below your gates,
  Thames along the silent level,
Streaming thro' his osier'd aits!

Emily now made what may seem the rather surprising request that

[79]

they should go directly to Hallam's grave at Clevedon, as 'a kind of consecration' of their marriage. Perhaps she felt obscurely that it needed Hallam's blessing; at any rate, the request must have touched Tennyson deeply. From Clevedon they went to Glastonbury, another hallowed spot. There they lunched at what had once been the refectory of the Old Hospital for pilgrims, built by Abbot John de Selwoode, an ancestor of Emily's who was reputed to have been buried beside the tomb of King Arthur in the chancel of the abbey.

From Glastonbury they went to Bristol and Bath; then to Cheltenham, to visit Alfred's mother and his Aunt Russell, who gave them a generous gift of money and offered Brancepeth Castle for for their honeymoon. Monckton Milnes had already offered them Fryston. By the end of July they were at Mary Marshall's Tent Lodge, Coniston, in the Lake District. Mrs Marshall was the sister of Tennyson's Cambridge friend Stephen Spring Rice.

'Dearest Aunt,' he wrote to Mrs Russell from Coniston, 'We have been making a little tour about these lakes, and have spent the last few days with my friends the Speddings at Bassenthwaite water. We only arrived here last night. Mrs. Marshall's park looked as lovely as the Garden of Eden, as we descended the hill to this place. We have a very beautiful view from our drawing-room windows, crag, mountain, woods and lake, which look especially fine as the sun is dropping behind the hills. I wish you could see it. The Marshalls themselves are not here but expected daily. . . . I send you this little note just to tell you where we are, and how much your bounty has enabled us to enjoy ourselves among the mountains.'

At the Marshalls', Emily met Carlyle for the first time. He slowly scanned her from head to foot, then gave her a hearty handshake. Soon afterwards she silenced one of his wilder tirades by remarking: 'That is not sane, Mr Carlyle,' which increased his respect for her. 'Mrs. Tennyson also pleased me,' he said later. 'The first glance at her is the least favourable. A freckly *round* faced woman, rather tallish and without shape, a slight lisp too . . . so very delicate in health, sick without disorder.' Though he found her unpromising at first glance, he praised her 'bright glittering blue eyes'. Emily suffered all her life from a severe spinal disorder, which often confined her to her couch or to a bath chair. Her fine acquiline features, we are told, often wore a saintly expression. One evening Venables and Aubrey de Vere called and sat with Tennyson after Emily had gone to bed. After puffing at his pipe for some moments in silence, he said: 'I have known many women who were excellent, one in one way, another in another way, but this woman is the noblest I have ever known.' Coventry Patmore also came to stay at Tent Lodge in August. 'I like

Mrs. Tennyson more and more every day,' he wrote to his wife. 'She seems to like me, as she talks more freely than a woman of such character would without considerable faith in her hearer. Yesterday it was too wet to go to church and Tennyson read prayers, lessons and a sermon by Maurice. The more I talk to him the more I discover that he has given a defective notion of his faith in *In Memoriam*. He is far above the pantheistic "religious faculty" humbug that taints so many half geniuses in this day.'

After dinner at two o'clock, Tennyson and Patmore would sit for an hour or so over their wine, then set out for a long walk until dark, while Emily lay on the sofa. Of Emily, Patmore wrote again: 'She has instruction and intellect enough to make the stock-in-trade of half-a-dozen literary ladies, but she is neither brilliant nor literary at all. She seems to understand him thoroughly and, without the least ostentation or officiousness of affection, waits upon and attends to him, as she ought to do. I cannot enough value my advantage in seeing so much of Tennyson. It is a great good to me to find that I have my superior, which I have never found in the company of anyone else. In the society of nearly tip-top men, Thackeray, Carlyle, Allingham, I feel an inferiority only in the means of expressing myself – but in Tennyson I perceive a nature higher and wider than my own and at the foot of which I sit happily and with love.'[1] Such tributes from other people at this time were not uncommon. Tennyson seems to have impressed nearly everyone he met with this essential quality of power and nobility. It is a quality that often impresses one when looking at the portraits of other men of his age. The Marshalls even offered him Tent Lodge as a permanent home, and the Ashburtons offered him their house at Croydon. He declined both offers, and he and Emily went for a time to the Lushingtons at Park House in order to look for a house of their own near London.

*In Memoriam* was an overwhelming success with most of the critics and with the public. Two of its most ardent admirers were the Prince Consort and the Queen, who said, after the Prince's death that it was her comfort next to the Bible. Men like F. D. Maurice and F. W. Robertson, the famous preacher of Trinity Chapel, Brighton, 'thought that the author had made a definite step towards the unification of the highest religion and philosophy with the progressive science of the day, and that he was the one poet who "through almost the agonies of a death-struggle" had made an effective stand against his own doubts and difficulties and those of the time', on behalf of a faith in a God of love and a firm belief in immortality. 'Scientific leaders like Herschell, Owen, Sidgwick and Tyndall regarded him as a champion of Science, and cheered him with words of genuine admiration for his love of Nature, for the eagerness with which he welcomed all the latest scientific discoveries, and for his trust in the truth.'[2]

Nevertheless there were some reservations about the moral tone of *In Memoriam* and the kind of love it celebrated. *The Times*, for instance, remarked nastily that 'a great deal of poetic feeling had been wasted' and 'much shallow art spent on the tenderness shown to an Amaryllis of the Chancery Bar'. After quoting section LXXIV, the reviewer remarked: 'Very sweet and plaintive these verses are, but who would not give them a feminine application?' Another reviewer wrote: 'These touching lines evidently come from the full heart of the widow of a military man.' With such remarks, which touched on a sensitive area, in mind perhaps, Tennyson wrote: 'It must be remembered that this is a poem, *not* an actual biography. It is founded on our friendship, on the engagement of Arthur Hallam to my sister, on his sudden death in Vienna, just before the time fixed for their marriage, and on his burial at Clevedon Church. It was meant to be a kind of *Divina Commedia*, ending in happiness.' Therefore, as a matter of fact, it *is* a biography—indeed, a spiritual autobiography.

As Christopher Ricks points out, 'Shakespeare's *Sonnets* are not only an important source for *In Memoriam*, they are its most important analogue.'[3] And, one might observe with as much relevance, with this same key Tennyson unlocked his heart. Arthur Hallam had worshipped Shakespeare's *Sonnets*, though some Victorian critics, among them Henry Hallam, regretted that Shakespeare had ever written them. For the most part, however, the critics passed over in silence the similarity between the kind of love celebrated in the *Sonnets* and in *In Memoriam*. But it is precisely this aspect of *In Memoriam* that is crucial to an understanding of Tennyson's nature, since his love for Hallam was the greatest emotional experience of his life. Like Shakespeare he writes of Hallam as his other self, his true love, addressing him as 'dearest'. But on this head Tennyson assures us: 'If anybody thinks I ever called him "dearest" in his life, they are much mistaken, for I never even called him "dear".' Nevertheless, he writes of his heart as 'widowed' by Hallam's death, of Hallam's 'manhood fused with female grace'. Tennyson glossed this line as asserting Hallam's likeness to Christ, 'that union of man and woman. . . . Man must grow more like woman, and vice versa. . . . More as the double-natured poet each.' But what construction is one to put upon these lines from section XCVII:

Two partners of a married life –
I looked on these and thought of thee
In vastness and in mystery,
And of my spirit as of a wife.

Tennyson notes of this: 'The relation of one on earth to one in the
other and higher world. NOT my relation to him here. He looked up
to me as I looked up to him.' But this argument hardly applies to the
lines which follow:

These two – they dwelt with eye on eye,
  Their hearts of old have beat in tune,
  Their meetings made December June,
Their every parting was to die.

An earlier draft in the Heath Notebook is more passionate:[4]

They madly drank each other's breath
  With breast to breast in early years.
  They met with passion and with tears,
Their every parting was a death.

These lines did not survive in the published version. In any case, it
would seem idle to pretend that they, or those which Tennyson more
cautiously substituted for them, refer to 'the spirit yet in the flesh but
united in love with the spirit out of the flesh resembles the wife of a
great man of science. She looks up to him – but what he knows is a
mystery to her.' The lines only too plainly reflect Tennyson's feelings
for Arthur Hallam, both in the flesh and out of it. One is hardly
convinced by the reference to 'the wife of a great man of science'.
Tennyson did his best to believe in an afterlife in which he would be
reunited with Hallam. Indeed, his friend Charles Kingsley envisaged
Paradise in Islamic terms as an eternity of sexual bliss, and even
illustrated this by a drawing of himself and his wife ascending to
heaven locked in each other's arms, free from all inhibitions at last.[5]
Similarly, Tennyson is certainly thinking of Hallam again in CXVII
when he exclaims:

O days and hours, your work is this
  To hold me from my proper place,
  A little while from his embrace,
For fuller gain of after bliss:

That out of distance might ensue
  Desire of nearness doubly sweet;
  And unto meeting when we meet,
Delight a hundredfold accrue. . . .

The wife of the great man of science is not in question here, though in
*In Memoriam* Tennyson frequently casts himself in the feminine role
in his relationship with Hallam, as in:

> My spirit loved and loves him yet,
> Like some poor girl whose heart is set
> On one whose rank exceeds her own.

Again:

> I loved thee, Spirit, and love, nor can
> The soul of Shakespeare love thee more,

where the parallel with the *Sonnets* is explicit. As the poem proceeds the invocation of Hallam's spirit becomes ever more passionate, as in XCIII:

> Descend, and touch, and enter; hear
> The wish too strong for words to name,

which in the first version in the Lincoln MS, reads:[6]

> Stoop Soul and touch me: wed me: hear
> The wish too strong for words to name.

Is this, in fact, 'the love that dare not speak its name'? As Christopher Ricks observes, the reading that Tennyson published 'is in some ways even more disconcerting. . . . Anyone who believes that Tennyson's feelings for Hallam were not homosexual should try to say why.'[7]

Ricks does say why, but his explanation does not really dispose of the homosexual element in Tennyson's love, though the fact that Hallam was to marry his sister and that he was to marry Emily Sellwood does, on the face of it, appear to do so. But seventeen years elapsed between Hallam's death and Tennyson's marriage. Nor does his infatuation with Rosa Baring, not so long after Hallam's death, mean that there was not a strong homosexual element in his love for Hallam. Confirmation is suggested, as Ricks points out, by Charles Kingsley's review which appeared in *Frazer's Magazine* for September 1850. In *In Memoriam* Kingsley finds a successor to 'the old tales of David and Jonathan, Damon and Pythias, Socrates and Alcibiades, Shakespeare and his nameless friend, of "love passing the love of woman".' Indeed, he was twice drawn to that perilous phrase – perilous, that is, at that time – praising *In Memoriam* again for 'a depth and vehemence of affection "passing the love of woman" . . . altogether rivalling the sonnets of Shakespeare.' But Shakespeare never went so far as to liken Mr W. H. to Christ. The very idea would probably have seemed to him blasphemous. But by addressing Hallam throughout his poem as a disembodied spirit, Tennyson largely obscures the homosexual element in their love. Nevertheless, this love is the core of the poem, though it is by no means the whole poem, which is very much preoccupied with the problem of religious

[84]

belief and the challenge presented to it by modern science. And this is the part of the poem which is usually stressed. 'It is rather a cry of the whole human race than mine,' Tennyson wrote. 'In the poem altogether private grief swells out into thought of, and hope for, the whole world. It begins with a funeral and ends with a marriage – begins with death and ends in a promise of new life – a sort of Divine Comedy, cheerful at the close' – though 'cheerful' is rather an under-statement applied to the *Paradiso*: 'It's too hopeful this poem,' he said, 'more than I am myself.'

Later critics, among them T. S. Eliot, have seen *In Memoriam* as 'a poem of despair, but despair of a religious kind', the doubt more evident than the faith.[8] As Professor Ryals observes: 'Tennyson makes of *In Memoriam* an autobiography, which traces, like *The Prelude*, the growth of a poet's mind and, like the *Essay on Man*, the spiritual character of an age.'[9] So Tennyson turns to Nature – Eliot calls it 'that strange abstraction'–for consolation by identifying himself with it in one of his greatest passages (II):

Old Yew, which graspeth at the stones
    That name the under-lying dead,
    Thy fibres net the dreamless head,
Thy roots are wrapt about the bones. . . .

O not for thee the glow, the bloom,
    Who changeth not in any gale,
    Nor branding summer suns avail
To touch thy thousand years of gloom:

And gazing on thee, sullen tree,
    Sick for thy stubborn hardihood,
    I seem to fail from out my blood
And grow incorporate in thee.

He then has doubts whether Nature is not governed by blind, mechanical laws, with an inner emptiness in which there can be no consolation. And, waking from troubled Sleep, he cries (IV):

Break, thou deep vase of chilling tears,
That grief hath shaken into frost!

One of the most haunting sections of the poem (VII) describes the poet standing before Hallam's house in Wimpole Street as the dawn is about to break, only to intensify his sense of loss which has temporarily deprived his life of all meaning, with its implied analogy between the breaking of the 'blank day' and the breaking of his heart:

And ghastly through the drizzling rain
On the bald street breaks the blank day.

D*                         [85]

In XIX Tennyson compares his grief to the tide which, twice a day, fills the Severn channel below Clevedon where Hallam is buried. Only when the silent tide of tears recedes can he speak:

> There twice a day the Severn fills;
>   The salt sea-water passes by,
>   And hushes half the babbling Wye,
> And makes a silence in the hills.
>
> The Wye is hushed nor moved along,
>   And hushed my deepest grief of all,
>   When filled with tears that cannot fall,
> I brim with sorrow drowning song.
>
> The tide flows down, the wave again
>   Is vocal in its wooded walls;
>   My deeper anguish also falls,
> And I can speak a little then.

*In Memoriam*, it hardly needs saying, is full of magnificent land-scapes. Such is section XI, with its evocation of an autumn morning on the Lincolnshire wolds:

> Calm is the morn without a sound,
>   Calm as to suit a calmer grief,
>   And only through the faded leaf
> The chestnut pattering to the ground: . . .
>
> Calm and deep peace in this wide air,
>   These leaves that redden to the fall;
>   And in my heart, if calm at all,
> If any calm, a calm despair.

This is followed by XV, five verses in one unbroken sentence, that is among the finest passages in the language:

> Tonight the winds begin to rise
>   And roar from yonder dropping day:

with its magnificent final verse about the cloud

> That rises upward always higher,
>   And onward drags a labouring breast,
>   And topples round the dreary west,
> A looming bastion fringed with fire.

For in the wind and cloud we have an image of the condition of the poet's own heart: 'The wild unrest that lives in woe'. In XVIII he takes what comfort he can from the fact that Hallam is at least buried in English earth; and the thought occurs to him momentarily, as in the hopeful inscription on a tombstone: 'He is not dead, but sleepeth':

Ah yet, even yet, if this might be,
    I, falling on his faithful heart,
    Would breathing through his lips impart
That life that almost dies in me;

That dies not, but endures with pain,
    And slowly forms the firmer mind,
    Treasuring the look it cannot find,
The words that are not heard again.

The second part of *In Memoriam*, which begins with the first Christmas after Hallam's death in XXVIII, is concerned mainly with the concept of personal immortality, which always had an overwhelming importance for Tennyson, for without it there could be no reunion with Hallam. The poetry becomes more moralistic and metaphysical in a way that appealed greatly to the Victorians. But could they have derived much comfort from LIV?

Oh yet we trust that somehow good
    Will be the final goal of ill,
    To pangs of nature, sins of will,
Defects of doubt, and taints of blood;

That nothing walks with aimless feet;
    That not one life shall be destroyed,
    Or cast as rubbish to the void,
When God hath made the pile complete:

That not a worm is cloven in vain;
    That not a moth with vain desire
    Is shrivelled in a fruitless fire,
Or but subserves another's gain.

Behold, we know not anything;
    I can but trust that good shall fall
    At last – far off – at last, to all,
And every winter change to spring.

So runs my dream: but what am I?
    An infant crying in the night:
    An infant crying for the light:
And with no language but a cry.

The helplessness of this is but reinforced by LV:

> I stretch lame hands of faith, and grope,
>     And gather dust and chaff, and call
>     To what I feel is Lord of all,
> And faintly trust the larger hope.

Shall Man, he asks despairingly in LVI:

> Who trusted God was love indeed
>     And love Creation's final law –
>     Though Nature, red in tooth and claw
> With ravine, shrieked against his creed –

> Who loved, who suffered countless ills,
>     Who battled for the True, the Just,
>     Be blown about the desert dust,
> Or sealed within the iron hills?

> No more? A monster, then, a dream,
>     A discord. Dragons of the prime,
>     That tare each other in their slime,
> Were mellow music matched with him.

Nihilism could hardly go further. But such were the implications of the scientific materialism of the nineteenth century, from which it was thought men could be saved only by belief in a God of love. It was a dilemma which Tennyson faced squarely and which tormented him all his life.

With the celebration of the second Christmas after Hallam's death in LXXVIII, with the new year, the pessimism, the anguish of loss, appreciably lifts; and sitting out on the lawn one summer night after the others had gone to bed, Tennyson read through Hallam's letters (XCV):

> So word by word, and line by line,
>     The dead man touched me from the past,
>     And all at once it seemed at last
> The living soul was flashed on mine,

> And mine in his was wound, and whirled
>     About empyreal heights of thought,
>     And came on that which is, and caught
> The deep pulsations of the world. . . .

> Till now the doubtful dusk revealed
>     The knolls once more where, couched at ease,
>     The white kine glimmered, and the trees
> Laid their dark arms about the field.

Addressing Emily Sellwood, he writes in XCVI:

> You say, but with no touch of scorn,
>     Sweet-hearted, you, whose light-blue eyes
>     Are tender over drowning flies,
> You tell me, doubt is Devil-born.
>
> I know not: one indeed I knew
>     In many a subtle question versed,
>     Who touched a jarring lyre at first,
> But ever strove to make it true:
>
> Perplext in faith, but pure in deeds,
>     At last he beat his music out.
>     There lives more faith in honest doubt,
> Believe me, than in half the creeds.

A paradox indeed! But surely George Eliot was right when she wrote: 'Whatever was the immediate prompting of *In Memoriam*, whatever the form under which the author represented his aim to himself, the deepest significance of the poem is the sanctification of human love as a religion.' Swinburne remarked, after quoting from XLVIII:

> If these brief lays, of Sorrow born,
>     Were taken to be such as closed
>     Grave doubts and answers here proposed,
> Then these were such as men might scorn,

'To say that these effusions of mortal sorrow make no pretence, and would be worthy of contempt if they pretended, to solve or satisfy men's doubts – and then to renew the appearance of an incessant or even a fitful endeavour after some such satisfaction – is surely so incongruous as to sound almost insane.' This is wittily put, but is too captious and hardly affects the nobility of the poem as a whole, which expressed for most readers what Charles Kingsley in *Alton Locke* called 'the terrible questionings, the terrible strugglings of this great, awful, blessed time'. For, taken together, these 'short swallow-flights of song', as Tennyson called the stanzas of *In Memoriam*, undoubtedly constitute the greatest poem of the Victorian age.

However, FitzGerald was moved to a certain impatience. 'We have surely had enough of those reporting their sorrows,' he wrote, 'especially when one is aware all the time that the poet wilfully protracts what he complains of, magnifies it in Imagination, puts it into all the shapes of Fancy: and yet we are to condole with him, and be taught to ruminate our losses and sorrows in the same way. I felt that if Tennyson had got on a horse and ridden twenty miles, instead of moaning over his pipe, he would have been cured of his sorrows in half the time. As it is, it is about three years before the Poetic Soul walks itself out of the darkness and Despair into Common Sense.' Certainly, Tennyson spent many years weaving a crown of thorns for his own head, and yet what a crown it is!

At any rate it was *In Memoriam* which won him Emily Sellwood, and also won him the laureateship. The night before he received the offer of the post, he told James Knowles, he dreamed that the Prince Consort came to him and kissed him on the cheek, and in his dream he said: 'Very kind but very German'. The letter came the next morning and he thought about it all day, not being able to make up his mind whether to accept or to refuse. At last he wrote two letters, one accepting the post and the other declining it, left them on the table and settled to decide which one he would send after he had had his dinner and a bottle of port. Then, flushed with port and confidence, he decided to accept and was officially appointed Poet Laureate in the place of Wordsworth, who had died the previous April, on 19 November 1850. When his Uncle Charles heard of his appointment, he remarked of his nephew's poetry: 'Horrid rubbish indeed! What a discredit it is that British taste and Poetry should have such a representative before the Nations of the Earth and Posterity! . . . Posterity will, it is hoped, have a sound judgement on such matters, and if so what an age *this* must appear when such trash can be tolerated and not only tolerated but enthusiastically admired!'

Tennyson's first publication as Laureate, the seventh edition of his *Poems* in 1851, bore a graceful dedication to the Queen:

Revered Victoria, you that hold
  A nobler office upon Earth
  Than arms, or power of brain, or birth
Could give the warrior kings of old,

I thank you that your Royal Grace
  To one of less desert allows
  This laurel greener from the brows
Of him that utter'd nothing base:

And should your greatness, and the care
  That yokes with empire, yield you time
  To make demand of modern rhyme,
If aught of ancient worth be there,

Take, Madam, this poor book of song:
  For though the faults are thick as dust
  In vacant chambers I could trust
Your sweetness. May you rule us long

[90]

And leave us rulers of your blood
   As noble till the latest day!
   May children of our children say,
'She wrought her people lasting good:

'Her court was pure; her life serene;
   God gave her peace; her land reposed;
   A thousand claims to reverence closed
In her as Mother, Wife and Queen;

'She brought a vast design to pass,
   When Europe and the scatter'd ends
   Of our fierce world were mixt as friends
And brethren in her halls of glass.'

But, of course, it was the Prince Consort who planned the Great Exhibition of 1851, when the Crystal Palace reared its glittering halls of glass among the trees of Hyde Park. Tennyson visited the exhibition and was, his son tells us, delighted with Millais's *Ophelia* and *The Huguenot*, but he liked *The Huguenot* best. No one was more proud of her son's success than Elizabeth Tennyson. Whenever she heard his name mentioned in shop or bus at Cheltenham, she could not resist saying: 'It may interest you to know that I am the *mother* of the Laureate.' And sometimes she would add: 'My sons Frederick and Charles have also written some very beautiful verses.'

# 7

The early part of 1851 was spent house-hunting. In January Tennyson took a very old house at Warninglid, Sussex. But almost immediately as he and Emily were settling in, there was a violent storm: the fires smoked, doors banged and draughts drove through doors and windows, making the dining-room uninhabitable. The thundering wind in the chimney made sleep impossible at night; and when the wind finally blew down part of their bedroom wall, 'so that the rain streamed in upon them as they lay in bed', they decided that they would have to move. They discovered, too, that a notorious gang of thieves and murderers, known as the Cuckfield Gang, was still living in their lodge. The nearest doctor and butcher were seven miles away at Horsham, and the postman never called. So, seating Emily, who was expecting a baby, in her bath chair, Alfred dragged her over two miles of a very rough road to Cuckfield, where they put up at the Talbot Inn. From there they took themselves and their troubles to Drummond Rawnsley at Shiplake. Here they met Charles Kingsley, who impressed them powerfully with his Christian Socialism and his tirades against sweated labour and insanitary housing in the industrial cities, as he strode up and down the vicar's study, brandishing his long clay pipe, and calling somewhat unrealistically for an alliance between the Church, the gentry and the workers against the shopkeepers and the Manchester Radicals.

A fortnight later they went to Edmund Lushington. On the way, Emily fell down some steps and Alfred became seriously worried about her condition for several days after their arrival at Park House. Leaving her in the care of his sister Cecilia, he went up to London to attend the Queen's *levée* on 6 March; for this he borrowed Samuel Rogers's Court dress, which had also been worn by Wordsworth for another occasion. It was rather a tight fit, but Alfred was delighted with the cocked hat and the appearance of his fine legs in silk stockings. While in town he was inevitably drawn into a round of social engagements. At Lord John Russell's party he met George Campbell, eighth Duke of Argyll, with whom he became very friendly, for the duke was a great admirer of his poetry and spoke of his pleasure at meeting him. 'You won't find much in me, after all,' was Alfred's characteristic reply. He also met Henry Taylor, poet and civil servant, again; it was from him that he heard of Chapel House, Montpelier Row, Twickenham, which was to let. As soon as he saw it, Tennyson decided to take it without waiting to consult Emily. He signed the lease on 6 March, the day of his first appearance at Court. Five days later he and Emily moved in, and that first evening James Spedding and Coventry Patmore dined with them. Montpelier Row is one of the finest Georgian terraces in England. Overlooking the grounds of Marble Hill, it was built at about the same time as Lord Burlington's Chiswick House and Pope's villa nearby

On 20 April Emily gave birth to a dead boy. 'My poor boy died being born,' Tennyson wrote to John Forster. 'My wife is safe as yet, but I rather dread the third day. The nurse dressed up the little body in pure white. He was a grand massive manchild, noble brow and hands, which he had clenched in his determination to be born. Had he lived the doctor said he would have been lusty and healthy, but somehow he got strangled. I kissed his poor pale hands and came away and they buried him last night in Twickenham churchyard.'

As soon as Emily had recovered enough to receive visitors, many friends came out from London to see them: the Carlyles, Tom Taylor, Henry and Julia Hallam, the Patmores, Brookfield, John Millais. A new friend, the Irish poet William Allingham, came with an introduction from Patmore in June. His *Diary* gives a vivid account of this first meeting with Tennyson.

> I was admitted, shown upstairs into a room with books lying
> about, and soon came in a tall, broad-shouldered swarthy man,
> slightly stooping, with loose dark hair and beard. He wore
> spectacles and was obviously very near sighted. Hollow cheeks
> and the dark pallor of his skin gave him an unhealthy
> expression. He was a strange and almost spectral figure. The
> Great Man peered close at me, and then shook hands cordially,
> yet with a profound quietude of manner. He was then about
> forty-five, but looked much older, from his bulk, his short-sight,
> sloping shoulders, and loose careless dress. He looked tired,
> and said he had been asleep and was suffering from hay-fever.
> Mrs. Tennyson came in, very sweet and courteous, with low
> soft voice, and by and by when I rose to take my leave she
> said, 'Won't you stay for dinner?' which I was too happy to do.

Then Tennyson took Allingham upstairs to his study and picking up the volume of poems Allingham had sent him said: ' "You can see it is a good deal dirtier than most of the books." Here he began to read from the book. The rich slow solemn chant of his voice glorified the little poems. The pieces never seemed to me so good before or since.' Doubtless the chant was not unlike the hieratic chant of W. B. Yeats.

At dinner Tennyson complained of the amount of poetry he had sent to him, though he had recently received a critical work in which he had read, 'We exhort Mr Tennyson to abandon the weeping willow with its fragile earth-tending twigs, and to adopt the poplar, with one heaven-pointing finger.' Over his port, with the arrival of Patmore, Tennyson said that his belief rested on two things, a Chief Intelligence and Immortality. 'I could not eat my dinner without a belief in immortality. If I did not believe in that I'd go down immediately and jump off Richmond Bridge.' This made Allingham laugh. 'Why do you laugh?' said Tennyson shortly. Allingham explained that there was something ludicrous in the image of him jumping off Richmond Bridge. 'Well,' said Tennyson, 'in such a case I'd as soon make a comic end as a tragic.'

When tea was served in another room Tennyson went in muttering 'We exhort Mr Tennyson . . .'. When he left, Allingham felt as though he had been familiar for years with 'this great and simple man'.

Before his next visit Allingham received a note from Tennyson which said: 'As my wife is not very well you must tread softly and speak low.' Allingham found Mrs Tennyson, 'sweet, pale and kind', reclining on the drawing-room sofa. Then there arrived Frederick Tennyson and FitzGerald, who 'told droll stories with a quiet gravity, much amusing Mrs Tennyson in particular'. After dinner FitzGerald stood up for Pope's *Homer* and tried in vain to get Tennyson's approval. Allingham spilt some of his port on the table-cloth and Tennyson calmly put salt on it, remarking: 'I believe it never comes out.' Then he complained that nothing would grow in his garden but stones. 'I pick up all I can see, and the next time I come there are just as many!' Then he observed: 'England ought to keep her colonies and draw them closer. She ought to have their representatives sitting in London, either in or in connection with the Imperial Parliament.'

The number of visitors who came to Chapel House now became rather trying for Emily, so early in July Alfred took her to Italy, the country he had always longed to visit. In Paris they met the Brownings on their way back to England, and Alfred offered them Chapel House during his and Emily's absence. He spoke of England as 'the greatest nation in the world and the most vulgar' and said that he was leaving England because they hunted him to death. From Paris they went straight to the Italian Riviera, driving by the coast road from Genoa. They stayed three weeks at Lucca and then went on to

Florence to stay with Frederick at the Villa Torrigiani, thence on 24 September to Leghorn, intending to continue south by boat. But the sea proved too rough for Emily. They therefore turned north, crossing the Lombardy plain in a continuous downpour of rain to Milan, where Alfred climbed at dawn to the roof of the cathedral to see Monte Rosa hanging with its 'shadowy-pencilled valleys/And snowy dells in the golden air'. They missed seeing Rome and Venice, the one being in too disturbed a condition and the other in the grip of fever, and returned to Paris via Como. In Paris they met the Brownings again, as they were on their way back to Italy. Emily and Elizabeth met 'like sisters', and on leaving, the Brownings gave them two little bunches of artificial flowers. They reached Chapel House at the end of October. Tennyson commemorated the Italian tour in 'The Daisy', written in 1853 during a visit to Edinburgh.

Soon after their return came the news of Louis Napoleon's *coup d'état*. William Bell Scott, the Pre-Raphaelite painter and poet, witnessed his triumph at the Madeleine. 'Then came Louis Napoleon with thousands of cavalry and brazen music,' he recorded in his diary, 'and the clergy streamed out of the sacred fane to congratulate their saviour from republicanism.' Many people now began to fear a French invasion of England. Tennyson thought the invasion would take us by surprise and be successful. Nevertheless, he said, the whole country would rise against the invaders and the end of the historic chapter 'would be the combined European invasion of France, the destruction of Paris and its suppression for ever, with the final dismemberment of France.' 'Such was Tennyson's map of immediately coming events at that day,' wrote Bell Scott. 'His brother, Patmore, and others agreed with him. He hated the French with a hatred that made me love him, and he has been true to this feeling to the present, I believe; at least, when the Swinburnian passion for French things, for Victor Hugo and others, had infected nearly all the young writers, he warned us against degrading our own art with "the poisonous honey stolen from France".'[1]

In those days, of course, it was the fashion, a fashion set by the Queen, the Prince Consort and Carlyle, to admire everything German: Germany was the honest, wholesome, peace-loving country, whereas France was the whore of Europe, mendacious, immoral and militaristic, for which view there was during the Second Empire some excuse. 'By the holy living God,' exclaimed Tennyson, 'France is a loathsome state!' These fears resulted in the formation of the Volunteer Force, and Tennyson sent Patmore £5 for his rifle club, formed after Patmore's letter to *The Times* of 22 January 1852. The composition of patriotic songs followed: 'Rifle-Clubs ! ! !' 'Britons, Guard Your Own', 'For the Penny-Wise', 'The Third of February,

1852' and 'Hands All Round', which appeared in John Forster's *Examiner*. Tennyson wrote 'Hands All Round' with the tears streaming down his cheeks. It concluded with an invocation to America, such as we have become familiar with in more recent times:

> Gigantic daughter of the West,
>    We drink to thee across the flood,
> We know thee most, we love thee best
>    For art thou not of British blood?
> Should war's mad blast again be blown,
>    Permit not thou the tyrant powers
> To fight thy mother here alone,
>    But let thy broadsides roar with ours.
>    Hands all round!
>    God the tyrant's curse confound!
>    To our great kinsmen of the West, my friends,
>    And the great name of England round and round.
>
> O rise, our strong Atlantic sons,
>    When war against our freedom springs!
> O speak to Europe through your guns!
>    They *can* be understood by kings.

In writing this, Tennyson was not, of course, writing in his official capacity as Poet Laureate. He, therefore, published his martial verses either anonymously or signed 'Merlin'. Another anonymous piece 'Suggested by Reading an Article in a Newspaper' contained a reference to the Catholic Church as 'that half-pagan harlot kept by France'. The astonishing violence of Tennyson's political pronouncements was largely the violence of the sedentary man who knew he would not have to fight himself, though they are an indication of the innate violence of his nature, which later burst forth again in the final stanzas of *Maud*, celebrating the outbreak of the Crimean War.

Very different is the noble 'Ode on the Death of the Duke of Wellington', published as a two-shilling pamphlet to be sold on the day of the funeral in November 1852. This was his first great utterance as Laureate. He attended the funeral and was struck by 'the look of sober manhood of the British soldier', as he wrote to Fitz-Gerald. But the ode was generally abused by the critics, though Henry Taylor wrote: 'It has a greatness worthy of its theme and an absolute simplicity and truth, with all the poetic passion of your nature moving underneath.' Tennyson was fond of reading it aloud with his broad Lincolnshire accent, 'mouthing out his hollow oes and aes':

[96]

Bury the Greaaat Duke
  With an empire's lamentaaation,
Let us bury the Greaaat Duke
  To the nooise of the moourning of a mighty naaation.

About this time Tennyson was invited by F. T. Palgrave to meet Benjamin Jowett, the great tutor of Balliol, who was staying with Palgrave at Kneller Hall, the experimental training college at Twickenham. After their meeting he brought Jowett back to Chapel House to dine, and Jowett and Tennyson later became intimate friends. Jowett was already a far-sighted educational reformer whose aim was to throw Oxford open to young men of all classes, though at that time there was little chance of any working-class man going up to Oxford, any more than there was for Thomas Hardy's Jude. Jowett was already being persecuted for his liberal religious views by the entrenched conservatism of Oxford and worked for years as Classical Tutor for a ludicrously small salary. A few years later he became tutor to the obstreperous young Swinburne, and his treatment of him was remarkably understanding. He shared his persecution with the Christian Socialist F. D. Maurice, who was dismissed from his post at University College, London, for rejecting the doctrine of eternal punishment! Maurice, who founded the Working Men's College in Great Ormond Street, Bloomsbury, where Ruskin and Rossetti taught in the evenings, was also to become one of Tennyson's closest friends.

It was during the Chapel House period that a veteran of Waterloo brought Tennyson an epic poem on the battle in twelve cantos. He had taught himself to read and write in order to compose it, and Sir Charles Tennyson tells us that his grandfather 'suffered much under the author's reading from his work and particularly in the unwelcome task of advising on its merit, for alas! it was utterly worthless.' Tennyson was continually being sent manuscripts by would-be poets with requests for money, to which he generally succumbed. 'I don't suppose old Wordy paid attention to such,' he once remarked. 'He was too canny!'

Hallam Tennyson was born this year (August 1852) and his father wrote to John Forster: 'I have seen beautiful things in my life, but I never saw anything more beautiful than the mother's face as she lay by the young child an hour or two after, or heard anything sweeter than the little lamb-like bleat of the young one. I had fancied that children after birth had been all shriek and roar.' Elizabeth Barrett Browning wrote to congratulate him; the godfathers were Henry Hallam and F. D. Maurice. Dickens wrote excusing himself from attending the christening of the young one

[97]

'born in sin', as the baptism service has it. But among those present were Henry Taylor, Palgrave, Edmund Lushington, Drummond Rawnsley, Robert Browning and Charles and Julia Cameron, the formidable photographer. After the service Tennyson took Palgrave and Browning up to his study for a whisky toddy, talk about poetry, and abuse of Louis Napoleon.

The constant stream of visitors, combined with the river floods of the late autumn and winter, made it impossible for Tennyson to settle down to any substantial new work. Moreover, he heard that a woman was spreading rumours in Richmond that he had married her some years before at Cheltenham and then deserted her, and she was using this story to collect subscriptions to enable her to become matron of an emigrant ship. Tennyson said that this was 'only one of the fraudulent schemes for raising the wind which rogues and harlots have resort to' and that 'instead of being elected matron of an emigrant ship, she ought to be chucked overboard.' He offered to meet the woman any day she chose. After that he heard no more of it, and during the autumn he and Emily first moved to Seaford, then to Brighton, then to Farnham. Early in the next year Tennyson was asked whether he would allow himself to be nominated as Rector of Edinburgh University. He declined and wrote that while 'gratefully sensible of the honour intended me . . . I could neither undertake to come to Edinburgh nor to deliver an inaugural address at the time specified. You will doubtless find another and worthier than myself to fill this office.'

In May he and Emily visited Charles Kingsley at Eversley; towards the end of July they met Palgrave at York and went to Scotland to visit Alfred's old Cambridge friend Robert Monteith at his house on the Clyde. But he was beginning to find Palgrave's devotion distinctly trying. 'Poor fellow,' he wrote to Emily, after parting from him at Glasgow, 'I really believe he has a liking for me, which he thinks is not fully returned.' However, they once more joined forces and went to the Sound of Mull to spend several days with Palgrave's friend William Sellar, the Virgilian scholar and Professor of Latin at Edinburgh University, with whom they took long tramps on the moors. 'No one could have been more easy, simple and delightful,' Mrs Sellar wrote to Hallam Tennyson when he was compiling the *Memoir*. 'In the evening he read to us, and no one who heard him could ever forget his reading of the "Ode on the Death of the Duke of Wellington"; to this day I never read it without hearing his voice.' But Tennyson was not always so easy. '*In Memoriam* was on the table and he said: "I shan't read this." It happened to be open at "Calm is the Morn", and my remarking that it was an especial favourite of mine, he turned round quickly and demanded *"Why?"* . . . He and Mr Palgrave left us by boat, a long row of fifteen miles to Oban; and on my husband saying to the old Gaelic boatman, "Robert, you are taking over one of the greatest men in England," he replied "That black-a-vise Mr Tinsmith that came with Mr Pancake? Well, well!" ' From Oban Tennyson and Palgrave visited Loch Fyne, Inveraray, Staffa and Iona. He arranged with Palgrave that 'whenever the two of them came to any scene or building of any particular interest or grandeur, he himself should be allowed to withdraw entirely alone and out of sight, so that he could enjoy the beauty undisturbed.' He also refused to make any plans for their next day's expedition, saying that 'this 'often resulted in missed trains or other inconveniences', though on the day he left all arrangements to Palgrave.[2]

After parting from his too assiduous companion, Tennyson fell ill for three weeks in Edinburgh. One evening, turning over the pages of the book he had borrowed from Emily, he came upon the daisy he had given her during their Italian tour two years before, dry and flattened. This gave rise to one of his most charming lyrics, 'The Daisy', which concludes:

I found, though crushed to hard and dry,
This nurseling of another sky
 Still in the little book you lent me,
And where you tenderly laid it by:

And I forgot the clouded Forth,
The gloom that saddens Heaven and Earth,
 The bitter east, the misty summer
And gray metropolis of the North.

Perchance, to lull the throbs of pain,
Perchance, to charm a vacant brain,
 Perchance, to dream you still beside me,
My fancy fled to the South again.

# 8

It was while staying with friends at Bonchurch, Isle of Wight, that Tennyson first heard of Farringford; and in November 1853 he and Emily went to look at it. Having missed the ferry, they crossed the Solent in an open rowing-boat, when 'one dark heron flew over the sea backed by a daffodil sky'. They spent the night at an hotel and next day went to look over the house standing in its small park, where they were to spend the rest of their lives.

Farringford is a rambling late-Georgian house with Gothic trimmings, even the interior woodwork being carved in imitation of Gothic tracery. At that time the exterior was thickly overgrown with ivy and magnolias, half-obscuring the windows and making the interior rather dark, though the great west window of the drawing-room commanded a magnificent view of the downs and the sea at Freshwater Bay. To Mrs Thackeray Ritchie, who often stayed there in later years, 'the house at Farringford itself seemed like a charmed palace, with green walls without, and speaking walls within. There hung Dante with his solemn nose and wreath; Italy gleamed over the doorways; friends' faces lined the passages, books filled the shelves, and a glow of crimson was everywhere; the oriel drawing-room windows was full of green and golden leaves, of the sound of birds and the distant sea.' Farringford was, indeed, a veritable palace of the Sleeping Beauty and suited in every way to Tennyson's temperament, surrounded as it was by 'dense copses of pine, elm, holly and laurel, and carpeted with flowers in continual succession from snowdrop to foxglove.'[1]

'I wrote on Friday to accept the house,' writes Tennyson on 14 November. 'I also wrote today to Moxon to advance one thousand four hundred pounds he owes me, the odd six hundred to be paid if he will in March when I get my moneys in. Why I did it? Because by buying safe debentures in the East Lincolnshire Line for two thousand five hundred pounds, with that and five hundred a year I think we ought to get on.' On 24 November, having taken the house furnished on trial, they left Twickenham and next day came into possession of

Farringford. It did not take them long to decide to lease the house with an option of purchase. The property also included a small farm. Their two maids, however, did not relish the solitude and on the evening of their arrival were found in tears. The remainder of the lease of Chapel House Tennyson handed over to his mother.

He now became an enthusiastic bird watcher and amateur geologist. Visitors to Farringford usually had to walk the three miles from Yarmouth. There was, of course, no public transport and Tennyson did not as yet possess a carriage, though the gardener had a donkey cart. But it was not long before friends began to arrive: Edmund and Franklin Lushington, Patmore, Tom Taylor. Fitz-Gerald stayed a fortnight, read Persian poetry with Alfred, and played Mozart. These were soon followed by Spedding, Clough, Jowett, Lear, Dickie Doyle, and Millais, who had been commissioned by Moxon to illustrate Tennyson's poems. The poet himself did not care for the idea, but allowed himself to be persuaded by Moxon on the ground that it would bring him an extra £2,000 towards the purchase of Farringford. Otherwise he was kept busy rolling the lawn, cutting new glades through the copses, making a little summer house out of rushes in the kitchen garden, gravelling the paths and helping the farm workers to load the waggons, and taking Emily for walks with him in her bath chair. The varying moods of the sea were a constant delight and he would take long walks at night on the downs, and had a platform built on the roof so that he could study the stars. He made friends with the coastguards and the shepherds and went out at night with the fishermen in their boats, reading his poems to them as they rowed. These simple men were, he said, among the best listeners he ever had, and he was deeply interested in their lives and beliefs.

In March 1854 Lionel was born. Tennyson chose this name for his second son because he was at the time looking through his study window at the planet Mars as 'he glowed like a ruddy shield on the Lion's breast'. In April he dragged Emily out in her garden chair to see the 'wealth of daffodils and the ruby sheaths of the lime leaves'. During FitzGerald's stay he sketched and Tennyson began wood-carving. One day Fitz brought back from one of his walks bunches of horned poppies and yellow iris, 'over which like a boy he was ecstatic'. Tennyson studied Persian grammar so assiduously that he began to see the Persian letters 'stalking like giants round the walls of his room'. After that Hafiz and the Persian grammar had to be hidden away.

In June 1855 Tennyson went up to Oxford to receive his D.C.L. As he sat waiting in the Master's garden at Balliol, he said that the shouts of the undergraduates in the Sheldonian were like the shouts of the Roman crowd: 'Christiani ad leones'. He was very nervous, but as he entered the theatre in his borrowed scarlet gown with Sir John Burgoyne and Sir de Lacy Evans, two of the more successful commanders in the Crimea, a voice was heard to ask: 'Did your mother call you early, Alfred dear?', which he answered with a grim smile. Otherwise he was greeted with a tremendous ovation and there was cries of '*In Memoriam*! Alma! Inkerman!' After the ceremony he was so pleased with his scarlet gown that he continued to wear it all the evening.

In July *Maud or The Madness* was published. It had its origin, we are told, when his friend Sir John Simeon, the Roman Catholic squire of Swainston Hall, near Newport, came upon the lines in an old copy of *The Tribute* of 1837:

> Oh! that 'twere possible,
>   After long grief and pain,
> To find the arms of my true-love
>   Round me once again!

which had been written soon after the death of Arthur Hallam. Simeon was so moved that he urged Tennyson to weave a story round them. Other contributing factors were his old love for Rosa Baring, his talks with Kingsley and Maurice about the terrible conditions in the new manufacturing towns, with their dirt, disease and sweated labour, and the war fever that was sweeping the country during the summer and autumn of 1854. The complex strands of this poem have been illuminatingly disentangled by R. W. Rader in his *Tennyson's 'Maud': The Biographical Genesis* (1963). Many other things went to the making of *Maud*: Tennyson's grief at his father's death, which practically amounted to suicide, his brother Edward's incurable insanity, the loss of his money in Dr Allen's Pyroglyphs, his ten years' separation from Emily during which he sometimes felt that he was going mad himself, 'marriage-hindering Mammon', and his resentment at the attitude of the Tennyson d'Eyncourts. 'Alfred had thrown the whole passion of his being into *Maud*, which remained throughout his life his favourite poem, the one which he could best read aloud and read with the most overwhelming effect. He had never written with more fire and originality.'[2]

On 28 September 1855, Tennyson noted in his diary: 'I dined yesterday with the Brownings and a very pleasant evening. The two Rossettis came in during the evening.' It was on this occasion that Gabriel Rossetti did his sketch of the poet reading *Maud*. Afterwards Rossetti wrote to Allingham: 'He is quite as glorious in his way as

Browning in his, and perhaps of the two men even more impressive on the whole personally.'

The critics were utterly bewildered by *Maud*, for nothing could have been more different from *In Memoriam*, with its grave, controlled emotion and metaphysical speculation. *Maud*, with its free, irregular metres, fragmentary construction and wild outbursts of emotion, was not at all 'Tennysonian'. They were as bewildered as the critics of the 1920s were by *The Waste Land*. One critic said that one of the two vowels should be omitted from the title, and that it did not much matter which; another called it 'dead level prose run mad'. 'If our author pipe of adultery, fornication, murder and suicide,' wrote another, 'put him down as a practiser of those crimes.' This vastly amused Tennyson, who remarked: 'Adulterer I may be, fornicator I may be, murderer I may be, suicide I am not yet.' But Moxon wrote that Browning considered *Maud* a great poem and had already read it four times. In his own theatrical declamation of the poem, which invariably reduced both himself and his audience to tears, Tennyson, like Dickens in his public readings of his novels, exhibited all his latent histrionic talent. It was said of him that had he not been a poet he could have been a remarkable actor.

His son tells us that he thought so well of Dr Mann's '*Maud*' *Vindicated* that he wanted its opening passage setting the scene inserted among the notes to the poem. Tennyson realised that some explanation was necessary, for the first impression of the poem can be rather confusing.

'Although still a young man,' wrote Dr Mann of the protagonist, 'he has lost his father some years before by a sudden violent death – following immediately upon unforseen ruin brought about by an unfortunate speculation in which the deceased has engaged. Whether the death was the result of accident or self-inflicted in a moment of despair, no one knows, but the son's mind has been painfully possessed by a suspicion of villainy or foul play somewhere, because an old friend of the family became suddenly and unaccountably rich by the same transaction that had brought ruin to the dead. Shortly after the decease of his father, the bereaved young man, by the death of his mother, is left quite alone in the world. He continues henceforth to reside in the retired village in which his early days have been spent, but the sad experiences of his youth have confirmed the bent of his mind, constitutionally prone to depression and melancholy. Brooding in loneliness upon miserable memories and bitter fancies, his temperament as a matter of course becomes more and more morbid and irritable. He can see nothing in human affairs that does not awaken in him disgust and contempt. Evil glares out from all social arrangements, and unqualified meanness and selfishness appear in every human form, so he keeps to himself and chews the cud of cynicism and discontent apart from his kind. . . .'

Tennyson said of *Maud*: 'This poem is a little *Hamlet*, the history of a morbid poet-soul under the blighting influence of a recklessly speculative age. He is the heir of madness, an egoist with the makings of a cynic, raised to sanity by a pure and holy love which elevates his nature, passing from the height of triumph to the lowest depth of misery, driven into madness by the loss of her whom he has loved and when he has at length passed through the fiery furnace, and has recovered his reason, giving himself up to work for the good of mankind through the unselfishness of his great passion.' To this Hallam Tennyson adds: 'My father pointed out that even Nature at first presented herself to the man in sad visions:'

> And the flying gold of the ruined woodlands
>   drove through the air.

The 'blood-red heath', too, is an exaggeration of colour, and his suspicion that all the world is against him is as true to his nature as the mood when he is 'fantastically merry'. Today we should probably call him a manic-depressive. 'The passion of the first Canto was given by my father in a sort of rushing recitative, through the long sweeping lines of satire and invective against the greed for money, and of horror at the consequences of the war of the hearth.'[3]

This is followed by a certain longing for 'a philosopher's life in the quiet woodland ways'; but then come disturbing thoughts of Maud, though the protagonist tries to persuade himself that she is insipid.

> Long have I sighed for a calm: God grant I may find it at last!
> It was never broken by Maud, she has neither savour nor salt,
> But a cold and clear-cut face, as I found when her carriage past,
> Perfectly beautiful: let it be granted her: where is the fault?
> All that I saw (for her eyes were downcast, not to be seen)
> Faultily faultless, icily regular, splendidly null,
> Dead perfection, no more; nothing more, if it had not been
> For a chance of travel, a paleness, an hour's defect of the rose,
> Or an underlip, you may call it a little too ripe, too full,
> Or the least little delicate aquiline curve in a sensitive nose,
> From which I escaped heart-free, with the least little touch of
>   spleen.

Evidently he has observed her very closely, a perfect Victorian cameo. But he is by no means so 'heart-free' as he would like to think, and as the next Canto makes plain:

Cold and clear-cut face, why come you so cruelly meek,
Breaking a slumber in which all spleenful folly was drowned,
Pale with the golden beam of an eyelash dead on the cheek,
Passionless, pale, cold face, star-sweet on a gloom profound;
Woman-like, taking revenge too deep for a transient wrong
Done but in thought to your beauty, and ever as pale as before,
Growing and fading and growing upon me without a sound,
Luminous, gemlike, ghostlike, deathlike, half the night long
Growing and fading and growing, till I could bear it no more,
But arose, and all by myself in my own dark garden ground,
Listening now to the tide in its broad-flung shipwrecking roar,
Now to the scream of a maddened beach dragged down by the
    wave,
Walked in a wintry wind by a ghastly glimmer, and found
The shining daffodil dead, and Orion low in his grave.

The protagonist's emotional state is perfectly objectified in the
scream of the maddened beach, the intensity of his desire and its
frustration, while the last two lines seem to portend not only the
withering and death of his love, but his own death. But he still
deceives himself, and it is at night that his unconscious reveals to
him not only the intensity of his love but its doom. Meanwhile the
village 'bubbles o'er like a city, with gossip, scandal, and spite', and
all around him in Nature the murderous struggle for survival goes
on, one species preying upon another:

For nature is one with rapine, a harm no preacher can heal;
The Mayfly is torn by the swallow, the sparrow speared by the
    shrike,
And the whole little wood where I sit is a world of plunder and
    prey.

We are puppets, Man in his pride, and Beauty fair in her flower;
Do we move ourselves, or are moved by an unseen hand at a game
That pushes us off from the board, and others ever succeed?
Ah yet, we cannot be kind to each other here for an hour;
We whisper, and hint, and chuckle, and grin at a brother's shame;
However we brave it out, we men are a little breed.

Such pessimism foreshadows Thomas Hardy:

For the drift of the Maker is dark, an Isis hid by the veil.

But the thought of Maud returns obsessively:

And most of all I would flee from the cruel madness of love,
The honey of poison-flowers and all the measureless ill.

[105]

Ah Maud, you milkwhite fawn, you are all unmeet for a wife.
Your mother is mute in her grave as her image in marble above;
Your father is ever in London, you wander about at your will;
You have but fed on the roses and lain in the lilies of life.

Another day he hears her singing to herself up at the Hall:

A passionate ballad gallant and gay,
A martial song like a trumpet's call!
Singing alone in the morning of life,
In the happy morning of life and of May. . . .

Maud with her exquisite face,
And wild voice pealing up to the sunny sky.

But no, no, it is not her he adores, 'Not her, not her, not a voice.'
Even when he meets her in the village and she smiles tenderly at him
and touches his hand, he finds any reason for her action but the
obvious one, imagining that perhaps her brother, 'That jewelled
mass of millinery,/That oiled and curled Assyrian Bull/Smelling of
musk and of insolence', had told her to smile on him to catch his vote
at the next election. Then he thinks that perhaps she pities him,
which is worse. Tennyson's picture of a neurotic state of mind is
perfect:

Living alone in an empty house,
Here half-hid in the gleaming wood,
Where I hear the dead at midday moan,
And the shrieking rush of the wainscot mouse,
And my own sad name in corners cried,
When the shiver of dancing leaves is thrown
About its echoing chambers wide,
Till a morbid-hate and horror have grown
Of a world in which I have hardly mixt,
And a morbid eating lichen fixt
On a heart half-turned to stone.

O heart of stone, are you flesh, and caught
By that you swore to withstand?

And he thinks of the new-made lord, Maud's suitor, whom he had
lately seen riding with her and her brother on the moor:

whose splendour plucks
The slavish hat from the villager's head?
Whose old grandfather has lately died,
Gone to a blacker pit, for whom
Grimy nakedness dragging his trucks

[106]

And laying his trams in a poisoned gloom
Wrought, till he crept from a gutted mine
Master of half a servile shire,
And left his coal all turned into gold
To a grandson, first of his noble line,
Rich in the grace all women desire,
Strong in the power that all men adore,
And simper and set their voices lower,
And soften as if to a girl, and hold
Awe-stricken breaths at a work divine,
Seeing his gewgaw castle shine,
New as his title, built last year,
There amid perky larches and pine,
And over the sullen-purple moor
(Look at it) pricking a cockney ear.

So Tennyson evidently felt about his uncle's newly-built Bayons Manor.

Maud could be gracious too, no doubt,
To a lord, a captain, a padded shape,
A bought commission, a waxen face,
A rabbit mouth that is ever agape –
Bought? what is it he cannot buy?
And therefore splenetic, personal, base,
A wounded thing with a rancorous cry,
At war with myself and a wretched race,
Sick, sick to the heart of life, am I.

It is a little surprising that all this bitterness and fury should burst out of Tennyson so soon after a happy marriage, when, as he said, the peace of God had entered his life at the altar. Evidently his old miseries and resentment were still boiling deep within him. He may not have even been aware of them as he dragged Emily about in her invalid chair or blew soap bubbles for his children. But the old wounds of half a lifetime had gone too deep to be healed so soon, or, perhaps, to be ever healed. Cries the 'hero' of *Maud*:

And ah for a man to arise in me,
That the man I am may cease to be.

And yet, contrary to all his fears and bitterness, he declares his love to Maud and is accepted. Yet an astonishing moment of bathos accompanies his declaration:

I kiss'd her slender hand –
    She took the kiss sedately:

[107]

Maud is not seventeen,
    But she is tall and stately.

Why this sudden artificiality, when all his passion resolves itself into a genteel Victorian keepsake? and when so much in this poem arises from deeply buried autobiographical sources. As R. W. Rader points out, there is every reason to connect the Hall of *Maud* with Harrington Hall, the home of Rosa Baring, who, like Maud, had 'her own little oak room'. Tennyson's lover goes up to the Hall at dawn and to his morbid imagination the drawn curtains seem to him like the curtains in a house of the dead, for death and the fear of madness have haunted the poem from its opening lines. But there is a moment of blessedness after Maud has returned his love, 'a blessedness so intense,' comments Hallam Tennyson, 'that it borders on sadness, and my father's voice used to break down when he came to:

I have led her home, my love, my only friend.
There is none like her, none.
And never yet so warmly ran my blood
And sweetly, on and on
Calming itself to the long-wished-for end,
Full to the banks, close on the promised good.

None like her, none.
Just now the dry-tongued laurels' pattering talk
Seemed her light foot along the garden walk,
And shook my heart to think she comes once more;
But even then I heard her close the door,
The gates of Heaven are closed, and she is gone.

There is none like her, none.
Nor will be when our summers have deceased.
O, art thou sighing for Lebanon
In the long breeze that streams to thy delicious East,
Sighing for Lebanon,
Dark cedar, though thy limbs have here increased,
Upon a pastoral slope as fair,
And looking to the South, and fed
With honeyed rain and delicate air,
And haunted by the starry head
Of her whose gentle will has changed my fate,
And made my life a perfumed altar-flame.

But his state of mind is still a morbid one: the strained idealism of these lines is but the reverse of the neurotic dread and anguish of the earlier part of the poem. Hallam Tennyson continues: 'Joy

[108]

1   George Clayton Tennyson the Younger, father of the poet

2  a Somersby Rectory

b Bayons Manor

3   Tennyson aged about 22, from a drawing attributed to James Spedding

4 Arthur Hallam, from
a drawing by James
Spedding

5 Rosa Baring, from a
portrait by R. Buikner

6  Tennyson in about 1840, from the portrait by S. Laurence

7    Emily Tennyson, with Hallam (left) and Lionel (right), in about 1864

8    Tennyson with the Howard family at Naworth Castle, Cumberland, in
1871

9   a  Farringford

b  Aldworth

original M.S. of the epilogue to the "Idylls of the King"
To the Queen.

O loyal to the royal in thyself,
And loyal to thy land, as this to thee—
Bear witness, that rememberable morn
When pale from fever yet the goodly Prince
Who scarce had pluck'd his flickering life again
From halfway down the shadow of the grave,
Past with thee Thro' thy people & their love,
And London roll'd one tide of joy Thro' all
Her trebled millions, & loud leagues of man
And welcome: witness too, thus silent cry,
The prayer of many a people, creed & clime—
Thunderless lightnings striking under sea
From sunset & sunrise of all thy realms,
And that true North, whereof we lately heard
A strain to shame us "Keep ye to yourselves;
So for, here we sicken of your loyalty:
Your love is as a burthen; get you gone?
Is this the tone of empire? this the faith
That made us rulers? this, indeed, her voice
And meaning, whom the roar of Hougoumont
Left mightiest of all peoples in the west?
What shock has fool'd her since, that she should speak
So feebly? — wealthier - wealthier - hour by hour:
The voice of Britain, or a sinking land,
Some thirdrate isle half-lost among her seas?
There rang her voice, when the full city peal'd
Thee & thy Prince! the loyal to their crowns
Are loyal to their own far sons, who love
This ancient Ocean-empire, & her throne

10   The Epilogue to *Idylls of the King* in Tennyson's manuscript

11  *The Beguiling of Merlin,* from the painting by Sir Edward
Burne-Jones

THE IMPERIAL INSTITUTE

AN ILLUSTRATED RECORD OF THE

Opening Ceremony by Her Majesty the Queen

12 The opening of the Imperial Institute by Queen Victoria in 1893. From a print first published in a commemorative supplement of *The Graphic*

13 Tennyson in 1864, from the drawing by M. Arnault

14 Tennyson in 1866, photographed by Julia Margaret
Cameron

15 G. F. Watts at work on his statue of Tennyson in 1903

16   Tennyson in 1884, from the drawing by Frederick Sandys

culminates in "Come into the garden, Maud", and my father's eyes, which were through the other love-passages veiled by his drooping lids, would suddenly flash as he looked up and spoke these words, the passion in his voice deepening in the last words of the stanza:

> She is coming, my own, my sweet,
>   Were it ever so airy a tread,
> My heart would hear her and beat,
>   Were it earth in an earthy bed;
> My dust would hear her and beat,
>   Had I lain for a century dead;
> Would start and tremble under her feet,
>   And blossom in purple and red.'

It is symptomatic of his neurotic state of mind that Tennyson's protagonist should think of himself as lying in the grave at the very moment when his love is about to be fulfilled and his life has become 'a perfumed altar-flame'. But his heart has virtually lain dead for so long that he can scarcely believe that a new life is now opening before him and he is still aware of some 'dark undercurrent of woe' which he tries in vain to banish. The 'woe' materialises all too soon in the return of Maud's father, the 'ponderous squire', who gives

> A grand political dinner
> To half the squirelings near,

followed by a dance at the Hall 'For the maids and the marriage-makers'. And standing in Maud's rose garden, her lover waits in a light-headed condition for her to come out to him on the terrace, while he communes with the flowers, who seem to be waiting for Maud too:

> But the rose was awake all night for your sake,
>   Knowing your promise to me;
> The lilies and roses were all awake,
>   They sighed for the dawn and thee.
>
> Queen rose of the rosebud garden of girls,
>   Come hither, the dances are done,
> In gloss of satin and glimmer of pearls,
>   Queen lily and rose in one;
> Shine out, little head, sunning over with curls,
>   To the flowers, and be their sun.
>
> There has fallen a splendid tear
>   From the passion-flower at the gate.

E                                       [109]

She is coming, my dove, my dear;
  She is coming, my life, my fate;
The red rose cries, 'She is near, she is near;'
  The white rose weeps, 'She is late;'
The larkspur listens, 'I hear, I hear;'
  And the lily whispers, 'I wait.'

There is evidently an echo of these lines in Swinburne's 'Interlude':

You came, and the sun came after,
  And the green grew golden above,
And the flag flowers lightened with laughter,
  And the meadowsweet shook with love.

If this is considered faintly absurd, it is no more absurd than Tennyson's talking flowers, parodied by Lewis Carroll in *Through the Looking-Glass*: 'She's coming!' cried the Larkspur, 'I hear her footstep, thump, thump, along the gravel walk!'

It has been pointed out that the song 'Come into the garden, Maud' has a latent waltz rhythm, echoing the sound of the dances from the Hall, a rhythm that quickens towards the close of the song with Maud's imminent arrival and the climax of Part I of the poem, when disaster strikes as Maud's brother discovers his sister and the protagonist in each other's arms on the terrace. This situation seems to have been something of an obsession of Tennyson's, for it recurs in *Locksley Hall*, *Edwin Morris* and *Aylmer's Field*, and had its origin in a similar situation in his own life, when he and Rosa Baring were discovered by her indignant relatives in each other's arms on the terrace of Harrington Hall. For Tennyson, like his own heroes, had been spurned by the family in favour of a more wealthy lover, a memory which still rankled. In this case, the protagonist challenges Maud's brother to a duel and shoots him, as we learn in Part II, when he has fled to Brittany. His memory of it is suitably melodramatic. Maud dies of shock and grief and her lover is haunted by her ghost as he temporarily loses his reason and fancies himself dead too.

Dead, long dead,
Long dead!
And my heart is a handful of dust,
And the wheels go over my head,
And my bones are shaken with pain,
For into a shallow grave they are thrust,
Only a yard beneath the street,
And the hoofs of the horses beat, beat,

The hoofs of the horses beat,
Beat into my scalp and my brain.

This is followed by ravings and fantasies of the madhouse, horribly
real and probably remembered from Tennyson's visit to Dr Allen's
hospital for the mentally deranged and perhaps, too, from Dr Allen's
*Essay on the Classification of the Insane* of 1837. But this is a grimness
very typical of Tennyson, who relished the macabre. Typical also
were the vitriolic attacks on the society of his time, very different
from the English Idyls that had at first made him popular with the
reading public. No wonder the poem was so disliked and abused
when it first appeared. Tennyson is writing partly of himself again
during the 1840s when the hero says, at the opening of Part III:

My life has crept so long on a broken wing
Through cells of madness, haunts of horror and fear. . . .

                          Yet it lightened my despair
When I thought that a war would arise in defence
    of the right,
That an iron tyranny now should bend or cease,
The glory of manhood stand on his ancient height,
Nor Britain's one sole God be the millionaire:
No more shall commerce be all in all, and Peace
Pipe on her pastoral hillock a languid note,
And watch her harvest ripen, her herd increase,
Nor the cannon-bullet rust on a slothful shore,
And the cobweb woven across the cannon's throat
Shall shake its threaded tears in the wind no more.

Tennyson was bitterly attacked for his enthusiasm for the Crimean
War, but he expressed the feelings of many people of his time, who
saw the war at its onset as a national awakening.

'It is time, it is time, O passionate heart,' said I
(For I cleaved to a cause that I felt to be pure and true),
'It is time, O passionate heart and morbid eye,
That old hysterical mock-disease should die. . . .'

Let it flame or fade, and the war roll down like a wind,
We have proved we have hearts in a cause, we are noble still,
And myself have awakened, as it seems, to the better mind;
It is better to fight for the good than to rail at the ill:
I have felt with my native land, I am one with my kind,
I embrace the purpose of God, and the doom assigned.

The purpose of God? Tennyson changed his views somewhat when the frightful suffering of the troops became known through Russell's *Times* dispatches from the Crimea, revealing how the lives of so many men were being thrown away through sheer callousness and incompetence. While an aristocrat like Lord Cardigan, who led the disastrous Charge of the Light Brigade, enjoyed champagne suppers on his yacht in the harbour with his mistress, the wounded lay in the crowded filth of the military hospital at Scutari. Tennyson got no nearer the seat of war than watching the troop ships sailing out of the Solent, and considerable resentment was felt at his martial enthusiasm, when, as the author of *Anti-Maud* pointed out, he had no intention of risking his own skin or embracing 'the doom assigned'. Abusive letters poured into Farringford. One began: 'Abhorred Sir!', and an anonymous correspondent wrote: 'Sir, Once I worshipped you – now I loathe you! So you've taken to imitating Longfellow, you BEAST!' Emily intercepted as many letters as she could and burned them, but inevitably some reached the Laureate, and he was bitterly hurt.

Nevertheless many other people felt differently about *Maud*, especially Jowett, who wrote to Tennyson in December: 'I want to tell you how greatly I admire *Maud*. No poem since Shakespeare seems to show equal power of the same kind, or equal knowledge of human nature. No modern poem contains more lines that ring in the ears of man. I do not know any verse out of Shakespeare in which the ecstacy of love soars to such a height.' And Ruskin wrote on 12 November: 'I hear so many stupid and feelingless misunderstandings of *Maud* that I think it may perhaps give you some little pleasure to know my sincere admiration of it throughout.' Admiration was not confined to intellectuals. One day a workman from Nottingham turned up at Farringford in the hope of hearing the Laureate read *Maud*. Tennyson invited him to dinner and afterwards read the whole poem to him at a sitting.

Though he never went to the Crimea, Tennyson's imaginative identification of himself with the disasters and triumphs, the suffering and heroism of the troops, was shown by the enormous popularity of 'The Charge of the Light Brigade' among the survivors. In fact, there was a request for two thousand copies of the poem to be distributed among the men in the hospitals. 'Half are singing it and all want to have it in black and white, so as to read what has so taken them,' wrote the chaplain of the military hospital at Scutari. 'The poet can now make heroes, just as in days of yore, if he will' – sufficient evidence that Tennyson's work reached 'the masses'. One trooper of the Light Brigade said it was as though Tennyson had taken part in the charge himself. He could hardly have been paid a higher compliment. But it is a curious sign of his caution, or timidity, that he suppressed what became the most famous line in the poem: 'Someone had blundered', though he restored it in the final version. 'My heart almost burst with indignation,' he said, 'at the accursed mismanagement of our noble little Army, the flower of our men.' He wrote the poem in ten minutes after reading the report of the charge in *The Times* at breakfast, the tears running down his cheeks. It was published in one of his little green books with the Wellington Ode, *Maud* and 'The Daisy' in 1855. Nearly thirty years later, Tennyson wrote a companion piece, 'The Charge of the Heavy Brigade', which is not nearly so stirring. Its subject is the successful action of the Scots Grays and the Second Squadron of Inniskillings which routed a far superior Russian force.

A new friend came into Tennyson's life this summer of 1855, Granville Bradley, a housemaster at Arnold's Rugby, who was staying at Alum Bay with his family. Afterwards Bradley became Headmaster of Marlborough and Dean of Westminster. Tennyson's first meeting with Mrs Bradley took place when she slid down from a haystack on top of which she was picnicking with her children, to be confronted with the Laureate in person. She 'had to descend,' she observed in her diary, 'as gracefully as circumstances permitted.' Her birthday on 6 August happened to be the same as Tennyson's, and after that first occasion the two families regularly picnicked each year at Alum Bay on 6 August. 'I have seen a great deal of Tennyson,' Bradley wrote to a friend. 'I made bold to call on him. . . . A genial note next day and an invite to meet Lear, the artist. Two days after another dinner – five o'clock with long evenings – and since then sundry talks, culminating in a whole day yesterday spent *tête-à-tête* with him. We walked early to see the Wealden strata five miles off and spent all the day walking and sitting. I found I could talk to him as to an old friend on all subjects, high and low, and I believe that even if he had never written a line I should think him one of the finest specimens of the *genus humanum*.' So attractive did Bradley find Tennyson that he built a house near Farringford: 'earnest, simple, real, truth-loving, evil-hating, noble hearted,' that, he discovered was the man when he came to know him.

When in London, Tennyson frequented Little Holland House in Kensington, an old farmhouse surrounded by fields, where Mrs Princep, one of the beautiful Pattle sisters, dispensed tea on the lawn, clothed in long richly-coloured robes of aesthetic design. Here were to be met all the celebrities of the age: Ruskin, Newman, Gladstone, Maurice, George Eliot, Browning, Holman Hunt, Burne-Jones and everybody who was somebody. Du Maurier complained that at Little Holland House 'the women offer Tennyson, Browning and Thackeray cups of tea almost kneeling'. It all sounds rather like *Patience*. Here Tennyson inevitably found himself the centre of a circle of adoring ladies. On one occasion, unable to stand it any longer, he took the arm of one of the ladies and cried: 'Wilt thou fly with me to Araby the Blest?' and waltzed her out of the room and escaped from the house. His shyness and social *naïveté* caused much amusement, as when he was introduced to a lady admirer and could find nothing to say to her. Later the same evening he went up to her in the drawing-room and, wishing to make amends for his former *gaucherie*, said: 'I couldn't find anything to say to you before dinner, but now that I have a bottle of port inside me, I can talk to you as much as you like.' On another occasion when Mrs Princep introduced him to the editor of *The Midnight Beacon* with the words, 'Mr Tennyson is delighted to make your acquaintance,' he turned to her and said: 'What made you say that? I didn't say that I was delighted to make his acquaintance.'

It was while Watts was living at Little Holland House that he painted what came to be known as 'the great moonlight portrait' of the Laureate, who was at that time writing 'The Fair Maid of Astolat', subsequently called 'Lancelot and Elaine'. At Little Holland House Burne-Jones too first met him. 'It was there in the days when he was fiercely attacked and reviled by people: afterwards when he wrote the Idylls of the King and gave them what they wanted they were pleased and praised him – but in the days of the Poems and Maud he was much abused by the English. Unfortunately he minded being abused and was very sensitive about it, and one evening at dinner he was in real distress about an anonymous letter he had received – which began "Abhorred Sir" and ended "yours in Aversion" – and one by one he took the guests apart and said "What would you do if you got a letter like this?" '[4]

The famous illustrated edition of the poems was issued by Moxon in 1857. As we have seen, the poet himself was against the idea, until Moxon told him it would bring him a lot of money. Rather surprisingly, Tennyson wanted Rossetti's mistress Elizabeth Siddall, who had become a great admirer after finding a pound of butter wrapped up in one of his poems, to do some of the illustrations. He also stipulated that one or two of the older academicians should be asked to contribute. The result was an incongruous mixture of engravings by Creswick, Mulready, Maclise, Stanfield and others, alongside work in a totally different manner by Millais, Rossetti, and Hunt. Thus we have Creswick's delicate and nostalgic 'Claribel' followed by Millais's powerful 'Mariana', Hunt's strong 'Oriana' and Horsley's conventionally pretty 'Circumstance'. Tennyson disliked Hunt's 'Lady of Shalott'. 'My dear Hunt,' he complained, 'I never said the young woman's hair was flying all over the shop.' 'No,' replied Hunt, 'but you never said it wasn't.' His opinion of Rossetti's first plate for 'The Palace of Art', where a sinister-looking creature, certainly not an angel as in the poem, is taking a bite out of St Cecily's forehead, is not recorded. This was apparently the fault of Dalziel the engraver, and disgusted Rossetti when he saw it. Millais's engraving of Cleopatra pointing to her bared breast where the asp had bitten it in 'A Dream of Fair Women' is somewhat unexpected, and Hunt's 'Godiva' makes strange company with Horsley's anaemic 'Gardener's Daughter', particularly inappropriate for so lush a poem. Tennyson also objected to the flight of steps in Hunt's illustration to 'The Beggar Maid': 'I never said that there were a lot of steps: I only meant one or two,' he grumbled. 'But,' Hunt explained, 'the old ballad says there was a flight of steps.' 'I daresay it does,' said Tennyson, 'but I never said I got it from the old ballad.' 'Well,' replied Hunt, 'the flight of steps does not contra-dict your account – you merely say "in robe and crown the king stept down".' But Tennyson continued to grumble that he had only meant 'two steps at the outside'. The argument would appear to be irrelevant, though Tennyson might well have objected that the king and the beggar maid should not have been shown waltzing *up* the steps to the throne. And what is the mysterious occupation of the man and the boy in the right-hand corner? On the other hand Millais's deathbed scene for 'The Lord of Burleigh' is a strikingly fine engraving, for Millais was still a Pre-Raphaelite at this time. Equally striking is his 'Edward Gray' illustrating the lines

Bitterly weeping, I turned away;
'Sweet Emma Moreland, love no more
Can touch the heart of Edward Gray.

'Ellen Adair she loved me well,
Against her father's and mother's will:
To-day I sat for an hour and wept,
By Ellen's grave, on the windy hill. . . .

'Bitterly wept I over the stone,
Bitterly weeping I turned away:
There lies the body of Ellen Adair!
And there the heart of Edward Gray!'

One is struck by the amount of weeping in Tennyson's earlier poems occasioned by the failure of so many of his lovers to come together, prevented either by their parents or by sudden death, while the two Marianas weep for lovers that never come back to them at all. But then the Victorian public dearly loved a pathetic story of pining maids, the most spectacular being Elaine, who pined and died of love for Sir Lancelot and had herself laid out on a bier in her wedding-dress and went floating down the river to Camelot with a note to Lancelot in her dead hand. Like Elaine, the unfortunate Lady of Shalott also floated down to Camelot in a barge, singing till she died. But doubtless this reflected the feelings, in an idealised form, of many unwed middle-class maids in the nineteenth century. Yet on rare occasions Tennyson's young women could be quite startling in their abandon, like Fatima, who exclaims:

> My whole soul waiting silently,
> All naked in a sultry sky,
> Droops blinded with his shining eye:
> I *will* possess him or will die.
> > I will grow round him in his place,
> > Grow, live, die looking on his face,
> > Die, dying clasp'd in his embrace.

From an oriental woman, such abandon was to be expected, but why should she die? 'Mariana in the South' is also notably passionate. But then she is a French girl. English girls simply pined away. Mariana and Œnone suffer from the same frustration, while the lover's song in 'The Miller's Daughter' can only be described as coyly suggestive:

> It is the miller's daughter,
> > And she is grown so dear, so dear,
> That I would be the jewel
> > That trembles at her ear:
> For hid in ringlets day and night,
> > I'd touch her neck so warm and white.

> And I would be the girdle
> > About her dainty, dainty waist,
> And her heart would beat against me,
> > In sorrow and in rest:
> And I should know if it beat right,
> > I'd clasp it round so close and tight.

> And I would be the necklace,
> > And all day long to fall and rise
> Upon her balmy bosom,
> > With her laughter or her sighs,
> And I would lie so light, so light,
> > I scarce should be unclasped at night.

Once more it is made plain that the young man is marrying 'beneath him', as the well-to-do William Morris married the Oxford groom's daughter, as Rossetti married the shop-girl Lizzie Siddall and as Holman Hunt planned to marry Annie Miller – after she had been taught to behave more like a lady. So in 'The Miller's Daughter':

> And slowly was my mother brought
> > To yield consent to my desire:
> She wish'd me happy, but she thought
> > I might have looked a little higher.

In Millais's illustration we see the poor girl drooping before her lover's lady mother, quite unable to look her in the face, even though her father the miller is described as wealthy. This is the side of Tennyson which most readers today find most difficult to take seriously, though it was precisely such coyness and snobbery that endeared him to readers of his own age.

The distinguished American writer Bayard Taylor visited Tennyson at Farringford in June 1857. 'I spent two days with him,' wrote Taylor, 'and you may take my word for it he is a noble fellow, every inch of him. He is as tall as I am, with a head which Read capitally calls that of a delapidated Jove, long black hair, splendid dark eyes, and a full moustache and beard. The portraits don't look a bit like him; they are handsome, perhaps, but haven't half the splendid character of his face. We smoked a pipe together, and talked of poetry, religion, politics and geology. I thought he seemed gratified with his American fame; he certainly did not say one unkind word about us.'[5] But why should he?

In July of the same year Nathaniel Hawthorne saw Tennyson at the exhibition of National Art Treasures in Manchester, and recorded his impressions in his *English Notebooks*.

> The most picturesque figure without affectation that I ever
> saw, of middle size, rather slouching, dressed entirely in black,
> and with nothing white about him except the collar of his
> shirt, which methought might have been clean the day before.
> He had on a black wideawake hat, with round crown and wide
> irregular brim, beneath which came down his long black hair,
> looking terribly tangled; he had a long pointed beard, too, a
> little browner than the hair, and not so abundant as to
> encumber any of the expression of his face. His frock-coat was
> buttoned across his breast though the afternoon was warm.
> His face was very dark, and not exactly a smooth face, but
> worn, and expressing great sensitiveness; though not at
> the moment the pain and sorrow which is seen in the bust. He

E*                                    [117]

seemed as if he did not see the crowd nor think of them, but as if he defended himself from them by ignoring them altogether. There was an entire absence of stiffness in his figure; no set-up in him at all, no nicety or trimness. Gazing at him with all my eyes, I liked him well, and rejoiced more in him than in all the other wonders of the Exhibition.

Standing near, Hawthorne also heard him speak: 'a bass voice, but not of resounding depth; a voice rather broken, as it were, and ragged about the edges, but pleasant to the ear. . . . I was indescribably sensible of a morbid painfulness in him, a something not to be meddled with. Very soon he left the saloon, shuffling along the floor with short irregular steps, a very queer gait, as if he were walking in slippers too loose for him. I had observed that he seemed to turn his feet slightly inward, after the fashion of Indians.'

Hawthorne adds that Tennyson 'might well enough pass for a madman at any time, there being a wildness in his aspect which doubtless might readily pass from quietude to frenzy. He is exceedingly nervous, and altogether un-English as possible; indeed an Englishman of genius usually lacks the national characteristics, and is great abnormally, and through disease. Un-English as he was, and sallow, and unhealthy, Tennyson had not, however, an American look . . . there was something more mellow in him, softer, broader, more simple, than we are apt to be.'

Somewhat earlier Hawthorne had observed of Emily that she seemed to be 'a good person, not handsome, but cheerful, capable of appreciating him and fit to make him comfortable. Her mode seems to be a gentle and good-humoured raillery of his peculiarities. Allingham says that they have a fine boy and that it would have been better for Tennyson to have been married fifteen years ago, instead of three or four.'

Lewis Carroll met Tennyson at Tent Lodge, Coniston, in September, when he came to take photographs of the family. 'The door opened, and a strange shaggy-looking man entered,' Carroll notes in his *Diary* under 22 September 1857. 'He was dressed in a loosely-fitting morning coat, common grey flannel waistcoat and trousers, and carelessly tied black silk neckerchief. His manner was kind and friendly from the first . . . there is a dry lurking-humour in his style of talking.' Carroll's next meeting with Tennyson was two years later at Farringford, when he found the Laureate in a wideawake and spectacles mowing the lawn. But when he wrote to Tennyson to ask if he might circulate a copy of one of his unpublished poems, he received a freezing reply from Emily: 'It would be well that a gentleman should understand that when an author does not give his works to the public he has his own reasons for it.' After that Carroll did not approach Tennyson again, but took a sly revenge in his parody 'The Three Voices'[6] and by making fun of the talking flowers of *Maud* in chapter 2 of *Through the Looking Glass*.

# 9

As Kathleen Tillotson observes in a notable essay,[1] *Idylls of the King* was 'a life-work, prepared for by study and meditation and slowly perfected'. The uniting theme is the antithesis between 'the True and the False' – Tennyson's original title for the first four books published in 1859: 'Enid', 'Vivien', 'Elaine' and 'Guinevere'. As Geraint muses:

> How many of us at this very hour
> Do forge a life-long trouble for ourselves,
> By taking true for false, or false for true
> Here, through the feeble twilight of this world
> Groping. . . .

As Tennyson sees it, the corruption which finally destroys Arthur's Round Table has its roots in Guinevere's adulterous love for Lancelot – 'the rumour [that] rose about the Queen' – which, by her example, develops into 'the common sewer of the realm'. After the Prince Consort's death in 1861, Tennyson next year dedicated a new edition of the *Idylls* to his memory in a noble tribute:

> These to His Memory – since he held them dear,
> Perchance as finding there unconsciously
> Some image of himself – I dedicate,
> I dedicate, I consecrate with tears –
> These Idylls.
>        And indeed He seems to me
> Scarce other than my king's ideal knight,
> 'Who reverenced his conscience as his king;
> Whose glory was, redressing human wrong;
> Who spake no slander, no, nor listened to it;
> Who loved one only and who clave to her –'
> Her – over all whose realms to their last isle,
> Commingled with the gloom of imminent war,
> The shadow of His loss drew like eclipse,
> Darkening the world. We have lost him: he is gone:

We know him now: all narrow jealousies
Are silent; and we see him as he moved,
How modest, kindly, all-accomplished, wise,
With what sublime repression of himself,
And in what limits, and how tenderly;
Not swaying to this faction or to that;
Not making his high place the lawless perch
Of winged ambitions, nor a vantage-ground
For pleasure; but through all this tract of years
Wearing the white flower of a blameless life,
Before a thousand peering littlenesses,
In that fierce light which beats upon a throne,
And blackens every blot; for where is he,
Who dares foreshadow for an only son
A lovelier life, a more unstained, than his? . . .
Sweet nature gilded by the gracious gleam
Of letters, dear to Science, dear to Art,
Dear to thy land and ours, a Prince indeed,
Beyond all titles, and a household name,
Hereafter, through all times, Albert the Good.

Break not, O woman's heart, but still endure;
Break not, for thou art Royal, but endure,
Remembering all the beauty of that star
Which shone so close beside Thee that ye made
One light together, but has past and leaves
The Crown a lonely splendour.

No wonder the Queen loved her Poet Laureate! Their friendship was
founded on a true mutual sympathy and regard.
Swinburne wrote in *Under the Microscope* in 1872:[2]

> The enemies of Tennyson . . . are the men who find in his
> collection of Arthurian idylls – the Morte d'Albert as it might
> perhaps more properly be called, after the princely type to
> which (as he tells us with just pride) the poet has been fortunate
> enough to make his central figure so successfully conform, – an
> epic poem of profound and exalted morality. Upon this moral
> question I shall take leave to intercalate a few words. . . . It
> seems to me that the moral tone of the Arthurian story has
> been on the whole lowered and degraded by Mr. Tennyson's
> mode of treatment. Wishing to make his central figure the
> noble and perfect symbol of an ideal man, he has removed not
> merely the excuse but the explanation of the fatal and tragic
> loves of Lancelot and Guinevere. The hinge of the whole legend

of the Round Table, from its first glory to its final fall, is the
incestuous birth of Modred from the connexion of Arthur with
his half-sister, unknowing and unknown; as surely as the hinge
of the Oresteia from first to last is the sacrifice at Aulis. From
the immolation of Iphigenia springs the wrath of Clytaemnestra,
with all its train of evils ensuing; from the sin of Arthur's youth
proceeds the ruin of his reign and realm through the falsehood
of his wife, a wife unloving and unloved. Remove in either case
the plea which leaves the heroine less sinned against indeed than
sinning, but yet not too base for tragic compassion and interest,
and there remains merely the presentation of a vulgar
adulteress. . . . Treated as he has treated it, the story is rather a
case for the divorce-court than for poetry. . . . In the old story,
the king, with the doom denounced in the beginning by Merlin
hanging over his toils and triumphs as a tragic shadow, stands
apart in no undignified patience to await the end in its own good
time of all his work and glory, with no eye for the pain and
passion of the woman who sits beside him as Queen rather than
as wife. Such a figure is not unfit for the centre of a tragic
action; it is neither ignoble nor inconceivable; but the besotted
blindness of Mr. Tennyson's 'blameless king' to the treason of a
woman who has had the first and last of his love and the whole
devotion of his blameless life is nothing more or less than pitiful
and ridiculous. All the studious and exquisite eloquence of the
poet can throw no genuine halo round the sprouting horns of a
royal husband who remains to the very last the one man in his
kingdom insensible to his disgrace. . . . The Vivien of Mr.
Tennyson's idyll seems to me, to speak frankly, about the most
base and repulsive person ever set forth in serious literature.
Her impurity is actually eclipsed by her incredible, incomparable
vulgarity ('*Oh ay,*' *said Vivien,* '*that were likely too!*') She is
such a sordid creature as plucks men passing by the sleeve. . . .
I do not remember that any modern poet who has been assailed
on the score of sensual immorality – say for instance the author
of 'Mademoiselle de Maupin' or the author of 'Fleurs du Mal' –
has ever devoted an elaborate poem to describing the erotic
fluctuations and vacillations of a dotard under the moral and
physical manipulation of a prostitute.

Swinburne somewhat overstates his case, as usual; but he is
basically right, though it is amusing to find the author of 'Anactoria',
'Faustine' and 'Dolores' taking up this moral stance. But was it,
perhaps, due to his own twisted sexual nature that Vivien's perfectly
normal blandishments struck him as so repellent? For Vivien is

certainly the most vividly portrayed woman in the *Idylls*, the perfect foil to the innocent Elaine, the Lily Maid of Astolat. It is interesting to observe that Benjamin Jowett told Tennyson that 'Vivien' ('the naughty one', he called it) was his favourite book of the *Idylls*. Vivien is drawn with an unerring hand, snake-like in her seduction of the aged Merlin:

> And lissome Vivien, holding by his heel,
> Writhed toward him, slided up his knee and sat,
> Behind his ankle twined her hollow feet
> Together, curved an arm about his neck,
> Clung like a snake; and letting her left hand
> Droop from his mighty shoulder, as a leaf,
> Made with her right a comb of pearl to part
> The lists of such a beard as youth gone out
> Had left in ashes.

Vivien is Tennyson's prime example of the destructive power of sex. 'My father,' says Hallam Tennyson, 'created Vivien with much care – as the evil genius of the Round Table – who in her lustfulness of the flesh could not believe in anything either good or great. The story of the poem is essentially original.' For the name Vivien – he had originally called her Nimuë – Tennyson was indebted to the old *Romance of Merlin*. In this version, Vivien is presented with considerable charm. It is also the source of Burne-Jones's masterpiece *The Beguiling of Merlin*, where Vivien is shown standing in front of the flowering whitethorn bush in which the enchanter is imprisoned, holding the great book of his magic spells. Referring to the 'decorous eroticism' that hangs over much of the poem, G. M. Young quotes an American schoolboy who remarked, aptly enough: 'There is some pretty hot necking in Lord Tennyson, only they never quite make it!'[3] This criticism applies to nearly all Tennyson's lovers, of whom Swinburne remarked: 'There is always a latent if not patent propensity in many of his very lovers to scold and whine after a fashion that makes even Alfred de Musset seem by comparison a model or a type of manliness. His Enids and Edith Aylmers are much below the ideal mark of Wordsworth, who has never, I believe, been considered a specially great master in that kind: but his "Little Letties" were apparently made mean and thin of nature to match their pitifully poor-spirited suitors.'[4]

It must be admitted that here Swinburne puts his finger on the main weakness of Tennyson's amatory poems. One is reminded of Meredith's remark in this context about Morris's *Love is Enough*: 'Our public seems to possess the fearful art of insensibly castrating its favourites.'[5] Certainly Tennyson's knights and ladies are Victorian

[123]

rather than medieval, though they could scarcely be otherwise. 'To find fault with the poet for making his heroes think and speak the language of the nineteenth century,' observed Macaulay, 'is as much out of place as to find fault with the authors of the romances of *Merlin* and *Lancelot* for making their heroes, whom they imagine to have lived in the fifth century, think and speak like men and women of the thirteenth and fourteenth.'

The point is, however, that Malory's King Arthur is not nearly so grieved for the loss of his queen as for the loss of Lancelot and his other knights, remarking somewhat unchivalrously:

> And therefore, said the king, wit you well my heart was never so heavy as it is now, and much more sorrier for my good knights' loss than for the loss of my fair queen; for queens I might have enow, but such a fellowship of goodly knights shall never be together in no company. And now I dare say, said King Arthur, there was never Christian king held such a fellowship together: and alas that ever Sir Lancelot and I should be at debate. Ah Agravaine, Agravaine, said the king, Jesu forgive it thy soul for thine evil that thou and thy brother Sir Modred hadst unto Sir Lancelot hath caused all this sorrow: and ever among these complains the king wept and swooned.

That is the real accent of the Middle Ages, the sorrowful beauty of Malory. Nor does Malory's Arthur go to Amesbury to lecture the repentant Guinevere 'like a curate', said Meredith, as she grovels at his feet, as in Tennyson's poem. There is nothing in *Idylls of the King* to equal Sir Ector's noble and haunting threnody on the death of Sir Lancelot, who, for all his adultery, remains for Malory the peerless knight.

> Ah Launcelot, he said, thou were head of all Christian knights. . . . And thou were the courteoust knight that ever bore shield. And thou were the truest friend to thy lover that ever bestrad horse. And thou were the truest lover of a sinful man that ever loved woman. And thou were the kindest man that ever struck with sword. And thou were the goodliest person that ever came among press of knights. And thou was the meekest man and the gentlest that ever ate in hall among ladies. And thou were the sternest knight of thy mortal foe that ever put speare in the rest. Then there was weeping and dolour out of measure. Thus they kept Sir Lancelot's corpse on loft fifteen days, and then they buried it with great devotion (Book XXI, chapter XIII),

Malory makes it quite plain, as Swinburne points out, that the ruin of the realm and the destruction of the Round Table is due to Arthur's incest. For Merlin warns him:

> You have done a thing of late that God is displeased with you, for you have lain by your sister, and on her ye have gotten a child that shall destroy you and all the nights of your realm.

That child was, of course, Modred. Also Merlin warns Arthur that 'Guinevere was not wholesome for him to take to wife, for Lancelot should love her and she him again'. Why, then, did Arthur, knowing this, persist in taking her for his queen? Loving Lancelot as he did, why did he deprive him of the woman he loved? But, in fact, he did not deprive him; he was content to wink at his wife's adultery until forced by Agravaine and others to acknowledge it. His attitude is curious, for even when told that Lancelot had been caught in the queen's chamber and had killed thirteen knights getting out of it, he exclaims only: 'Jesu mercy, he is a marvellous knight of prowess.' Just as when Dinas is told that his wife has absconded with another knight, taking his brachets, or greyhounds, with her, 'then was he wrother for his brachets than for his lady'. From which it appears that in the age of chivalry the relationship between knights, and even between knights and their dogs, was closer than between knights and their fair ladies. It is precisely here, as Betty Miller has argued, that the great appeal of the *Morte d'Arthur* lay for Tennyson, who in many ways identified King Arthur with Arthur Hallam: 'For the purposes of Victorian morality, he succeeded in the feat of creating an ideal Arthur, "blameless king and stainless man", by the simple expedient of transferring all the blame and stain to the women of the piece.'[6]

It was William Morris who gallantly took up arms for her in *The Defence of Guinevere* (1858), where the queen is given more life than in any other modern poem. In his treatment of Merlin's relationship with Vivien, Tennyson also differs radically from Malory, who tells us that the magician 'always lay about the lady to have her maidenhead, and she was ever passing weary of him, and fain would have been delivered of him . . . and she could not put him away by no means.' But had he followed his source too closely it would have conflicted with his view of the wise old man, with whom he came to identify himself, though he commented that 'some even among the highest intellects become slaves of evil which is at first half-disdained'. It is hardly necessary to point out that here and elsewhere 'evil' is equated with what we today call sex. Arthur, whom Guinevere describes as 'cold, high, self-contained, and passionless', says that his knights should 'lead sweet lives in purest chastity'.

Tennyson composed 'Vivien' first and then the unpleasant 'Enid', which he based on the *Mabinogion*. In 1869 *The Holy Grail and Other Poems* appeared (though the edition is marked 1870), with 'The Coming of Arthur', 'Pelleas and Ettarre', and 'The Passing of Arthur' (the old 'Morte d'Arthur' of 1833–4 expanded with a new beginning and a new end). Of the earlier *Idylls* republished at this time, some were given new titles: 'Merlin and Vivien', 'Lancelot and Elaine', with 'The Coming of Arthur' and 'The Passing of Arthur' framing the six other poems, to which Tennyson gave the collective title of *The Round Table*, showing the founding and the breaking of the 'goodly fellowship of knights'. Here Tennyson's narrative power is plain enough, though Eliot said that he could not tell a story, for the pellucid verse carries one forward with all the enchantment of the most accomplished story-teller. But the poem as a whole was not yet finished. 'The Last Tournament' and 'Gareth and Lynette' (begun ten years earlier) were published separately, and the reader was told that 'the whole series would shortly be published in their proper shape and order'. When this finally appeared in 1872 as the Imperial Library edition of the *Works*, with a new Epilogue 'To the Queen', many of the poems had been revised and the text archaised to bring it closer to the style of the early 'Morte d'Arthur'. In 1804 Tennyson wrote 'Balin and Balan', but this did not appear until 1886, when 'Enid' was expanded into 'The Marriage of Geraint' and 'Geraint and Enid', to make up the twelve books.

Tennyson had carried the whole scheme of *Idylls of the King* in his head for thirty years. He said he could have written it all much earlier, haunted all his life by what he called 'the greatest of all poetical subjects', but the reviews of his first volumes stopped him. The greater part of the *Idylls* was written at Farringford, though the end of 'Enid' was done during two months spent in Wales in 1856. His son tells us that '*Idylls of the King* gives his [Tennyson's] innermost being, though not more truthfully than *In Memoriam*. My father strongly felt that only under the inspiration of ideals and with his sword "bathed in heaven", can a man combat the cynical indifference, the intellectual selfishness, the sloth of will, the utilitarian materialism of the transition age.'[7] But what ideal is it that inspires the unchivalrous Geraint to subject his 'simple, noble-natured' wife to such cruel humiliations in order to discover whether she is 'tainted' or not by the example of Guinevere? Though the tale is taken from the *Mabinogion*, Tennyson retells it with evident relish, even expanding the original 'Enid' into two parts to make it the longest of the *Idylls*. In 'Pelleas and Ettarre', a tale of female lubricity brought to book, R. W. Rader argues that Tennyson associated this poem 'consciously or unconsciously with memories of Rosa Baring' – no doubt a long-delayed revenge for her humiliation of him thirty-five years ago!

'We do not know where to look in history or in letters for a nobler or more overpowering conception of man as he might be, than in the Arthur of this volume,' trumpeted Gladstone. 'Whenever he appears it is as the great pillar of the moral order, and the resplendent top of human excellence. But even he only reaches to his climax in those two really wonderful speeches [at the close of "Guinevere"].'[8] Indeed, it was these very speeches that Swinburne, anticipating contemporary opinion, stigmatised as 'the acme, the apogee, the culmination of all imaginable cant'. But, as a matter of fact, it is the quest for the Grail, the futile search for 'wandering fires', as the king somewhat surprisingly calls it, that breaks up the Round Table, no less than Modred's treason and Guinevere's adultery, since several of the knights renounce the world to become monks. The lesson of the *Idylls* therefore would seem to be that a life-denying asceticism is as destructive in its effect as a surrender to sensual passion. While Tennyson's ideal was married love, a tranquil ordering of the senses, in his most moving work he celebrated 'a lost or unrealisable love in a personal or legendary past'.[9]

Perceptive, as usual, Ruskin wrote to Tennyson: 'I am not sure but I feel the art and finish of these poems a little more than I like to feel it. Yet I am not a fair judge quite, for I am so much of a realist as not by any possibility to interest myself much in an unreal subject to feel it as I should, and the very sweetness and stateliness of the words strike me all the more as *pure* workmanship.

'As a description of various nobleness and tenderness the book is without price: but I shall always wish it had been nobleness independent of a romantic condition of externals in general.

'*In Memoriam, Maud,* "The Miller's Daughter", and such like will always be my pet rhymes – yet I am quite prepared to admit this to be as good as any for its own peculiar audience. Treasures of wisdom there are in it, and word-painting such as never was yet for concentration, nevertheless it seems to me that so great power ought not to be spent on visions of things past but on the living present.'

Thackeray's delightful letter came in October 1859:

My Dear Old Alfred,
I owe you a letter of happiness and thanks. Sir, about three weeks ago, when I was ill in bed, I read the *Idylls of the King,* and I thought, 'Oh I must write to him now, for this pleasure, this delight, this splendour of happiness which I have been enjoying.' But I should have blotted the sheets, 'tis ill writing

on one's back. The letter full of gratitude never went as far as the post-office and how comes it now?

*D'abord*, a bottle of claret. (The landlord of the hotel asked me down to the cellar and treated me.) Then afterwards sitting here, an old magazine, *Frazer's Magazine*, 1850, and I came on a poem out of *The Princess* which says 'I hear the horns of Elfland blowing, blowing', no, it's 'the horns of Elfland faintly blowing' (I have been into my bedroom to fetch my pen and it has made that blot), and, reading the lines, which only one man in the world could write, I thought about the other horns of Elfland blowing in full strength, and Arthur in gold armour, and Guinevere in gold hair, and all those knights and heroes and beauties and purple landscapes and misty gray lakes in which you have made me live. They seem like facts to me, since about three weeks ago (three weeks or a month was it?) when I read the book. It is on the table yonder, and I don't like, somehow, to disturb it, but the delight and gratitude! You have made me as happy as I was as a child with the *Arabian Nights*, every step I have walked in Elfland has been a sort of Paradise to me. (The landlord gave *two* bottles of his claret and I think I drank the most.) And here I have been lying back in my chair and thinking of those delightful *Idylls*, my thoughts being turned to you: what could I do but be grateful to that surprising genius which has made me so happy? Do you understand that what I mean is all true and that I should break out were you sitting opposite with a pipe in your mouth? Gold and purple and diamonds, I say, gentlemen and glory and love and honour, and if you haven't given me all these why should I be in such an ardour of gratitude? But I have had out of that dear book the greatest delight that has ever come to me since I was a young man; to write and think about it makes me almost young, and this I suppose is what I'm doing, like an after-dinner speech.

P.S. I thought the 'Grandmother' quite as fine. How can you at 50 be doing things as well as at 35?

Though much of this generous enthusiasm may have been due to the claret, it must have been refreshing for Tennyson to read after the somewhat pernickety criticism of Ruskin.

The appreciation of the royal family must have been considerably gratifying to Tennyson. Prince Albert had already called at Farring-ford in 1856, before the Tennysons had properly moved in, and had taken away a large bunch of cowslips for the Queen. 'It is such a pretty place,' the Prince had said. 'I shall certainly bring the Queen to see it.' But Victoria never came to Farringford, though on two occasions she had announced her intention of doing so and then, at the last moment, had been prevented by bad weather. But one day, on coming home from one of his walks on the downs, Tennyson saw a small, dumpy figure seated with her back to him and talking to Emily. Convinced it was the Queen at last, he began in a deeply respectful voice: 'Madam, this is indeed an honour . . .' only to realise, when the figure turned to look at him, that it was only Mrs Cameron after all.

In 1857 Tennyson sent the Queen a copy of the illustrated edition of his *Poems* and received a formal acknowledgment through the Lord Chamberlain. The next royal message, just before Christmas 1857, was a request for an additional verse to *God Save the Queen*, to be sung at the state concert at Buckingham Palace on the evening of the wedding day of the Princess Royal to the Crown Prince Frederick William of Prussia. Promptly, he sent two additional verses for the Queen to choose from. In the event, both verses were sung. Tennyson had no greater admirer than Prince Albert.

On receiving his dedication of *Idylls of the King* to her father, Princess Alice wrote: 'If words could express *thanks* and *real* appreciation of lines so beautiful, so truly worthy of the great pure spirit which inspired the Author, Princess Alice would attempt to do it. Mr. Alfred Tennyson could not have chosen a more beautiful and true testimonial to the memory of him who was so really good and *noble*, than the *Idylls of the King*, which he so valued and admired. Princess Alice has transmitted the lines to the Queen, who desired her to tell Mr. Tennyson with her warmest thanks how much moved she was in reading them and that they soothed her aching bleeding heart. She knows also how *he* would have admired them.'[10]

The Crown Princess of Prussia also wrote from Germany in February 1862 that the first time she had heard the *Idylls* was 'last year when I found both the Queen and the Prince in raptures about them. . . . I cannot separate the idea of King Arthur from the image of him whom I most revered on earth! I almost know the *Idylls of the King* by heart now: they are really sublime!'[11]

The Queen then asked the Duke of Argyll to tell Mr Tennyson how much she loved to dwell on *In Memoriam*, and gave him her copy to show how many passages she had marked. She had even changed 'widower' to widow', 'he' to 'she' and 'Her' to 'His' in Elegy XIII:

Tears of the widower, when he sees
  A late-lost form that sleep reveals –
  And moves his doubtful arms, and feels
Her place is empty, fall like these;

[129]

which only goes to show how similar Tennyson's feelings for the loss of Arthur Hallam were to the Queen's for the loss of Albert.

Soon after that, on 25 March 1862 Tennyson received the Queen's command to visit her at Osborne. He was alarmed and wrote to the Duke of Argyll: 'I am a shy beast, and like to keep to my burrow – two questions – what sort of salutation to make on entering Her private room? and whether to retreat backward? or sidle out as I may.' The Duke replied that 'all formality and mere ceremony breaks down in the presence of real sorrow, and what is *natural* is right with Her. Don't let yourself be a "shy beast" and "come out of your burrow." Talk to her as you would to a poor woman in affliction – that is what she likes best. She dislikes very much the word "late" applied to the Prince. I only mention it in connection with the strong reality of Her belief in the *life presence* of the Dead. There are some bits in *In Memoriam* which are specially soothing to Her in this matter.'

Tennyson went to Osborne on 14 April. Afterwards the Queen wrote in her diary: 'I went down to see Tennyson who is very peculiar looking, tall, *dark*, with a fine head, long black flowing hair and a beard – oddly dressed, but there is no affectation about him. I told him how much I admired his glorious lines to my precious Albert and how much comfort I found in his *In Memoriam*. He was full of unbounded appreciation of my beloved Albert. When he spoke of his own loss, of that to the Nation, his eyes quite filled with tears!'

Tennyson was much affected by his visit to Osborne. Emily wrote an account of it immediately after his return: 'He said that the Queen "stood pale and statue-like before him, speaking in a quiet, unutterably sad voice. There was a kind of stately innocence about her." She said many kind things to him, such as "Next to the Bible *In Memoriam* is my comfort." She said, "I am like your Mariana now." She talked of the Prince, and of Hallam, and of Macaulay, and of Goethe, and of Schiller in connection with him, and said that the Prince was so like the picture of Arthur Hallam in *In Memoriam*, even to his blue eyes. When A. said that he thought that the Prince would have made a great king, she answered, "He always said that it did not signify whether *he* did the right thing or not, so long as the right thing was done." A. said, "We all grieve with your Majesty," and the Queen replied, "The country has been kind to me, and I am thankful." When she left she asked Tennyson if there was anything she could do for him and he replied, "Nothing, Madam, but shake my two boys by the hand. It may keep them loyal in the troublous times to come." ' Then Princess Alice came in with Princess Beatrice. Tennyson liked Princess Alice and said that she was 'true natured and true mannered'.[12]

The Queen continued to read Tennyson's poetry. She had also been moved by 'In the Valley of Cauteretz', with its memories of Hallam, which the Duke of Argyll had recited to her. She sent Tennyson some specially-bound volumes of German poetry, including the poems of Zeller, so that he could read and admire what she admired. Their relationship was becoming funereally romantic. In January 1863 Lady Augusta Bruce brought to Farringford a copy of *The Principal Speeches and Addresses of His Royal Highness the Prince Consort*, with an inscription in the Queen's hand: 'To Alfred Tennyson Esquire –/Who so truly appreciated/This greatest purest and best of men/ from/the beloved Prince's/broken-hearted widow Victoria/Osborne Dec. 9 1862.' Emily noted ecstatically in her diary: 'What is to us beyond price, *The Prince Consort*, a gift from the Queen with kind words written by H.M.'s own hand, also a beautiful photograph of herself and three of her children with A's lines written under it "May all love" &c., also the prayers used at the anniversary [of the Prince's death] and the sermon preached.'

The next duty that devolved upon Tennyson as Poet Laureate was a royal request to compose some lines celebrating the marriage of Princess Alexandra of Denmark and the Prince of Wales. The Queen became very fond of Alexandra, who, it was hoped, would have a stabilising influence on Bertie, whose 'irregular' behaviour, even before Prince Albert's death, had, she felt, greatly contributed to her husband's collapse. And now there were rumours that Bertie was involved with an Irish actress in Dublin. So Tennyson sat down and dutifully wrote his 'A Welcome to Alexandra', which appeared in *The Times* on 10 March 1863:

Sea-king's daughter from over the sea,
               Alexandra!
Saxon and Norman and Dane are we,
But all of us Danes in our welcome to thee,
               Alexandra!
Welcome her, thunders of fort and of fleet!
Welcome her, thundering cheer of the street!
Welcome her, all things youthful and sweet,
Scatter the blossom under her feet!
Break, happy land, into earlier flowers!
Make music, O bird, in the new-budded bowers!
Blazon your mottoes of blessing and prayer!
Welcome her, welcome her, all that is ours!
Warble, O bugle, and trumpet, blare!
Flags, flutter out upon turrets and towers!
Flames, on the windy headland flare! . . .

O joy to the people and joy to the throne,
Come to us, love us and make us your own.

The Queen sent a message thanking her Laureate warmly for these lines: 'how much she rejoices that the sweet and charming Princess should be thus greeted.' The royal wedding was celebrated with a great bonfire on the Down above Farringford and a torchlight procession. Hallam and Lionel waited on the guests at dinner and, Emily notes, 'Ally proposed the health of the happy couple, saying the simple words "The Queen and God bless her" very grandly and impressively.' To Bertie marriage meant £100,000 a year and freedom from the sour, pedantic tutelage of Colonel Bruce, freedom to take advantage of the uninhibited night-life of London and Paris, which in the 1860s was very free indeed. Alexandra of Denmark had been Albert's choice for his son and the choice could hardly have been a better one. But at the wedding the Queen refused to show herself to the people and sat muffled up in the deepest mourning, unobserved in a gallery above the chancel of St George's Chapel, Windsor.

In May the whole Tennyson family visited Osborne, so that Hallam and Lionel might be presented. The invitation was prompted by a gift of snowdrops gathered by Hallam and sent by Lady Augusta Bruce to the Queen, who kept them on her dressing-table for a week and sent a message to Hallam saying that 'she was very glad that he had that name and that he had such good and great godfathers as F. D. Maurice and Henry Hallam.' Emily wrote in her diary:

A., the boys and myself to Osborne. We lunch with Lady Augusta Bruce and afterwards drive with her in the grounds. We see the dairy. Very pretty it is, lined with Dutch tiles with a wreath of convolvulus round a fountain in the middle; then the kitchen where the Princesses amuse themselves with cooking, also lined with tiles. The little garden where Prince Arthur has made [sic] the pet donkey that draws the gun-carriage, the Swiss Cottage where they have their Museum and another where they come to tea.

Soon after we return Lady Augusta is sent for and she comes to fetch us to the Queen. We wait in the Drawing-room and after a little we heard a quiet shy opening of the door and the Queen comes in and I kissed her hand.

She shook hands with the boys and made a very low reverence to Ally. All the Princesses came in by turns, Prince Leopold also.

All shook hands very kindly with us. . . .

The Queen's face is beautiful. Not the least like her portraits

but small and child-like, full of intelligence and ineffably sweet
and of a sad sympathy.

A. was delighted with the breadth and freedom and
penetration of her mind. One felt that no false thing could stand
before her. We talked of all things in heaven and earth it
seemed to me. I never met a lady with whom I could talk so
easily and never felt so little shy with any stranger after the
first few minutes.

She laughed heartily at many things that were said but
shades of pain and sadness passed over her face that seemed
sometimes all one smile. . . .

One feels that the Queen is a woman to live and die for. . . .

Hallam, ten years old, remarked that 'Her Majesty has a beautiful
little nose and soft blue eyes. . . . Princess Beatrice's cat died at seven
o'clock tonight.'

In her diary the Queen recorded under 9 May 1863: '. . . . saw Mr.
and Mrs. Tennyson and their 2 sons. Had some interesting conversation with him and was struck by the greatness and largeness of
his mind, under a certainly rough exterior.

'Speaking of the immortality of the soul and of the scientific
discoveries in no way interfering with that, he said, "If there is no
immortality of the soul, one does not see why there should be any
God" and that "you cannot love a Father who strangled you" &c.'

The Queen then asked Tennyson to compose four lines for the
statue of her mother, the Duchess of Kent, at Frogmore.

But *Idylls of the King*, what do we feel about them today? As usual,
T. S. Eliot summed up the general consensus of critical opinion of his
time, when he wrote that one only need compare them with Malory
'to admire the skill with which Tennyson adapted this great British
epic material – in Malory's handling hearty, outspoken and magnificent – to suitable reading for a girls' school: the original ore being
so refined that none of the gold is left.' Carlyle expressed much the
same opinion: 'We read, at first, Tennyson's *Idylls*, with profound
recognition of the finely elaborated execution, and also of the inward
perfection of *vacancy*, – and, to say the truth, with considerable
impatience at being treated so very like infants, though the lollipops
were so superlative.' They are, indeed; so that while one reads these
poems for the many beautiful isolated passages, and the charm of
their stories, the moral scheme as a whole falls down, and there
remains at the heart of the work a peculiar emptiness as of a world
of ghosts. There is, as Ruskin saw, 'the very sweetness and stateliness
of the words', the 'nobleness and tenderness' (in 'Lancelot and Elaine'

especially), the delicate sensuality of 'Merlin and Vivien', and such
marvellous descriptive passages as we have in 'The Last Tournament', in which Tennyson is remembering the sea at Mablethorpe:

as the crest of some slow-arching wave,
Heard in dead of night along that table-shore,
Drops flat, and after the great waters break
Whitening for half a league, and thin themselves,
Far over sands marbled with moon and cloud,
From less and less to nothing.

And, above all, the original 'Morte d'Arthur', which became 'The
Passing of Arthur', with its unforgettable lines:

And bore him to a chapel nigh the field,
A broken chancel with a broken cross,
That stood on a dark strait of barren land:
On one side lay the Ocean, and on one
Lay a great water, and the moon was full.

Such things will always be admired. But we can no longer see King
Arthur as Gladstone saw him, 'as the great pillar of the moral order,
and the resplendent top of human excellence'. He appears too much
of a prig for that, too much like any Victorian husband angrily
lecturing his erring wife in the last speeches of 'Guinevere', which to
the Victorians appeared so sublime.

In the Epilogue 'To the Queen' Tennyson tells us again how he
saw his Arthur:

Ideal manhood closed in real man,
Rather than that gray king, whose name, a ghost,
Streams like a cloud, man-shaped, from mountain peak,
And cleaves to cairn and cromlech still; or him
Of Geoffrey's book, or him of Malleor's, one
Touched by the adulterous finger of a time
That hovered between war and wantonness.

The twelve books of the *Idylls* follow the full cycle of the year. As
Tennyson said: ' "The Coming of Arthur" is on the night of the New
Year: when he is wedded "the world is white with May"; on a
summer night the vision of the Holy Grail appears; and the "Last
Tournament" is in the "yellowing autumn–tide." Guinevere flees
through the mists of autumn, and Arthur's death takes place at
midnight in mid-winter. The form of the *Coming of Arthur* and of the
*Passing* is purposely more archaic than that of the other idylls. The
blank verse throughout each of the twelve idylls varies according to
the subject.' And the poem as a whole closes in

[134]

The darkness of that battle in the West,
Where all of high and holy dies away,

which could be taken as prophetic. To his own age Tennyson
appeared not only as a great poet, but as a seer, and he came to
identify himself with Merlin, brooding on things to come:

So dark a forethought rolled about his brain,
As on a dull day in an Ocean cave
The blind wave feeling round his long sea-hall
In silence.

And finally we are left with:

The sad sea-sounding wastes of Lyonnesse . . .

the sound of the sea washing over a legendary land, the enchantment
of such lines temporarily drowning all critical objections.

# IO

In August 1860 Tennyson went to Cornwall again with Holman Hunt, Woolner, Val Princep and Francis Palgrave. His diary letters to Emily record the main events of the tour. The first entry is dated 'August 18th. All Soul's Reading Room, Oxford':

> Before my departure Palgrave called with his Syrian brother, a very interesting man in an Eastern dress with a kind of turban, having just escaped from his convent in the Syrian Desert where several of his fellow monks were massacred. Palgrave obliged to stop for a week at Hampstead till his brother goes to Paris, where he will have an interview with the Emperor on affairs in the East. . . . Woolner, like a good fellow, followed me here yesterday that I might not feel lonely; and this morning we breakfasted with Max Muller, and are going to dine with him at 7 o'clock. . . .
>
> August 25th. Tintagel. Black cliffs and caves and storm and wind, but I weather it out and take my ten miles a day walks in my weather proofs. Palgrave arrived today.
>
> August 28th. Tintagel. . . . We have had two fine days and some exceedingly grand coast views. Here is an artist, a friend of Woolner's (Inchbold): sketching now in this room. I am very tired of walking against wind and rain.

Inchbold, described by Palgrave as 'that ever graceful, ill-appreciated landscapist,' was also a friend of Swinburne, who stayed for several weeks with him at Tintagel, when he was finishing *Atalanta in Calydon* three years later.

Palgrave describes this as 'Tennyson's Arthurian Journey'. Near Camelford, on the edge of the river Camel, they saw the large block of stone on which King Arthur is said to have sat after the last fatal battle in the mist. It lies below the river bank, and Tennyson was so eager to sit down on it too, that he slipped and fell into the river.

August 31st. Union Hotel, Penzance. I have now walked
10 miles a day for 10 days, equal 100, and I want to continue
doing that for some time longer. I am going tomorrow to
Land's End, and then I must return here, and then I go to the
Scilly Isles and then return here.

At St Mary's, Scilly Isles, he noted: 'West Indian aloes 30ft high,
in blossom, and out all the winter, and vast hedges of splendid
geraniums, a delight to the eye, yet the peaches won't ripen. These
Islands are very peculiar and in some respects very fine. I never saw
anything quite like them.' At Falmouth he was disgusted by the
behaviour of the riflemen, 'who get drunk every night and squabble
and fight, and disgrace themselves and their corps'. Caroline Fox,
meeting him at this time, observed in her *Memories of Old Friends*:
'Tennyson is a grand specimen of a man, with a magnificent head set
on his shoulders like the capital of a mighty pillar. His hair is
long and wavy, and covers a massive head. He wears a beard
and moustache, which one begrudges, as hiding so much of that
firm, forceful, but finely chiselled mouth. I can quite understand
Sam Lawrence calling it the best balance of a head he had ever
seen.'
Tennyson benefited greatly from the tour in general health,
though he found Palgrave's attentions particularly trying. Not only
did Palgrave refer to him at hotels as 'the old gentleman', but he
followed him wherever he went with the perpetual cry of 'Tennyson,
Tennyson!', carrying out Emily's instructions, perhaps, never to let
him out of his sight in case he fell over the edge of the cliff or slipped
on the rocks of the shore. Finally, one evening there was a blazing
row. Tennyson said he could not stand it any longer and was going to
Falmouth to take the next train home. With that he went off with
his candle to bed. Presently, however, after Palgrave had gone up
too, he came down again in his dressing-gown to apologise to the
others: 'I've come to say to you young fellows that I am sorry if I
seem to be the cause of all the bickerings that go on between Palgrave
and myself. It is, I know, calculated to spoil your holiday, and that
would be a great shame. I don't mean to quarrel with anyone, but
all day long I am trying to get a quiet moment for reflection. Sometimes I want to compose a stanza or two and to find a quiet nook
where I can wind off my words; but before I have finished a couplet
I hear Palgrave's voice like a bee in a bottle, making the neighbourhood resound with my name, and I have to give myself up to escape
the consequences. I know he means well, but it worries me and I am
going away to-morrow morning . . . but I hope you will stay and
enjoy yourselves.'

But next morning, as Tennyson was driving away in a dog-cart, Hunt tells us, Palgrave was seen running and jumping up beside him, amid protests and explanations. Nevertheless, it was during this Cornish tour that the idea of *The Golden Treasury of the Best Songs and Lyrical Poems in the English Language* was born. Tennyson had a considerable share in the selection, but he refused to have any of his own poems included. The final selection took place during a ten-days' conference at Farringford in December, when Tennyson read each poem aloud twice before passing his final judgment. The book is valuable as an index to his taste, and was for long the most popular English anthology, until the vogue of the seventeenth-century metaphysical poets was introduced by T. S. Eliot. Palgrave originally intended to dedicate it to Henry Hallam before his death: 'But', he wrote in his Preface, 'he is beyond the reach of any human tokens of love and reverence: and I desire therefore to place before it a name united with his by associations which, whilst Poetry retains her hold on the minds of Englishmen, are not likely to be forgotten. Permit me then to inscribe to yourself a book which, I hope, may be found by many a lifelong fountain of innocent and exalted pleasure.' That name was, of course, Alfred Tennyson's.

Next August Tennyson took his family to the Auvergne and the Pyrenees. But, his son tells us, 'the difficulty of getting rooms, carriages, and even donkeys to ride in those days, and the impossibility of finding food not soaked in garlic, took away much of our pleasure. The difficulties were increased by the presence of two small children and an invalid. The cathedral at Bourges, its great pillars and its gorgeous windows, were what struck my father on the journey out. On our arrival at Clermont, the comet was flaring over the market place. Here we would have been content to stay, had it not been for the bad drainage.' Tennyson climbed the Puy du Dôme with Graham Dakyns, the boys' tutor. 'At Mount Dore, while my father was reading some of the *Iliad* out aloud to us, little boys came and stood outside the window in open-mouthed astonishment. He took long walks there by the Dordogne, and one day when he came in from his walk we heard him call "Clough, come upstairs," and in walked Mr. Clough. My father, Mr. Clough and Mr. Dakyns made many expeditions to waterfalls and up the mountains, Mr. Clough riding.'[1] They were delighted with the fields of forget-me-nots and yellow anemones.

Leaving Clough at Mount Dore, they drove to Tulle and Perigueux, 'a quaint place with its Roman Tower and Cathedral with grass-grown tower, church of St. Etienne, and city walls. Thence to Bordeaux, Tarbes, Bagnères de Bigorre where there was a magnificent thunderstorm at night, forked lightning of different colours striking the mountains on either hand. From this place my father and Mr. Dakyns made an expedition up the Pic du Midi. When the climbers reached the summit, three great eagles, they said, kept swooping round without any perceptible movement of wing.' No doubt they had come to salute the Laureate. 'My father walked with Mr. Dakyns to the Port de Venasque and into Spain, and to see the Cascade d'Enfer and other cascades, and the Lac D'Oo, and the Lac Vert, and up several mountains. . . . My father was enchanted with the torrent of the Gave de Pau, he sat by it and watched it, and seemed to be possessed by the spirit of delight. Mr. Dakyns and he climbed towards the Brèche de Roland, Mr. Clough meeting them on their return in the Cirque de Gavarnie, where my father said that the phrase "slow dropping veils of thinnest lawn" was taken from the central cataract which pours over the cliff. . . . On August 6th, my father's birthday, we arrived at Cauteretz, – his favourite valley in the Pyrenees. Before our windows we had the torrent rushing over its rocky bed from far away among the mountains and falling in cataracts. . . . He wrote his lyric "All along the valley" "after hearing the voice of the torrent seemingly sound deeper as the night grew" (in memory of his visit here with Arthur Hallam).'

> All along the valley, where thy waters flow,
> I walked with one I loved two and thirty years ago.
> All along the valley, while I walked today
> The two and thirty years were a mist that rolls away,
> For all along the valley, down thy rocky bed,
> Thy living voice to me was as the voice of the dead,
> And all along the valley, by rock and cave and tree,
> The voice of the dead was a living voice to me.

'Altogether – I like the little piece as well as anything I have written,' Tennyson said afterwards. Dakyns tactfully left him to wander off alone with his memories. 'Dakyns isn't a fool,' he afterwards commented to Emily. He climbed to the Lac du Gaube with Clough and Dakyns – the deep, still lake among the fir woods where Swinburne, visiting the place eight years later with Richard Burton, was to swim. After Burton's death, in his 'Elegy, 1869–1891' ('Auvergne, Auvergne, O wild and woeful land') he recalled their ascent of the Puy du Dôme, and in 'The Lake of Gaube' described his ecstasy as he dived into the dark ice-cold water.

'We had a sad parting from Mr. Clough,' Emily wrote in her journal. 'There could not have been a gentler, kinder, more unselfish man or more thoughtful companion than he has been. Among other kind things he corrected the boys' "little journals" for them: we called him the "child-angel".' On their return journey, Tennyson remarked to Emily: 'I have seen many things in this tour I shall like to remember.' Emily must have suffered from the hardships of the tour, but she put up with everything with her usual saintly patience.

Mrs Margaret Cameron, writing to her husband from Freshwater, where she had come to live in order to be near Tennyson in 1860, said:

> His place is in perfect beauty but it does not really satisfy him. His prairies are really enamelled with the purple orchis and golden cowslip. . . . He *sees* the beauty but he *feels* it not. His spirits are low, and his countenance serious and solemn. The buildings *getting* up are a nightmare to him, the workmen *not* getting on are very vexation to him. His furniture has not come. The sculptures for the hall have miscarried or been delayed. The tradesmen cheat him. The visitors look at him. Ladies pester and pursue him. Enthusiasts dun him for a bit of stone off his gate. These things make life a burden, and his great soul suffers from these stings. What is the cure? I believe there is no cure. I believe it is a matter of temperament – of blood and bile. . . .
>
> All that he has is so great and grand – if he would only live in his own divine powers and not suffer the merest terrestrial trifles to magnify themselves into misfortunes on him. . . .
>
> He won't give welcome to the Regiments here, or know either men or their officers. He will be so kind as to lend his stable to the Major, yet can never forgive me because I introduced him to that same Major, who sought an opportunity of thanking him and seeing him.
>
> The looking at him would be the most capital offence of all if he were Ruler of the universe.
>
> His health is much better. . . . But still the least variableness of the weather produces some oppression on his chest – and nothing but constant smoking keeps it down.

Tennyson could not have been easy to live with. He was a congenital grumbler and hypochondriac. But, as he had moved to Farringford for its seclusion, it is surprising to find how many people he regularly entertained there. On some days there were as many as ten people to dinner; there were friends and relations frequently staying in the house, FitzGerald, F. D. Maurice, Jowett, or Edward

Lear. To Lear he addressed one of the most charming of his occasional poems, 'To E. L. on His Travels in Greece':

> Illyrian woodlands, echoing falls
>   Of water, sheets of summer glass,
>   The long divine Peneïan pass,
> The vast Akrokeraunian walls,

which Lear echoed perhaps unconsciously in his 'Dong with a Luminous Nose' ('Over the great Gramboolian plain'), just as he adopted the metre of Tennyson's poem to Catullus:

> Row us out from Desenzano, to your Sirmione row!
> So they rowed, and there we landed – O venusta Sirmio!

in the 'Yonghy-Bonghy-Bo,' and the metre of 'The Lady of Shalott' in 'My Aged Uncle Arly'. This may have irritated the Laureate, if he noticed it, though the undertone of tragedy in Lear's nonsense verses is quite as genuine as anything in Tennyson's. But Lear, it seems, was more attached to Emily than to her husband, of whom his admiration was sometimes qualified. After setting out for a walk with Tennyson and Franklin Lushington on the downs one Sunday, he confided to his diary under 17 June 1860: 'A.T. was most disagreeably querulous and irritating and would return, chiefly because he saw people approaching. But F.L. would not go back, and led zigzagwise towards the sea – A.T. snubby and cross always. After a time he would not go on – but led me back by muddy paths (over our shoes), a shortcut home – hardly, even at last, avoiding his horror – the villagers coming from Church. . . . I believe that this is my last visit to Farringford – nor can I wish it otherwise all things considered.'

The next time Lear went to Farringford, it proved to be equally unfortunate for another reason. Horatio Tennyson and his family were expected and Lear felt that he was not really wanted, so he took a room in the Royal Albion Hotel at Freshwater and left without saying goodbye, after there had been some misunderstanding about an invitation to dinner. He returned, however, in 1866 and noted in his diary that he 'loathed the brutal and snubbing way in which he [Tennyson] treated Lionel and Hallam. . . . Emily T. is I think sadder than formerly. . . . Alfred is more expansive and offensive than usual.' As for his recent poetry, it seemed to Lear a repetition of the old. Things were even worse at his next visit in 1869. Tennyson had chosen two of Lear's drawings of Corsica and while Lear was putting the rest away in his portfolio, he said that he had changed his mind: he would rather a watercolour. Then he began to wonder whether he really wanted that either. After all, 'the money

F                    [141]

might be better used on the outside of the house.' Anyway, he said, it was Emily who wanted them. At this Lear lost his temper and Tennyson accused him of being irritable. Lear replied that he, Tennyson, 'was given to worry and that everybody knew it'. Both men then exploded with rage and Lear went upstairs to pack his bag. When he came down again, Emily had written out a cheque for £10 for a watercolour, and she persuaded him to stay. Before he left, Lear apologised for speaking angrily and Tennyson said 'how characteristic', it wasn't what Lear had said that worried him, but 'everyone called him a worrier'.[2]

It seems that the two men got on each other's nerves. They had never been really close, though they admired each other's work. Vivian Noakes conjectures that things began to go wrong between them when Lear turned to Emily for consolation about his frustrated love for Franklin Lushington, though Tennyson should have understood Lear's feelings. Perhaps he understood them well enough, for on the fly-leaf of his prayer book he had written:[3]

> Oh but alas for the smile of smiles that never but one face wore,
> Oh for the voice that has flown away like a bird to an unseen shore.
> Oh for the face the flower of flowers that blossoms on earth no
> more.

One does not need to be told to whom these lines were addressed. Then Lear's sense of humour was rather too acute for the atmosphere of veneration that surrounded Tennyson at Farringford, for when he wrote his 'Northern Farmers, Old Style' and followed it with the 'Northern Farmer, New Style', Lear remarked that if he wrote any more on the subject he might publish them in a Farmacopoeia, which, Lear notes, 'disgusted him'.[4] Lear admired Tennyson's poetry for its superb landscapes, but he found his harshness and egocentricity hard to bear. 'I would he were as his poems,' he remarked sadly on one occasion; on another, when he had just left Farringford, he wrote: 'I suppose it is the anomaly of high souled and philosophical writings combined with slovenliness, selfishness and morbid folly that prevents my being happy there.'[5]

But Emily he worshipped. She 'remained his perfect ideal of womanhood' and he felt more at home in her presence than anywhere else, let Tennyson growl as he would.[6] He wrote of her: 'Computing moderately, that 15 angels, several hundreds of ordinary women, many philosophers, a heap of truly wise and kind mothers, 3 or 4 minor prophets, and a lot of doctors and schoolmistresses, might be boiled down, and yet their combined essence fall far short of what Emily Tennyson really is.'[7]

John Addington Symonds visited Farringford, with an introduction from Jowett, in November 1864, during one of Tennyson's
absences in London. Afterwards he wrote to Graham Dakyns, now a
housemaster at Clifton: 'Mrs. Tennyson and the boys I saw, and the
rooms full of works of Art intense. She is a strange woman: I love her
from the little I have seen, almost monastic in her shy retirement,
plain drapery, and worn heavenly face. But the boys. . . . My heart
bled and my soul yearned to them. They filled me with a love sadly
deep even at first sight. . . . But there was something in the light
that ran over Hallam's face, in Lionel's grace, and in the delicate
fibre of both felt through their fingertips, which revealed them to
me. . . . Tell me about these boys. I will never forget them.'[8] Next
day he described the same occasion in a letter to his sister Charlotte,
waxing lyrical about the boys. 'We entered by passages and rooms,
low, small and dark, as in an old country house, covered with plaster
casts from Michael Angelo and antiques, with prints and photographs, some of them from well-known works of art. Some of them
Mrs. Cameron's portraits. . . . The furniture was plain and scanty,
but these ornaments all choice and of rare taste. I noticed Mr.
Kirkup's mask of Dante. . . . We found Mrs. Tennyson in a large
gloomy room, fitted up in Gothic style, a drawing-room and a study
with a big bow window all in one. She greeted us kindly, softly, and a
little shyly . . . and looked altogether monastic, worn in face, with
white features and a calm expression.' Lionel he describes as 'a
splendid creature, tall and lithe with long curls and a pear-shaped
face, extremely beautiful. He was curled up in an oak armchair
hanging his red legs over its side.' Hallam he describes as 'also
medieval but not so handsome as his brother. . . . Now they are
growing in a hot house, and are pale, feminine, and full of upward
striving, accordingly. . . . They are more noticeable than anything
else at Farringford.'[9]

Symonds first met Tennyson on 8 December 1865, after dinner at
Thomas Woolner's, and has left a revealing account of the evening in
his *Miscellanies* (1885).[10] As well as Tennyson, there were Gladstone,
Holman Hunt, Palgrave and Dr Symonds. He arrived late and found
everyone discussing the trial of Governor Eyre and his brutal
suppression of the Jamaica rising of October and November that
year.

> [Tennyson] defended any cruelty in the case of putting
> down a savage mob. . . . Tennyson did not argue. He kept
> asserting various prejudices and convictions. 'We are too tender
> to savages, we are more tender to a black man than to
> ourselves. . . . Niggers are tigers, niggers are tigers.' Gladstone

remarked that 'the Englishman is a cruel man – he is a
strong man.' Dr. Symonds then illustrated this with stories
of the Indian Mutiny. 'That's not like Oriental cruelty,'
said Tennyson. 'But I would not kill a cat, not the tom cat
who scratches and miaows over his disgusting amours and
keeps me awake' – thrown in with an indefinable impatience and
rasping hatred. Gladstone looked glum and iron at this speech,
thinking probably of Eyre.

The after-dinner conversation then turned to other
evidences of Eyre's 'nasty butchery', his hanging of a woman
for mutilating a corpse; stories of martial severity were
then told.[11] Gladstone mentioned a case where an Italian
soldier was shot by an Italian general for not wearing his
jacket, and Tennyson put in *sotto voce*: 'If they shot the paupers
they wouldn't tear up their clothes,' and laughed grimly. . . .
Tennyson all the while kept drinking glasses of port, and
glowering round the room through his spectacles. His
moustache hides the play of his mouth, but as far as I could
see that feature is as grim as the rest. He has cheek-bones
carved out of iron. His forehead is domed, quite the reverse of
Gladstone's, like an Elizabethan head, strong in the coronal,
narrow in the frontal regions, but very finely moulded. . . .
Soon after came coffee. Tennyson grew impatient, moved
his great gaunt body about and finally left to smoke his
pipe.

Symonds noticed his 'deep drawl rising into impatient falsetto
when put out'. Contrasting Gladstone with Tennyson, he observes:
'both of them humorous, but the one polished and delicate in re-
partee, the other broad and coarse and grotesque.' Gladstone's
hands, he noticed, 'white and not remarkable. Tennyson's are huge
and unwieldy, fit for moulding clay or dough. Gladstone is some sort
of a man of the world, Tennyson a child and treated by him as a
child.'

When they joined the ladies in the drawing-room, Tennyson was
asked by Woolner and several others to read his translations of the
*Iliad*, 'Achilles over the Trench'.

'No, I shan't,' said Tennyson, standing in the room with a
pettish voice and jerking his arms and body from the hips. 'No,
I shan't read it: it's only a little thing – must be judged
by comparison with the Greek – can only be appreciated by
the difficulties overcome' – then seeing the MS in Gladstone's
hand – 'This isn't fair – no, this isn't fair' – he took it

away and nothing would pacify him. 'I meant to read it to
Mr. Gladstone and Dr. Symonds.' My father urged him to no
purpose. 'Yes, you and Gladstone – but the rest don't
understand it.' Dr. Symonds said: 'Here's my son, an Oxford
first class man.' 'Oh, I should be afraid of him.' Dr.
Symonds then talked to him soothingly of his poems, 'Mariana',
and the Lincolnshire flats, and Tennyson talked of the universe,
imagining himself travelling from one galaxy to another
through infinity. Then he spoke of the nature of matter.
'I cannot form the least notion of a brick. I don't know what
it is. It's no use talking about atoms, extension, colour,
weight. I cannot penetrate the brick. But I have far more
distinct ideas of God – of love and such emotions. I can
sympathise with God in my poor way. The human soul seems
to be always in some way, how we do not know, identical
with God. That's the value of prayers. Prayer is like
opening a sluice between the great ocean and our little
channels. . . . Huxley says we may have come from monkeys.
That makes no difference to me. If it's God's way of
creation, he sees the whole past, present and future as one.'
(Entering on an elaborate statement of Eternity à la Sir
Thomas Browne) 'Why do mosquitoes exist? I believe that
after God had made his world the devil began and added
something.' (Cat and mouse and leopards). My father raised
moral evil. (Morbid art). The conversation turned on
Swinburne for the moment and then dropped.

In all this metaphysical vagueness about Matter, the
Existence of Evil, and the evidence of God there is something
childish. Such points pass with most men for settled and
insoluble, after a time. But Tennyson has a perfect simplicity
about him, which recognises the real greatness of such things
and regards them as always worthy of consideration. He
treats them with profound moral earnestness. . . . There is
nothing original or startling, on the contrary a general
commonplaceness, about his metaphysics, yet so far as they
go, they express real agitating questions, express in a poet's
language what most men feel and think about.

A move was made back to the dining-room, where Tennyson
agreed to read his translations to Gladstone and Dr Symonds.

He began reading in a deep bass growl the passage of
Achilles shouting in the trench. Gladstone continually
interrupted him with small points about words. Tennyson

[145]

replied: 'These lines are word for word. You could not have
a closer translation: one poet could not express another
better. There, these are good lines.' Gladstone would object:
'But you will say Jove and Greeks: can't we have Zeus
and Achaeans?' 'But the sound of Jove is much softer than
Zeus – Zeus – Zeus!' – and for that reason less Greek, Gladstone
might have replied. Later Tennyson exclaimed: 'Ah! there's
nothing more romantic than the image of those women
floating along the streets of Troy with their long dresses
flying out behind them – windy Troy. I daresay it was not
windier than other places, but it stood high open to the air.
As a schoolboy I used to see them.'

Symonds was most anxious to have Tennyson's view of Shakespeare's *Sonnets* and asked Dakyns to find out, if he could. He did
not have the courage to ask himself, since the subject touched him
so nearly. When Palgrave edited them in 1861 he left out Sonnet 20,
with its significant conclusion:

And for a woman wert thou first created,
Till Nature, as she wrought thee, fell adotinge,
And by addition me of thee defeated,
By adding one thing to my purpose nothing.
   But since she prickt thee out for women's pleasure,
   Mine be thy love and thy love's use their treasure.

This was foolish of Palgrave, because this conclusion seems, on the
face of it, to dispose of the idea that Shakespeare's love for his fair
friend was physical.[12] Missing the point entirely, Palgrave wrote:
'We cannot enter into the strange series of feelings which they paint;
we cannot understand how our great and gentle Shakespeare could
have submitted himself to such passions; we have hardly courage to
think that he really endured them.' Similarly, Samuel Butler in his
edition of the *Sonnets* said that he was 'almost afraid to turn the key
that unlocks the mystery of the poet's heart'. But he is anxious to
excuse Shakespeare on the ground that 'his offence' was 'a sin of
very early youth . . . towards which not a trace of further tendency
can be discerned in any subsequent sonnet or work during five and
twenty years of later prolific activity!' In any case, he adds, this
offence 'never went beyond intention and was never repeated. . . .
The marvel, however, is this: that whereas the love of Achilles for
Patroclus depicted by the Greek poet is purely English, absolutely
without taint or alloy, the love of the English poet for Mr. W. H.
was, though only for a short time, more Greek than English.'[13]

[146]

The remarkable thing is that while most Victorians tied themselves into knots about the *Sonnets*, Tennyson, far from being uneasy on this subject, thought them in some respects greater than the plays.

Returning to the close of the year 1861, Tennyson now interrupted his work on *Idylls of the King* to write *Enoch Arden*, which he finished in April the following year. It was just the kind of simple, touching story the Victorian public loved. Woolner had told him of a shipwrecked sailor, who, after years of isolation on a desert island, comes back to find his wife married to his best friend. Unwilling to spoil her happiness, he creeps away and dies. But though the story was a simple one, the verse in which Tennyson told it is elaborate. The poem contains some of his most famous descriptive lines:

> The lustre of the long convolvuluses,
> The sweep of some precipitous rivulet to the wave,

which are triumphs of his art. But its concluding lines are among the most banal he ever wrote:

> And when they buried him the little port
> Had seldom seen a costlier funeral.

as if the costliness of the funeral made up for Enoch's wasted life. It would be useless to look in *Enoch Arden* for anything approaching the realism of Crabbe, who knew fishermen all too well to sentimentalise them. For the reality of the fisherman's life we must go to *The Borough* and *The Parish Register*. Tennyson admired Crabbe, and would often read him aloud; but he avoided the grimness of his picture of Aldeburgh at the beginning of the century:

> Here joyless roam a wild amphibious race,
> With sullen woe displayed in every face;
> Who far from civil arts and social fly
> And scowl at strangers with suspicious eye.

*Peter Grimes*, one feels, is nearer the truth than *Enoch Arden*. Would such a man be likely to creep away to die, when he returned to find his wife living with another man, so as not to spoil an idyllic picture

of domestic peace? It is hard to credit. But Enoch, we are invited to
believe.

> . . . was not all unhappy. His resolve
> Upbore him, and firm faith, and evermore
> Prayer from a living source within the will,
> And beating up through all the bitter world,
> Like fountains of sweet water in the sea,
> Kept him a living soul . . .
>
> and he thought
> 'After the Lord has called me she shall know,'
> I wait His time.'

Perhaps the fishermen of the Isle of Wight were milder and more
pious than on the wild and desolate coast of Suffolk. But Crabbe had
grown up among the fishermen of Aldeburgh; he had worked among
them and knew them. Tennyson had indeed talked to his fishermen
and had gone out with them in their boats at night, not as one of
themselves, but as a gentleman poet, the Squire. He could only
sentimentalise them.

Walter Bagehot, writing in *The National Review*, remarked that
*Enoch Arden* was an example of ornate art. 'Many characters in real
life, if brought distinctly, prominently, and plainly before the mind,
as they really are, – shewn in their inner nature, their actual essence,
are doubtless very unpleasant. They would be horrid to meet and
horrid to think of. We fear it must be owned that Enoch Arden is
this kind of person. A dirty sailor who did *not* go home to his wife is
not an agreeable being: a varnish must be put on him to make him
shine. The dismal act of a squalid man needed many condiments to
make it pleasant.' And he concludes: 'So much has not often been
made of selling fish.'

Mrs Cameron was a constant visitor at Farringford, in and out of
the house with her photographic apparatus, with such gifts as legs of
Welsh mutton, rolls of expensive wallpaper, deep blue with a frieze of
the Elgin Marbles, even one day sending up her grand piano, carried
by eight men, when the piano at Farringford was out of tune, so that
Lear could play and sing his settings of Tennyson's poems. She
continually waylaid the shy Laureate, pestering him to pose for her,
but such was her enthusiasm and generosity that Tennyson put up
with much from her that he would never have put up with from
anyone else, and it is due to her persistence that we have such a fine
photographic record of him. No one was safe from Mrs Cameron:
Darwin, Browning, Henry Taylor, Carlyle, Watts, Trollope, they
were all forced to submit to 'the ordeal of her camera; or her house-
maids and the village girls would be posed as Sappho and the Virgin

Mary, her children as angels with swans' wings, fishermen as King Arthur, and Mrs. Watts and her sisters as the "Rosebud Garden of Girls".'[1] We are also indebted to Mrs Cameron for studies of those astonishing beauties Mrs Herbert Duckworth (later Mrs Leslie Stephen, the mother of Virginia Woolf), Ellen Terry and Marie Spartali, who was painted by Rossetti and Burne-Jones. Though she was of the Pattle sisters, Mrs Cameron was unfortunately no beauty herself. But she made up for it by her vitality and endearing eccentricity, 'a short stout figure, with gorgeous trailing draperies of crimson and violet and face and hands stained with chemicals'.[2]

Tennyson was much disturbed at this time by the new building in the neighbourhood, the plans for Freshwater, of which he wrote to the Duke of Argyll in 1861: 'I am sure the Duchess will sympathise with my disgust at having Freshwater (where I had pitched my tent taken with its solitariness) so polluted and defiled with brick and mortar, as is threatened; they talk of laying out streets and crescents, and I oscillate between my desire of purchasing land at a ruinous price in order to keep my views open, and my wish to fly the place altogether. Is there no millionaire who will take pity on the wholesome hillside and buy it all up?' The year before, Emily had complained to Frederick Goddard Tuckerman of Harvard: 'Our beautiful views will, I fear, be spoilt before long. People are seized with a building mania. Already a bit of our sea is built out from us and we are obliged to buy land at the rate of a thousand pounds an acre merely to prevent more of the bay being hidden by ugly brick houses. . . . If our down were no longer lonely we could not stay. We could only be here in the winter when it is too stormy for visitors.' One cannot help feeling that Tennyson was lucky to have enough money to buy land at a ruinous rate to preserve the view of 'our sea'. Ironically, many people moved to Freshwater in order to be near him. Such was the penalty of fame. But tourists and visitors increased each year, and finally things got so bad that in 1868 he built another house for the summer months at Blackdown, near Haslemere, on the edge of the pine woods, with a tremendous view of the Sussex Weald, a house that cannot be seen from the rough track through the woods that leads to it. The Tennysons continued to use Farringford during the winter.

In April 1864 Garibaldi visited the Isle of Wight and the Tennysons went to the Seelys of Brooke to pay their respects to the great Italian patriot. 'A most striking figure in his picturesque white poncho lined with red,' Emily observed in her diary, 'his embroidered red shirt and coloured tie over all. His face very noble, powerful, and sweet, his forehead high and square. Altogether he looked like one of the great men of our Elizabethan age. His manner was simple and kind.' And when he came to Farringford, 'people on foot and on horseback and in carriages had waited at our gate two hours for him. Some rushed forward to shake hands with him. He stood up and bowed. A. and I and the boys were in the portico awaiting his arrival. . . . A. and he went up to A.'s study together, and they talked on politics, A. advising the general not to talk politics in England. They repeated Italian poetry together. . . . Mrs. Cameron wanted to photograph Garibaldi, and dropped down on her knees before him, and held up her black hands, covered with chemicals. He evidently thought she was a beggar until we explained who she was.

'Then we went to plant the Wellingtonia. A. had the large screen put up to protect Garibaldi from the cold east wind. Several strangers were there, and when the tree was planted they gave a shout. On going away Garibaldi shook hands with all and kissed the boys. A. was charmed with simplicity, but thought that in worldly matters he seemed to have "the divine stupidity of a hero".' *The Illustrated London News* devoted a full page to this visit, with a picture of Tennyson and Garibaldi standing together at the door of Farringford.

In February 1865, there came the news that Tennyson's mother was seriously ill at Rose Lodge, Hampstead, where she had lived since 1855. For the last ten years, Rosemount, the adjoining and larger house in Flask Walk, where Emily lived with her husband Richard Jesse, had been the regular meeting place of the different members of the family when in London, though in those days Hampstead was still to all intents and purposes a village. But his mother died before Tennyson could reach her. 'My last thoughts of her,' he wrote to Dr Bickersteth, 'shall be as I saw her two or three weeks ago, sitting in her chair. That look is printed on my soul for ever.' On the morning of the funeral at Highgate, he wrote: 'We all of us hate the pompous funeral we have to join; black plumes, black coaches and nonsense. We should all like to go in white and gold rather, but convention is against us.' Frederick, Arthur, Horatio and Matilda were also there. When shaking hands with Dr Bickersteth, who had conducted the burial service, Tennyson said: 'I hope you will not think I have spoken in exaggerated terms of my beloved mother, but indeed she was the beautifullest thing God Almighty ever did make.' After her death Matilda, 'tall, dark and equine',[3] left Hampstead and went to live at Farringford. Her sister Emily continued to live at Rosemount.

Next year brought another distinguished guest to Farringford, Queen Emma of the Sandwich Islands, 'with Major Hopkins and a huge native Mr. Hoapli in attendance,' Emily Tennyson notes. 'The Queen's maid and her luggage lost on the road: they arrived at midnight. We had a throne chair made out of our ilex wood. It was

[151]

first used by the Queen. She, poor lady, wanted to stay quietly there but had to go to banquets, &c., about the Island. I collected money for the projected cathedral at Honolulu.

'A. went with the Queen up the Down. . . . Endless guests came to tea. A. took her out that she might read her letters; and hid her from the guests in the summerhouse in the kitchen garden ("among the cabbages," she said). A. and I pleased with her sweet dignity and manner, and a calmness that made one think of an Egyptian statue; her voice was musical. Mr. and Mrs. Hoapli sang Hawaiian songs. They sat on the ground and acted the songs as they sang. Then they chanted an ode to the young Prince, a wild monotonous chant.

'Oct. 2nd. A. gave her two large magnolia blossoms on her leaving. She has an affectionate nature; something very pathetic about her.'[4]

In July, when the boys returned from their first term at Marlborough, where Granville Bradley was now headmaster, Tennyson took the family for a tour of Belgium and Germany, making a special expedition to the field of Waterloo, where the wailing of the wind at night was like the dead lamenting. 'We saw the bank behind which our Guards lay when the last French attack was made by the "Old Guards",' notes Emily. 'Sergeant Mundy, who showed us round Hougemont, assured us that the Duke of Wellington did not say, "Up, Guards, and at them", but merely put his hand to his head and said "Ready". As A. observed, "That is infinitely more like him". We spent a week at the hotel, A. enjoying his study of the battlefield and his long walks.

'Thence we went to Luxembourg and Trèves – the last an enchanting place.' Early in September, they reached Weimar, where the people seemed rather stupid about Goethe and Schiller: 'In vain we tried to impress upon our driver that we wanted to see all which concerned them. . . . Went with Mr. Marshall – Secretary to the Grand Duchess – to see Goethe's town-house. . . . A. was touched by seeing "Salve" on the door-mat, and all Goethe's old boots in the entrance.' They were then taken to see Goethe's study: 'One cannot explain in words the saw and sadness with which this low dark room filled A. . . . door opened to his bedroom. Such a melancholy little place! By the bed was an arm-chair, to which at last he used to move from his bed for a little change. All round the wall, by the bed and chair, a dark green leafy carpet or tapestry was fastened half-way up the wall of the room. On the washing-stand was some of the last medicine he took. The window at the foot of the bed was partly boarded up.' At Dresden 'the Madonna and Child by Raffaelle struck A. and me as wonderfully "human and divine". We seemed to see the trouble of the world in the Virgin's eyes. . . . Next day to the

Gallery to see the Raffaelle Madonna again; we also looked at the Holbein Holy Family, which is very great, Titian's tribute money and Correggio's Magdalene, &c. . . . A German professor suddenly discovered A. and made him a long speech, which was very trying.' After a week at Dresden, they went to Brunswick and Aix-la-Chapelle and then sailed to Ryde. When they arrived back at Farringford, they found eighty letters to answer, which was also very trying.

'We are at present in a very knocked-up state,' Emily wrote to Woolner on their return. 'It is nearly ten and I am ordered to go to bed as soon as possible so I must not say much. . . . I hope he [Alfred] has stored some recollections when the (to him usual) unpleasant accompaniments of continental travel have worn away.' Then the usual stream of visitors began to arrive: the Brookfields, Spedding, Monckton Milnes, Edmund and Franklin Lushington, Lord Dufferin, the Duke of Argyll, F. D. Maurice, Holman Hunt, Norman Lockyer, Froude, Watts, Francis Doyle, Woolner, Palgrave, Kingsley, Lear, and others.

In September 1866 Alfred and Emily were in Haslemere, having heard of the Devil's Jumps as a possible site for a house. They called on Mrs Gilchrist, the widow of Blake's biographer and a friend of the Carlyles, who offered to help them to find a suitable site for building, which Tennyson was now well able to afford, with three editions of *In Memoriam*, three of *Maud* and two of *The Princess* having appeared during the years 1865–6. The sixth edition of *Idylls of the King* had come out in 1865. Next year they took rooms in a farm-house at Grayshott. Just before going here, on 23 March, Tennyson wrote to Palgrave:[5]

I suppose I may come up to town sometime after we are settled in our farm-house, where I have taken rooms for ourselves and three servants for two years. . . .

I don't give the name of the place because I wish it to be kept secret: I am not flying from the cockneys here to tumble in among the cockneys there I hope: tho' some of my friends assert that it will be so, and that there will be more cockneys and of a worse kind, but I don't believe them, for the house is quite solitary and five miles from town or village. You ask whether Doré's illustrations are a success. I liked the first four I saw very much, tho' they were not quite true to the text, but the rest not so well; one I hate, that where the dead lady [Elaine] is stuck up on a chair, with her eyes open, as if her father had forgotten to close them, or as if she had opened them again, for they are closed in the voyage down the river. On the whole I am against illustrators, except one could do with them as old Mr.

[153]

Rogers did, have them to breakfast twice a week and explain your own views to them over and over again.

My wife (thanks for your enquiries) has been shut up in the house for nearly three months, with cough and cold. The Queen sent her an invitation to go with me to Osborne, but I was obliged to make her excuses, and went alone. You say that you expect another little one in June: ought I to congratulate you or condole? Love to Mrs. Palgrave from us both.

The search for a suitable building site went on. 'Mrs. Gilchrist and Mr. Simmons, having taken endless trouble in communicating with Mr. Lucas about Black-horse Copse on Blackdown,' Emily notes in her diary, 'we went there in an odd procession, Lionel on a donkey with a lady's saddle, I driving in the basket-carriage, the rest walking. The wheels spun round on the axles without touching ground in some deep ruts, and the carriage had to be lifted over, William leading the pony carefully. At last we reached the charming ledge of the heathery down. This looks over an immense view bounded by the South-down, by Leith Hill on the north. Copse-wood surrounds the ledge, and the hill protects it from the north-west. The foxglove was in full bloom. A. helped me down the mountain path. We all enjoyed the day thoroughly.

'June 16th. The Blackdown land was bought. . . . A. met Mr. Knowles at the station. . . . and A. knowing that Mr. Knowles was an architect, said, "You had better build me my house on Blackdown."

'Mr. Knowles came to luncheon and looked at our sketch and plans, and took them home to put them in "working order", as he said.'

On 31 January next year Tennyson went to Blackdown to fix the exact site of the house, changing the name from Black-horse Copse to Aldworth, 'some of my mother's family having come from a village of that name near Streatley in Berks,' writes Hallam Tennyson, 'where there is a curious old church with the tombs of her Sellwood ancestors.' Blackdown is the highest hill of the Sussex North Down. Tennyson described the view from the front windows of Aldworth in the Prologue to 'The Charge of the Heavy Brigade':

> Green Sussex fading into blue
> With one grey glimpse of sea.

The property was about sixty acres and included Black-horse Copse, two or three fields and, at the foot of the hill, Roundhurst, a small farmhouse, three and a half miles from Haslemere.

James Knowles had agreed to build Aldworth on condition that he would not be paid. Originally Tennyson had intended it to be quite a small house, 'little more than a cottage', but, as his grandson observes, with his 'imaginative appreciation of the site and Knowles's youthful enthusiasm the scheme grew and grew until the cottage became a substantial mansion' with 'a colonnaded porch extending along the end in which the entrance door was set, so that the poet could walk up and down when the weather was bad; and inside a broad corridor was to run the entire length of the house from the front door, with a staircase rising from one side of it as far back as possible so as to give room for him to walk when the outdoor colonnade was unsuitable.' The principal room was the library, a large oblong room on the first floor, with tall windows overlooking the Weald. On the dining-room mantelpiece were to be carved devices emblematic of his favourite poets: Chaucer, Milton, Shakespeare, Wordsworth, Goethe and Dante; and round the cornice under the roof was to run a motto in the Welsh language meaning 'The Truth against the world'.[6] The lawn in front of the house was bordered by a terrace with a stone balustrade along which cypresses were planted, giving an Italian flavour to the garden. Later, Helen Allingham did her charming watercolours of the house and garden, reproduced in her *Homes and Haunts of Tennyson* (1905).

In February 1867 Tennyson drove over from Farringford to Osborne. 'He likes and admires the Queen personally very much,' Emily wrote to Amy Gilchrist, 'and he enjoys conversation with her. . . . The Queen's manner towards him is child-like and charming, and they both express their opinions freely. Even when his differ from the Queen's, she takes it with perfect good humour, and is very animated herself.' He made her 'very merry' telling her how his privacy was invaded by cockneys and when she said, 'We are not troubled much here', he replied, 'Perhaps I shouldn't be either, Your Majesty, if I could stick a sentry at my gates.' The Queen then drove him all over the Osborne estate, which had been laid out by Prince Albert, and he remarked that 'it would be very pretty in thirty years' time!'

With the plans for Aldworth settled, Tennyson took his usual summer holiday; he went this year to Dorset and Devon to join Palgrave and his family at Lyme. Meeting Allingham at Yarmouth pier, he persuaded him to come too, and they took the train to Dorchester, where they called on the Dorset poet William Barnes and then walked over the downs to Bridport. Next day they walked across the hills to Lyme. 'Now take me to the Cobb and show me where Louisa Musgrave fell,' said Tennyson, being a great admirer of Jane Austen. They then walked to the Undercliff and Tennyson observed that it exactly represented 'some of the romantic landscape before my mind's eye in the *Idylls* – little winding glades closed all

[155]

round with grassy mounds and wild shrubs where we might fancy the sudden appearance of a knight riding, or a spellbound damsel,' as Palgrave describes it. 'This peculiar character (which was partly suggested to him by the background of medieval illuminations) he also once pointed out in a certain field of his own beyond his summer house at Farringford.'[7] A little tame, perhaps, and certainly lacking the wild romantic glamour of Doré's illustrations.

Next day, much to Tennyson's disappointment, Allingham had to return to his customs office at Lymington. He offered to pay Allingham's expenses if he would stay. 'Most delicious,' Allingham observes in his *Diary*, 'that the man whose company I love best should care about mine. Most mortifying for I am tied by the leg.' So Tennyson set out on a walking tour to Dartmoor and Exeter with Palgrave.

At this time the sale of Tennyson's poems fell off to some extent owing to the growing popularity of Swinburne, and he began to publish single works in periodicals. For 'The Victim', which appeared in *Good Words*, he received £700. 'Lucretius' appeared in *Macmillan's Magazine* in May 1868 in a slightly expurgated condition, the editor, as we have seen, objecting to the rather too glowing description of the old Roman poet's bacchanalian dreams. As Harold Nicolson observes: 'There are indications that the advent of Swinburne was leading the Laureate to consider whether a little – very little – wine might not with advantage be added to the limpid waters of Camelot.'[8] He even thought of writing a poem on Tristram and Isolt, but confined himself, in 'The Last Tournament', to describing their pitiful last meeting at Tintagel, followed by Tristram's death at the hands of the treacherous King Mark. It was his summary treatment of the most beautiful and tragic love story of the Middle Ages that encouraged Swinburne to undertake his ambitious *Tristram of Lyonesse*.

Tennyson's study of metaphysics resulted in poems which, we are told, 'came in for a good deal of rough handling'. One such poem was 'The Higher Pantheism', written in December 1867 and read, though not by Tennyson, at the first meeting of the Metaphysical Society. Of this poem Swinburne wrote a deadly parody, 'The Higher Pantheism in a Nutshell', although he said 'I allow no one to laugh at Mr. Tennyson but myself.'

One, who is not, we see: but one, who we see not, is:
Surely this is not that: but that is assuredly this.

What, and wherefore, and whence? for under is over and under:
If thunder could be without lightning, lightning could be without
    thunder.

Doubt is faith in the main: but faith, on the whole, is doubt:
We cannot believe by proof: but could we believe without?

Why, and whither, and how? for barley and rye are not clover:
Neither are straight lines curves: yet over is under and over. . . .

Ask a man what he thinks, and get from a man what he feels:
God, once caught in the fact, shows you a fair pair of heels.

Body and spirit are twins: God only knows which is which:
The soul squats down in the flesh, like a tinker drunk in a ditch.

More is the whole than a part: but half is more than the whole:
Clearly, the soul is the body: but is not the body the soul? . . .

God, whom we see not, is: and God, who is not, we see:
Fiddle, we know, is diddle: and diddle, we take it, is dee.

'The subjects suggested for discussion at the Metaphysical Society,'
Hallam Tennyson tells us, 'were the comparison of the different
theories respecting the ultimate grounds for belief in the objective
and moral sciences, the logic of the sciences whether physical or
social, the immortality of the soul and its personal identity, the
personality of God, conscience and its true character, the material
hypothesis.'[9]
Swinburne's parody touches on most of these questions, to which,
of course, there can hardly be any satisfactory answer. The greatest
mind among the members of the Society, according to Tennyson,
was F. D. Maurice, though often 'his thoughts were too deep to be
easily understood'. Other members were Dean Stanley, James
Martineau, Henry Sidgwick, Edmund Lushington, Huxley, Bagehot,
Gladstone, Cardinal Manning, A. J. Balfour, Ruskin, Leslie Stephen,
John Morley, representing a cross-section of the Victorian intellectual
world. Tennyson, we are told, did not say very much at the meetings,
but usually sided with the more conservative speakers. 'Wages',
which appeared in *Macmillan's Magazine* in February 1868, sums up
his belief in the immortality of the soul and is the kind of poem upon
which his reputation as a seer was based.

The wages of sin is death: if the wages of Virtue be dust,
    Would she have heart to endure for the life of the worm and the
    fly?
She desires no isles of the blest, no quiet seats of the just,
    To rest in a golden grove, or to bask in a summer sky:
Give her the wages of going on, and not to die.

It is hardly surprising that the young were turning to the paganism
of Swinburne.

[157]

Tennyson's next important poem was 'The Holy Grail' of 1869. He felt that unless he could handle this subject worthily, he could not proceed with *Idylls of the King*. But a poem on this subject presented many difficulties. Chief among these was that he feared the charge of irreverence. In any case, as he confessed to Hallam, 'it could not be done better than by Malory'. But he had had the subject in mind for many years and had already composed a poem in his head on the Grail theme, but had not written it down. At last, however, he yielded to persuasion, not least Emily's. 'I doubt whether the *San Graal* would have been written but for my endeavour, and the Queen's wish, and that of the Crown Princess. Thank God for it,' she notes. Tennyson himself said of the poem: 'Faith declines, religion in many turns from practical goodness to the quest after the supernatural and the marvellous and selfish religious excitement. Few are those for whom the quest is a source of spiritual strength. . . . "The Holy Grail" is one of the most imaginative of my poems. I have exposed there my strong feeling as to the Reality of the Unseen. The end where the King speaks of his work and of his visions, is intended to be the summing up of all in the highest note by the highest of men.' It is interesting that the materialistic nineteenth century produced, as well as Tennyson's and Stephen Hawker's versions, Wagner's *Lohengrin* and *Parsifal*, the Morris–Burne-Jones tapestries for Stanmore Hall, and Rossetti's unfinished mural at the Oxford Union. There is a close similarity between the celestial Grail music of *Lohengrin*, written in 1847, and the following lines from Tennyson's poem:

> I heard a sound
> As of a silver horn from o'er the hills . . .
> and the slender sound
> As from a distance beyond distance grew
> Coming upon me – O never harp nor horn,
> Nor aught we blow with breath, or touch with hand,
> Was like that music as it came; and then
> Streamed through my cell a cold and silver beam,
> And down the long beam stole the Holy Grail,
> Rose-red with beatings in it, as if alive,
> Till all the white walls of my cell were dyed
> With rosy colours leaping on the wall;
> And then the music faded, and the Grail
> Past, and the beam decayed, and from the walls
> The rosy quiverings died into the night.

Tennyson was very much in tune with the mystical, transcendental feeling of the Grail legend, hence Emily's conviction that he was uniquely fitted by temperament to deal with it. 'There are moments when the flesh is nothing to me,' he said to Mrs Bradley in January 1869, 'when I feel and know the flesh to be the vision, God and the Spiritual the only real and true. Depend upon it, the Spiritual is real: it belongs to one more than the hand and foot. You may tell me that my hand and my foot are only imaginary symbols of my existence, I could believe you; but you never, never can convince me that the *I* is not an eternal reality, and that the Spiritual is not the only true and real part of me'.

Again: 'I have never had any revelations through anaesthetics, but a kind of waking trance – this for lack of a better word – I have frequently had, quite up from boyhood, when I have been alone. This has come upon me through repeating my own name to myself silently, till all at once, as it were out of the intensity of the consciousness of individuality, individuality itself seemed to dissolve and fade away into boundless being, and this not a confused state but the clearest, the surest of the surest, utterly beyond words – where death was an almost laughable impossibility – the loss of personality (if so it were) seeming no extinction, but the only true life. I am ashamed of my feeble description. Have I not said the state is utterly beyond words?. . . . By God Almighty! there is no delusion in the matter! It is no nebulous ecstasy, but a state of transcendent wonder, associated with absolute clearness of mind.'

It is curious, therefore, that King Arthur in Tennyson's poem is by no means in favour of his knights' departing on their quest for the Grail. He regarded this as the principal cause of the break-up of the Round Table. He wanted his knights to remain fighting men, not to become monks.

> 'Lo now,' said Arthur, 'have ye seen a cloud?
> What go ye into the wilderness to see? . . .
>                 O my knights,
> Your places being vacant at my side,
> The chance of noble deeds will come and go
> Unchallenged, while you follow wandering fires
> Lost in a quagmire! Many of you, yea most,
> Return no more.'

And as the knights depart on their quest

>                 the king could hardly speak
> For grief, and all in middle street the Queen
> Who rode by Lancelot, wailed and shrieked aloud,
> 'This madness has come upon us for our sins.'

But the quest, for most of them, was unsuccessful and proved the

[159]

king right: they were but following wandering fires. As for Lancelot, he ran mad.

When Tennyson's old friend FitzGerald read 'The Holy Grail' volume he was clearly disappointed. 'The whole myth of Arthur's Round Table Dynasty in Britain presents itself to me with a sort of cloudy, Stonehenge grandeur. I am not sure if the old knight's adventures do not tell upon me better, touched in some lyrical way (like your own "Lady of Shalott") than when elaborated into an epic poem. I never could care for Spenser, Tasso, or even Ariosto, whose epic has a ballad ring about it. But then I never could care much for the old prose Romances either, except *Don Quixote*. So as this was always the case with me, I suppose my brain is wanting in this bit of its dissected map. Anyhow, Alfred, while I feel how pure, noble and holy your work is, and whole phrases, lines and sentences of it will abide with me, and, I am sure, with men after me, I read on till the "Lincolnshire Farmer" drew tears to my eyes. I was got back to the substantial rough-spun Nature I knew; and the old brute, invested by you with the solemn humour of Humanity, like Shakespeare's Shallow, became a more pathetic phenomenon than the knights who revisit the world in your other verse. There! I can't help it, and have made a clean breast; and you need only laugh at one more of "old Fitz's crotchets", which I daresay you anticipated.' One wonders if Tennyson did laugh on reading this letter. 'I suppose you see that Tennyson is publishing another little lot of Arthurian legend,' William Morris wrote in October 1872. 'We know pretty well what it will be; and I confess I don't look forward to it.' For his part, Morris loved Malory too much to be interested in a dilution of the *Morte d'Arthur*. The whole of Tennyson was engaged in *In Memoriam* and *Maud*. The same cannot be said of *Idylls of the King*. In November 1868 he had read 'The Holy Grail' to Browning, who said that it was his 'best and highest'.

Nevertheless, the so-called reaction against Tennyson set in with this volume, and many people now began to feel as Morris felt. Sometimes, too, friends said the wrong thing. Visiting Jowett at Balliol on one occasion, Tennyson was asked after dinner to read them a manuscript poem. Chairs were arranged and the manuscript produced; the poem was listened to in respectful silence. But the silence continued after the reading had ceased. Then Jowett said in his high silvery voice: 'I wouldn't publish that, Tennyson, if I were you.' The strained apprehension on Emily's face changed to a look of panic. At last, the Laureate growled: 'If it comes to that, Master, the sherry you gave us at luncheon today was positively filthy!'

In June 1869, at the age of fifty-nine, Tennyson set off with Frederick Locker for a tour of Switzerland. They stopped at Paris for several days, visiting churches, museums, markets and the Louvre. On a previous visit the poet had been struck by a little Poussin depicting the death of Narcissus. 'He gazed at this picture with delight,' writes Locker in his account of their trip. At the falls of Schaffhausen it was so very hot that they took refuge in a shed 'pervaded by an atrocious odour of decayed cheeses, or some such horror. "This is my usual luck," says Tennyson. "I never go to see anything which is very impressive, without encountering something mean or repulsive. Now this sublime cataract, and this disgusting stench, will for ever dwell in my memory." He went on to say that the unpleasant odours of London were as offensive as those of Paris, but the latter were more pungent, piercing like the point of a lance; and then he added with grave emphasis: "It is an age of lies, and also an age of stinks."

'Grindelwald, Aigle, 20th June. To-day we bought two large carved wood bears, for which, after breaking a good deal of French over the dealer, we agreed that Tennyson should pay one hundred francs. These bears now stand in the entrance hall at Aldworth, keeping watch and ward, quite ready to welcome the arriving guest with a friendly hug.'

In the evenings they played battledore and shuttlecock in the *pension* attached to the Aigle. The account continues:

Just now the Aigle would be entirely deserted, but for ourselves and a young lately married couple. The pair much interest the poet. We sit opposite to them at breakfast and again at dinner at the extreme end of a vast expanse of bare, cold tablecloth. They nestle close to each other like love-birds on one perch, the perch being a short one. She is a bouncing *blonde* and frankly blue in her eyes and there is a coquetry, uncalculated, or calculated, in her dimples, her boots and her parasol: she has also an exasperating little hat and feather. Sad to say, none of these allurements seem lost on my gifted companion. As often as she addresses her swain, she gazes with innocent rapture into his mild eyes and every now and again, as if asserting her right of possession, with sympathetic fingers arranges and rearranges the bow of his cravat, and then sends a pretty appealing glance across the table in our direction. These lovers take pastoral walks together, and are often to be met with in twilight intervals, steeped in honeymoonshine. On such occasions they deem it expedient to affect an exquisite confusion.

Excepting for this, and you will allow this a large exception, our lovers may not be specially attractive, but surely they are beautiful in their *abandon*, loving and being loved. Thanks to

[161]

them the pension Aigle is an Arcadian hostelry, with green retreats and winding paths of dalliance, lawns, rocks and leafy trees.

The glacier nearest the hotel is much discoloured by the debris of the mountain. Tennyson's farewell words were: 'That glacier is a filthy thing; it looks as if a thousand London seasons had passed over it.' Such was our retrospect of Grindelwald.

Hotel d'Angleterre, Strasbourg, 3rd July. Tennyson does not like his eggs too lightly cooked. To-day at breakfast there was a pretty waitress, and he sent his eggs to be more boiled, and then, in the damsel's native tongue, expostulated with her as to the softness of the eggs and the apparent hardness of her heart. It was very pleasant to hear his grave but gallant remonstrance and her merry laugh. He is delightful.

Later, Locker wrote to Hallam Tennyson: 'Balzac's remark that "Dans tout homme de génie il y a un enfant" may find its illustration in Tennyson. He is the only grown-up human being that I know of, who habitually thinks aloud. His humour is of the dryest, it is admirable. Did anybody make one laugh more heartily than Tennyson? He tells a story excellently, and has a catching laugh' – a somewhat different picture from the usual one of the gloomy bard.

On his return from Switzerland, Tennyson and Emily settled in their new house at Blackdown. The Laureate was so delighted with the bath with its hot and cold water, that he at first took three baths a day. But the novelist Mrs Oliphant, meeting him in London this year, was struck by his 'roughness and acrid gloom'. Tennyson did not pay much attention to her, and when she was leaving she said to Emily how much she had enjoyed her visit, he stood 'glowering over them both and remarked: "What hypocrites you women are!" '

Tennyson's friend and neighbour in the Isle of Wight, Sir John Simeon, died next May; and when he went to the funeral, he asked Simeon's son to give him one of his father's pipes and one of his cloaks and hats. 'Come for me yourself when it is time to start,' he said, 'and do not send a servant.' When young Simeon came to fetch him, he found the poet lying full length on the ground, wearing the hat and cloak and smoking the pipe. Tears were running down his face and in his hand was a scrap of paper on which he had written a rough draft of his poem, 'In the Garden at Swainston', the last verse of which runs:

Two dead men have I known
  In courtesy like to thee:

Two dead men have I loved
  With a love that ever will be:
Three dead men have I loved and thou art last
  of the three.

The other two were, of course, Arthur Hallam and Henry Lushington. At the burial service Lady Simeon and her daughter clung to the coffin with heart-rending shrieks and sobs. The loss of his friend hung like a cloud over Tennyson all that summer. 'He is the only man on earth, I verily believe,' he wrote to Lady Simeon, 'to whom I could and have more than once opened my whole heart and he has also given me, in many conversations at Farringford in my little attic, his utter confidence. I knew none like him in tenderness and generosity.' Tennyson's depression affected his health, and he was much afflicted with eczema during the next few months. On 4 June 1870, his presence at Dickens's funeral in the Abbey caused an extraordinary commotion. People stood on their chairs to look at him and at the end of the service the crowd surging towards him and his companions was so great that special steps had to be taken to release him.

When the Franco–Prussian War broke out, Tennyson's sympathies, like most English people's, were with Prussia. He could not forgive Swinburne for praising *Mademoiselle de Maupin*, for 'the frightful corruption of French literature,' he said, 'makes one fear that they are going to hell.'

This year, too, there appeared a most vindictive attack on Tennyson's poetry by one James Friswell, who wrote of it as 'sugar-sweet, pretty-pretty, of womanly talk and feminine stuff'. Tennyson replied with some furious lines beginning:

Pisswell, Friswell – a clown beyond redemption,
  Brutal, personal, infinitely blackguard.

But having relieved his feelings, he fortunately did not publish these lines.

Early next year the Thoby Princeps settled near Farringford at 'The Briary', a house built for them free of charge by Philip Webb. Here Tennyson was an almost daily visitor, reading to the blind Thoby, who would recite to him Persian translations of his poems.

It was in 1871, too, that the young Edmund Gosse, then working as a junior assistant in the vaults of the British Museum library, first met Tennyson. He has left a charming account of this meeting in his *Portraits and Sketches* (1912). He met him in the long gallery that used to house busts of Roman emperors. Tennyson, he says, was 'every inch as imperial-looking as the best of them. He stood there as we approached him, very still, with slightly drooping eyelids, and made no movement, no gesture of approach.' When Gosse had been presented, Tennyson continued to stand there considering him in a silence 'which would have been deeply disconcerting if it had not, somehow, seemed kindly, and even, absurd as it sounds, rather shy.' As Gosse was understandably tongue-tied, Tennyson made conversation, even making 'vaguely generous remarks' about some of Gosse's verses. 'He seemed to accept me as a sheep of the fold of which he was, so magnificently, the shepherd.' Later, standing before the bust of Antinous, the Emperor Hadrian's lover, the great poet said, in his deep slow voice, as if speaking to himself: 'Ah! this is the inscrutable Bithynian. If we knew what he knew, we should understand the ancient world.'

1873 saw the publication of the Imperial Library Edition of the *Works* and its truly imperial dedication to the Queen, recalling the national thanksgiving at St Paul's after the Prince of Wales's recovery from typhoid fever in February 1872:

O loyal to the royal in thyself,
And loyal to thy land, as this to thee –
Bear witness, that rememberable day,
When, pale as yet, and fever-worn, the Prince
Who scarce had plucked his flickering life again
From halfway down the shadow of the grave,
Past with thee through thy people and their love,
And London rolled one tide of joy through all
Her trebled millions, and loud leagues of man
And welcome! witness, too, the silent cry,
The prayer of many a race and creed, and clime –
Thunderless lightnings striking under sea
From sunset and sunrise of all thy realm,
And that true North, whereof we lately heard
A strain to shame us 'keep you to yourselves;
So loyal is too costly! friends – your love
Is but a burthen: loose the bond and go.
Is this the tone of empire? here the faith
That made us rulers? this, indeed, her voice
And meaning, whom the roar of Hougoumont
Left mightiest of all peoples under heaven?
What shock has fooled her since, that she should speak
So feebly? wealthier – wealthier – hour by hour!
The voice of Britain, or a sinking land,
Some third-rate isle half-lost among her seas?
*There* rang her voice, when the full city pealed

[164]

Thee and thy Prince! The loyal to their crown
Are loyal to their own far sons, who love
Our ocean-empire with her boundless homes
For ever-broadening England, and her throne
In our vast Orient, and one isle, one isle,
That knows not her own greatness: if she knows
And dreads it we are fallen.

Tennyson foresaw and feared all that has actually happened to
Britain in our time, after the collapse of the Victorian empire. By
'that true North' he meant Canada, and the suggestion of *The Times*
that she should sever her connection with Great Britain as being
'too costly'. He goes on to mention all those things that could weaken
and bring down the greatness of England and destroy the *Pax
Britannica*:

For some are scared, who mark,
Or wisely or unwisely, signs of storm,
Waverings of every vane with every wind,
And wordy trucklings to the transient hour,
And fierce or careless looseners of the faith,
And Softness breeding scorn of simple life,
Or Cowardice, the child of lust for gold,
Or Labour, with a groan and not a voice,
Or Art with poisonous honey stolen from France. . . .
The goal of this great world
Lies beyond sight: yet – if our slowly-grown
And crowned Republic's crowning common-sense,
That saved her many times, not fail – their fears
Are morning shadows huger than the shapes
That cast them, not those gloomier which forego
The darkness of that battle in the West
Where all of high and holy dies away.

After this, the Queen invited her poet to Windsor, to visit the
Frogmore Mausoleum, where the Prince lies in his Wagnerian tomb,
in a setting that rivals the fantasies of Ludwig II of Bavaria. Soon
after Tennyson received the offer of a baronetcy. He replied to
Gladstone. 'I should rather we should remain plain Mr. and Mrs.
Tennyson, and that, if it were possible, the title should first be
assumed by our son at any age it might be thought right to fix it:
but like enough this is against all precedent, and could not be
managed and on no account would I have suggested it, were there
the least chance of the Queen's construing it into a slight of the
proffered honour. I hope that I have too much of the old worldly

loyalty left in me not to wear my lady's favours against all comers, should you think that it would be more agreeable to Her Majesty that I should do so.' Gladstone replied a week later formally offering the baronetcy and saying that this was in accordance with the Queen's personal desire. Tennyson replied, however, that he still did not want the honour conferred on him at that time.

Mrs Cameron now decided that Tennyson should 'wed the sea', like the old Venetian doges. She made up a red and white wreath, and a solemn procession from Farringford wound its way down to Freshwater, where the wreath was committed to the waves, while Tennyson intoned some words worthy of the occasion. The struggle to make him perform this odd ceremony had been a hard one, but as usual Mrs Cameron prevailed.

In August 1873 Tennyson and Hallam went for a tour of the Engadine and the Italian lakes. 'The Voice and the Peak', celebrating the spirit of Man, was begun in the Val d'Anzasca in September:

> The Peak is high and flushed
>   At his highest with sunrise fire;
> The Peak is high, and the stars are high,
>   And the thought of a man is higher.
>
> A deep below the deep,
>   And a height beyond the height!
> Our hearing is not hearing,
>   And our seeing is not sight.

It is not one of his best poems.

# 12

Alfred and Emily went to London in the autumn of 1874 to see Irving in *Hamlet* at the Lyceum. '*Hamlet* is a many-faceted gem,' he said to Irving after the performance, 'and you have given more facets than anyone I have seen.' In December he went with Hallam to see Helen Faucit in *As You Like It*.

For some time the English theatre had been putting on historical dramas, such as Willis's *Charles I* and *Mary Stuart* and Tom Taylor's *Axe and Crown, Jeanne d'Arc* and *Anne Boleyn*, plays which have been forgotten now but which gave Tennyson the idea of writing historical dramas. In 1875 he published *Queen Mary. Harold* followed in 1876 and *Becket* in 1884. Tennyson saw these plays as forming a historical trilogy portraying 'the making of England' and completing the line of Shakespeare's English chronicle plays, which end with the commencement of the Reformation in *Henry VIII*. Thus, at the age of sixty-four, Tennyson embarked on a new career as a dramatist, evidence of his astonishing creative vitality.

He was drawn to the subject of Mary Tudor as a counterblast to the growing influence of the Catholic Church with its dogma of Papal Infallibility and its reactionary attitude to liberalism, progress and modern civilisation in general, as laid down in Pope Pius IX's encyclical *Quanta Cura*; and this in spite of the fact that two of his closest friends, Aubrey de Vere and A. G. Ward, were devout Catholics, as indeed Sir John Simeon had been. He respected their faith and was anxious to be fair in his play, and to this end began a course of reading of Froude, Hooker, Neale, Strype, and Foxe's *Book of Martyrs*, works hardly calculated to endear to him either Mary or the Catholic Church. In *Queen Mary*, as his son tells us, are described 'the final downfall of Roman Catholicism in England, and the dawning of a new age; for after the era of priestly domination, comes the era of the freedom of the individual.'

*Queen Mary* was put on at the Lyceum on 18 April 1976, with Mrs Crowe in the name part and Irving as Philip of Spain. The incidental music was composed, at Tennyson's insistence, by a young and unknown composer, Charles Villiers Stanford, and, in order to accommodate the enlarged orchestra, Tennyson offered to pay for the loss of those stalls which had to be removed. The audience at the first night largely consisted of his admirers, but Tennyson himself refused to attend in case he should be called for at the end of the performance. The play was at first an uproarious success, though after about five weeks the interest waned and it was taken off. The text, which is longer than the complete *Hamlet,* had to be drastically cut.

The draft of *Harold* was finished by June the same year. The figure of Harold appealed to Tennyson as the English champion against the Norman invasion. He visited Battle, the scene of the Battle of Hastings, and then went for a tour of East Anglia with Hallam, visiting FitzGerald at Woodbridge, when Fitz advised him to give up writing poetry, 'A.T. should rest upon his Oars, or ship them for good now, I think,' wrote Fitz. 'And I was audacious enough to tell him as much. . . . I think he might have stopped after 1842, leaving Princesses, Ardens, Idylls, &c. all unborn.' In 1881 he complained to Cowell: 'The Old Dear will go on – like some of Aristophanes' Elders.'

*Harold* proved to be a good deal more concise than *Queen Mary* and better adapted to the stage, but no one offered to produce it. Unfortunately it contained no striking part for any leading actor or actress, and was really as undramatic as *Queen Mary.* Henry James described it as 'a somewhat graceless anomaly in the record of a poet whose verse has, in large degree, become part of the civilisation of his day.' *Becket* carried on the theme, first announced in *Queen Mary,* of England's struggle with the Papacy. While writing it, Tennyson was much helped by conversations with the historian J. R. Green, whom he described as 'vivid as lightning'. Green, on his side, had an enormous admiration for Tennyson and said that at one time in his life he could not have gone on living without the quiet half hour before breakfast spent in reading *In Memoriam.* But his plays did Tennyson's reputation no good; and people began to say that he was written out and no match for Rossetti and Swinburne. As a graceful gesture he dedicated *Harold* to Bulwer Lytton's son, then Viceroy of India. 'My Dear Lord Lytton,' he wrote, 'After old world records – such as the Bayeux tapestry and the Roman de Rou – Edward Freeman's *History of the Norman Conquest,* and your father's Historical Romance treating of the same times, have been mainly helpful to me in writing this Drama. Your father dedicated his *Harold* to my father's brother; allow me to dedicate my *Harold* to yourself.'

The next play of Tennyson's to be produced was *The Falcon,* a one-act comedy founded on a story by Boccaccio, which the Kendals put on at the St James's Theatre in December 1879. 'He attended rehearsals,' Dame Madge Kendal remembered, 'and sat in the stalls with a screen round him, a rug over his knees and a hot-water bottle at his feet. I think he was, without exception, the most complimentary man I ever met.' *The Falcon* ran for sixty-seven nights, and the Prince of Wales went to see it.

At a dinner given by Lord Houghton, Henry James was much struck by Tennyson's appearance, which he likened to 'a creature of some primordial British stock – swarthy and with a certain rustic simplicity of manner'. The conversation, he said, was mostly about tobacco and wine. But when James Knowles took Tennyson to the ballet on another evening, the sight of the short-skirted *corps de ballet* was altogether too much for him and he immediately left the box and 'walked up and down the corridor behind in an agony at "the degradation of the age" and refused to return to see the rest of the performance.'

At the end of 1874 Disraeli, now Prime Minister in place of Gladstone, renewed the offer of a baronetcy. 'A government should recognise intellect,' he wrote. 'It elevates and sustains the spirit of a nation.' But Tennyson replied as before: he would like his eldest son to have the honour; as for himself he did not really want it. Disraeli replied that this would be contrary to precedent, and there the matter was allowed to rest. 'I hate the blare and blaze called fame,' Tennyson said at this time. 'Why should the public be allowed to poke into all a man's private life? What business have they to want to hear about Byron's wildnesses? He has given them fine work and they ought to be satisfied. It is all for the sake of *babble* – I often wish I had never written a line and that I had been born a little squire just comfortably off, following my own country pursuits in peace and quiet.'[1]

Tennyson now felt that, as he was to devote himself to poetic drama, he should be near the theatres, so from 1875 onwards he and Emily regularly spent a considerable part of February, March and April in London, taking houses either in Upper Wimpole Street, Belgrave Square, Eaton Place or Eaton Square. He told Thomas Hardy that he hated it, but that 'they all got so rusty in the Isle of Wight'. Other people seemed to have feared for Emily's health. 'I don't much like the notion of London,' wrote Horatio, 'with the street door a complete sluice and the knocker a protracted cannonade all day long.' But for Emily there was some mollification in the fact that in 1876 Lionel secured an appointment in the India Office, which meant that they would be near him for at least part of the year. As for Alfred, he took long silent walks through the streets with little Elspeth Thompson, whom he had originally met with her mother at Pontresina during his tour of the Italian lakes with Hallam in 1874, skipping along beside him. They excited a good deal of attention from passers-by, and Tennyson said to his small companion: 'Child, your mother should dress you less conspicuously, people are staring at us.' He took her to Westminster Abbey, remarking that one day he would perhaps lie there.

In February 1878 Lionel was married to Eleanor Locker. Emily was too feeble to walk to her place in the Abbey, where the ceremony took place, and was carried in Hallam's arms. The wedding was a great social event and attended by the greater part of literary London. The American press described Tennyson, much to his annoyance, as stumbling over some steps on the way, and he wrote to Whitman describing every third word of the report as a lie.

Meanwhile, with Browning his affectionate friendship was unbroken; Ruskin also visited Tennyson to discuss the education of the poor; General Gordon came too, with his scheme for training homes for young soldiers all over the country, which he wanted Tennyson to help him to establish. When Thomas Hardy came to lunch in Belgrave Square, he was surprised to find Emily lying flat on her back in the drawing-room 'as in a coffin'. He found that the Laureate had 'a genial human face' which belied his portraits, a briar-like tangle of beard and hair, and a shirt with a loose collar and old steel spectacles. At lunch he told riddles and funny stories. He said that he liked *A Pair of Blue Eyes*, the best of Hardy's novels and invited him to Farringford. But Hardy never availed himself of this invitation, to his great regret.[2]

Henry James has recorded in *The Middle Years* a memorable occasion during a luncheon party at Eaton Place. Tennyson, who had been sitting silent next to Lowell, fiercely concentrating on his plate, suddenly looked up and said: 'Do you know anything about *Lowell*?' 'Why, my dear,' Emily quavered, 'this *is* Mr. Lowell.' At another luncheon at Aldworth, 'a large and simple and almost empty occasion' when it seemed to James 'that nothing but the blest obvious, or at least the blest outright, could so much as attempt to live,' Mrs Greville happened to mention one of her French relatives, a Mademoiselle Laure de Sade. 'De Sade?', Tennyson exclaimed at once with interest, so that James wondered 'in an ecstasy of curiosity to what length he would proceed. He proceeded admirably – admirably for the triumph of simplification – to the very greatest length imaginable.' And the comedy of the situation consisted in the fact that no one there, except James, seemed to know what he was talking about, 'least of all,' adds James, 'the gentle relative of Mademoiselle Laure, who listened with the blankest grace to her friend's enumeration of his titles to infamy.' But the interesting thing is that Tennyson evidently knew perfectly well what he was talking about.

After lunch, James went upstairs to hear his host read *Locksley Hall*. As he read, James sat at 'one of the windows that hung over space, noting how the windy, watery autumn day, sometimes sheeting it with rain, called up the dreary, dreary moorland or the long dun wolds. I pinched myself for the determination of my identity and hung on the reader's deep-voiced chant for the credibility of his: I asked myself in fine why . . . I failed to swoon away under the heaviest pressure I had doubtless ever known the romantic situation bring to bear.' Regretfully, James had to admit to himself that, though 'it was all interesting, it was at least all odd, but why in the name of poetic justice had one anciently heaved and flushed with one's own recital of the splendid stuff if one was now only to sigh "oh dear, oh dear"?' He came to the conclusion that in his reading of the poem, Tennyson 'lowered the whole pitch, that of expression, that of interpretation above all. I heard him in a cool surprise, take even more out of his verse than he put in to it, and so bring one back to the point I had immediately and privately made, that he wasn't Tennyson.' Indeed, as James listened to 'the long organ-roll of monotonous majesty', he could only conclude that Tennyson's reading 'lacked the intelligence, the play of discrimination, I should have taken for granted in it.' James goes on to contrast Tennyson's way of reading poetry with Browning's: 'his extraordinary vivacity, vividness and life' as if 'he had to *prove* himself a poet, *almost* against all presumption, and with all the assurance and all the character he could use,' whereas with Tennyson playing the part of the Bard, 'with all the resonance of the chant, the whole thing was yet *still*, with all the long swing of its motion it yet remained where it was – heaving doubtless grandly enough up and down and beautiful to watch as through the superimposed veils of its long self-consciousness.' Was it, James concludes, 'that I had preconceived him . . . as pale and penetrating, as emphasising in every aspect that he was fastidious? was it that I had supposed him more fastidious than he really could have been?'[3]

It is curious that this uncomfortably penetrating account is almost totally at variance with almost everybody else's. But James's view is supported by Edmund Gosse, who heard Tennyson reading 'Boadicea' one evening at Baron de Tabley's in April 1877. 'We sat in awe and silence when dinner began, the Bard being dreadfully grim, but he warmed up over some excellent port wine, and we soon forgot to be frightened. His reading is worse than anyone's I ever heard, less animated than Swinburne's, less distinct than W. B. Scott's. He hangs sleepily over the syllables in a rough monotonous manner, sacrificing everything to the quantity. Had I not known the poem well beforehand, it would have been entirely unintelligible. Afterwards Tennyson spoke a good deal about Swinburne, "with his marvellous facility". He begged us not to repeat this, which he found impossible to explain, namely that he always began Swinburne with enthusiasm, but became bored directly and almost failed to finish a poem. He thought *Atalanta* the best. In *Erechtheus* he found himself borne along on a great wave, but he could not finish it. At the same time Swinburne was a born singer. . . . He considered it a mistake to write Greek plays in English, – "it is so very easy and so very useless."

'Later he became very amusing. Apropos of Walt Whitman we got on lighter themes. He said "What a queer barbarian he is, but I think he's a good honest fellow. What do you say to his things?" He expressed wonder at his obscenities and repeated an astounding passage, highly Whitmanian, about a woman praying to be filled with "albescent albumen", which he reproved very properly. But I am almost sure it was his own invention on the spur of the moment.' But Tennyson was not so far out. Whitman's 'Faces' reads: 'Fill me with albescent honey . . . bend down to me.' 'I said Whitman was like a man walking naked in the street, and then Tennyson eagerly asked us all round to tell him truly would we consent to walk down St. James's Street stark naked at 3 p.m. for £2,000. We had no answer to that, but he left us with the impression that he himself would think of it very seriously for such a sum. He then began to tell epigrams and stories, and listened with great forbearance and amusement to some of ours.' Tennyson then went on to tell a story about Skittles, the well-known Victorian tart. 'Somebody offered a bet that no one could successfully chaff that lady. The man who took on the bet accosted her on her entering a room. "Why, Skittles, what a fine arse you have!" She, affecting modesty, replied: "Oh! you shouldn't kiss and tell!"'

'Tennyson drank a bottle and a half of old port, besides champagne and sherry, without the slightest perceptible change of manner, except perhaps more geniality. He smoked six pipes. At 11 the carriage arrived and Hallam tried to get him away, but he was not anxious to go, and stayed on chatting for half an hour longer. . . . He was throughout very genial and accessible, full of humour, and at times even childishly playful and apt for quips and cranks. He left on my mind an impression wholly charming. I forgot to say that he recited, with great appreciation, several poems of Burns and Landor.'[4]

During one of his London visits, Tennyson saw much of Joachim, who would play Handel, Mozart and Beethoven to him, and in return Tennyson would read out his poems. He was conscious of not really understanding classical music, though he enjoyed old Scottish and Irish airs played and sung to him by Edward Lear and such songs as 'John Brown's Body'. And it was Lear's settings of his poems he liked best. Maud Valerie White once tried to interest him in Lohengrin as a subject for a poem, and outlined Wagner's musical and dramatic treatment of the theme, but when she had finished all he said was: 'What a remarkably sharp nose you've got!' His reaction to her settings of some stanzas from *In Memoriam*, which she got a friend to sing to him, was equally disconcerting. 'I couldn't hear a word she said,' he exclaimed at the end of the recital, 'and I have entirely forgotten the poem.'

By his seventieth year Tennyson was still taking his 'clockwork constitutional' each morning between eleven and one o'clock up and across the Down at Freshwater. He was usually accompanied by whoever was staying at Farringford. Often the walks were conducted in silence. One windy day his companion was a rather nervous little Eton master, who trotted at his side, trying to make himself heard through the blast. After striding along in silence for some time, Tennyson suddenly bellowed: 'I don't know who you are and I can't hear what you say.' He was still very active and vigorous, though Sir Charles Tennyson tells us that he had been in a nervous and unsatisfactory state of health since his favourite brother Charles Tennyson Turner's death in April 1879; he suffered much from eczema, from his liver, and from hearing perpetual ghostly voices.

In May 1880 he suddenly went off on a short tour with W. E. Lecky to Salisbury, Wilton, Stonehenge, Amesbury and George Herbert's country. Next month he went to Venice with Hallam on his doctor's advice. They broke their journey at Munich and stayed with Lord Acton at Tegernsee. Acton, a devout Catholic, was not particularly predisposed towards the author of *Queen Mary*, but Tennyson soon endeared himself to his family and, after he left, Acton wrote: 'Even I was tamed at last. There was a shell to crack, but I got at the kernel, chiefly at night, when everyone was in bed. His want of reality, his habit of walking on the clouds, the airiness of his metaphysics, the indefiniteness of his knowledge, his neglect of transitions, the looseness of his political reasoning, all these make up an alarming *cheval de frise*. But there was a gladness, not quickness, in taking a joke or story, a comic impatience of the external criticism of Taine and others, coupled with a simple dignity when reading impatient attacks, a grave groping for religious certainty and a generosity in the treatment of rivals – of Browning and Swinburne, not of Taylor – that helped one through.'

G
[173]

The travellers then went by way of Innsbruck to Cortina, where the valleys were brilliant with spring flowers. At Pieve di Cadore, the birthplace of Titian, Tennyson recognised the background of many of his favourite pictures; in Venice itself he delighted in the great paintings of Titian, Tintoretto and the Bellinis. Even more he enjoyed wandering by himself on the then solitary shore of the Lido and the Jews' burial place, overgrown with poppies and thistles. From Venice they returned home via Verona and the Lago di Garda, where they visited Catullus' Sirmio. Tennyson celebrated this visit in one of his best lyrics 'Frater Ave atque Vale', in which he also remembered his own dead brother Charles.

> Row us out from Desenzano, to your Sirmione row!
> So they rowed, and there we landed – 'O venusta Sirmio!'
> There to me through all the groves of olive in the summer glow,
> There beneath the Roman ruin where the purple flowers grow,
> Came that 'Ave atque Vale' of the Poet's hopeless woe,
> Tenderest of Roman poets nineteen-hundred years ago,
> 'Frater Ave atque Vale' – as we wandered to and fro
> Gazing at the Lydian laughter of the Garda Lake below
> Sweet Catullus's all-but-island, olive-silvery Sirmio!

After his return to Farringford in July, Tennyson often read through his Catullus after dinner with his bottle of port. He would go through the Latin lines with whatever guest chanced to be present, 'moving his finger from word to word,' his grandson tells us, 'and dwelling with deep satisfaction on the beauty of the expression and sound, and the masterly handling of the rhythm.' But Catullus is, after all, not so much 'the tenderest of the Roman poets' as the most passionate and at times the most wittily obscene. One wonders quite how many of his poems Tennyson read aloud, though, presumably, much was forgiven Catullus since he was a classic, even though he wrote love poems to girls and boys promiscuously in the old Roman way.

December saw the publication of *Ballads and Other Poems*, which contained 'The Revenge', 'The Defence of Lucknow', 'The Northern Cobbler', 'Rizpah', 'The Voyage of Maeldune', 'The Village Wife' and 'De Profundis'. The volume was received with delight as a return to themes of common life. Tennyson also wrote a short play, *The Cup*, which was produced with great splendour by Irving at the Lyceum in June next year, with Irving himself and Ellen Terry in the cast. 'The age which gave us the Grosvenor Gallery,' said *Truth*, 'must necessarily adore Ellen Terry, for she is the embodiment of the aspirations of modern art. With her waving movements and skill giving life to drapery, she is the actress of all others to harmonize with gold backgrounds and to lounge under blossoming apple trees' – in other words, the embodiment of a painting by Albert Moore.

At Irving's suggestion, Tennyson now wrote a pastoral play on the legend of Robin Hood, paying a visit to Sherwood Forest to get the local colour. Unfortunately Irving did not accept *The Foresters*, objecting that it was not sensational enough for a modern audience. Tennyson had a few copies privately printed, but did not publish it otherwise.

He was depressed this year by the death of his old Cambridge friend James Spedding, who had only recently been staying with him, and when he called at the hospital Spedding was too ill to see him, though shortly before he had repeatedly asked if Tennyson had called. Other deaths of friends that were keenly felt by Tennyson at this time were those of Carlyle, Dean Stanley and Drummond Rawnsley, who had been to stay with him every year since his marriage. He joined the Society for Psychical Research, hoping that it would provide some clue to personal survival after death. But the séances he attended were disappointing, although he would say that 'he *felt* the reality of the spirit world as a great ocean pressing round us on every side and only leaking in by a few chinks'.

In November he published 'Despair' in *The Nineteenth Century*, the powerful monologue of a man who has lost his faith in God and all hope of the life to come and who determines to put an end to his life by walking out to sea with his wife, an incident taken from a newspaper. The wife is drowned, but the man is saved by a Calvinist minister, the very sect to which he attributed his ruin.

O we poor orphans of nothing – alone on that lonely shore –
Born of the brainless Nature who knew not that which she bore!
Trusting no longer that earthly flower would be heavenly fruit –
Come from the brute, poor souls – no souls – and to die with the
brute. . . .

Why should we bear with an hour of torture, a moment of pain,
If every man die for ever, if all his griefs are in vain,
And the homeless planet at length will be wheeled through the
silence of space,
Motherless evermore of an ever-vanishing race,
When the worm shall have writhed its last, and its last brother-
worm will have fled
From the dead fossil skull that is left in the rocks of an earth that
is dead?

This was a return to the pessimistic mood of *Maud* and foreshadowed 'Vastness' and *Locksley Hall Sixty Years After*, written five years later.

At the request of Sir Frederick Young, Tennyson recast his patriotic poem 'Hands All Round'. Emily's musical setting was arranged by Stanford, and it was sung throughout the country and the empire on the Queen's birthday. Its exhortation to drink to the cause of freedom brought protests from the temperance party, who suggested that 'a cheer for freedom' would be 'more suitable for cottage and drawing-room and less likely to have an inebriating effect'. When this was followed by a formal resolution and protest from the Society of Good Templars, Hallam replied that 'the common cup has in all ages been the sacred symbol of unity'. But it was not only temperance societies that disliked the jingoism of 'Hands All Round'; there was a spate of parodies in the press of which that of *Truth*, with its title 'The Laureate Rampant, or Patriotism Gone Mad', is perhaps nearest to our feeling today.

Next drink to all the loyal hearts
  Who, to maintain our Empire's might,
By fraud or force in foreign parts
  Induced poor savages to fight!

To Lytton drink, who did his share
  To vex a friendly race full sore:
To Bartle Frere, that man of power,
  Who deluged Zululand with gore.

To India drink, won long ago;
  Still held, for India's sake, of course;
To China, sodden, feeble, low
  With opium we upon her force;

To Canada a borrower great,
  That always will be *dear* to us;
And to the Cape, ordained by fate
  Always to be an incubus. . . .

Then glasses round! God the Traitor's hope confound!
  And we will drink to our Colonies, my friends,
*Whilst* they pay twenty shillings in the pound.

Such liberal, even socialistic, sentiments were growing in the 1880s, and Tennyson was perfectly right in deploring them as a danger to the empire.

In June 1882 the Virgilian Academy of Mantua asked Tennyson to write a poem for the nineteenth centenary of Virgil's death, and he duly wrote his noble salutation, concluding:

I salute thee, Mantovano,
  I that loved thee since my day began,

Wielder of the stateliest measure
    ever moulded by the lips of man.

When the Queen's privileged gillie, John Brown, died in March
1883, Tennyson wrote sympathising with her grief. In reply she
asked his advice about a suitable inscription for the memorial she
proposed to erect at Balmoral, 'as well as for a small drinking
fountain which I am placing to his memory in Frogmore gardens
near the small cottage where I used to sit in summer.' Tennyson sent
her lines from Shakespeare, Byron and Pope and two lines of his own.

Friend more than servant, loyal, truthful, brave!
Self less than Duty, even to the grave.

News of this leaked out to the press and several papers, among them
*The Weekly Despatch* and *Truth*, organised competitions among their
readers for parodies, reflecting on the strange relationship between
the 'Empress Brown' and her rude Scottish servant. In August
Tennyson received a message through Victoria Baillie, a lady-in-
waiting, that the Queen would very much like to see him again, as
she had been reading *In Memoriam* and was most touched by his
letters of sympathy when she had injured herself by a fall earlier
that year, and that if he would make the journey from Aldworth to
Osborne, she would see him 'in Her room without any form'. Afterwards the Queen recorded their meeting in her *Journal*:

Osborne. Tuesday, Aug. 7th 1883. After luncheon saw the
great Poet *Tennyson* in dearest Albert's room for nearly an
hour; – and most interesting it was. He is grown very
old – his eyesight much impaired *and he is very shaky on his legs*.
But he was v.kind. Asked him to sit down. He talked of the
many friends he had lost [in June FitzGerald had died]
and what it would be if he did not feel and know there was
another World, where there would be no partings; and
then he spoke with horror of the unbelievers and philosophers
who would make you believe there was *no* world, no
immortality – who tried to explain all away in a miserable
manner – We agreed that were such a thing possible,
God, Who is Love, would be far more cruel than any human
being. He quoted some well-known lines from Goethe whom
he so much admires – Spoke of the poor Lilly of Hanover so
kindly – asked after my grandchildren. He spoke of Ireland
with abhorrence, of the wickedness of ill-using poor Animals.
'I'm afraid I think the world is darkened; I daresay it will
brighten again.'

[177]

I told him what a comfort *In Memoriam* had again
been to me, which pleased him, but he said I could not believe
the number of shameful letters of abuse he had received about
it. Incredible! When I took leave of him, I thanked him for
his kindness and said I needed it, for I had gone through
so much – and he said 'You are so alone on that terrible
height, it is Terrible. I've only a year or two to live, but I
shall be happy to do anything for you I can. Send for me
whenever you like.' I thanked him warmly.[5]

The Queen followed this with a long letter to Tennyson written in
her own hand, in which she told him of all her troubles and her
loneliness, now that her 'dear faithful Brown' had gone after thirty
years of service, and eighteen years of intimacy: 'He did for me
what no one else can. The comfort of my daily life is gone – the
void is terrible – the loss is irreparable! The most affectionate children, no lady or gentleman can do what he did.'[6] It is said that
Brown was a medium and put the Queen in touch with Albert's
spirit.

Tennyson replied: 'Dear and Honoured Lady, My Queen. . . .I will
not say that "I am loyal", or that "Your Majesty is gracious", for
these are old hackneyed terms used or abused by every courtier, but
I *will* say that during our conversation I felt that touch of true
friendship which binds human beings together, whether they be
kings or cobblers.

'Madam, when I left your presence, those lines of our Shakespeare
in his *Henry V* came across my memory:

O hard condition twin-born with greatness . . .
What infinite heart's-ease must kings neglect
Which private men enjoy!'

'In a sense, and in part,' observed Sir Charles Tennyson, 'Tennyson,
during this last phase, filled Brown's place.'[7]

Next year, on 12 February 1884, the Queen sent her Laureate her
*More Leaves from a Journal in the Highlands* – 'Though a very humble
and unpretending author I send you my new book which perhaps
you may like to glance at. Its only merit is its simplicity and truth.'[8]
After that, in his next interview, Tennyson spoke endearingly of 'We
authors, Mam.' In December, with Gladstone's persuasion, he
accepted a peerage: 'But for my part,' he added, 'I shall regret the
step, and my simple name all my life.' Nevertheless, this was one in
the eye for the Tennyson d'Eyncourts. Gladstone was only worried
that Tennyson might wear his sombrero in the House of Lords. But
when the news of this honour became known, there was an imme-

diate outburst of nasty parodies in the press; the most virulent
appeared in *The Secular Review*:

> You must wake and call me early, call me early, Vicky dear;
> To-morrow will be the silliest day we've seen for many a year,
> For I'm a lackey and prig, Vicky, that sham and shoddy reveres,
> And I'm to be one of the Peers, Vicky, I'm to be one of the Peers.

The virulence of Victorian journalism is always surprising, but this
particular outburst seems to have been inspired largely by jealousy.
After all, Tennyson deserved a peerage if anyone did, and certainly
no one was less of a lackey and time-server. He accepted a peerage
with great reluctance and then only as an honour due to literature,
rather than to himself. He took his seat in March 1884. 'What can
I do?' he wrote to a friend. 'How can I take off my cocked hat and
bow three times in the House of Lords? I don't like this cocked hat
business at all.' In the event, he made an impressive and dignified
figure.

At Aldworth Tennyson and William Allingham took long walks
together with the dogs, but when Allingham lent him some numbers
of *Justice*, the Social Democratic organ with which William Morris
was associated, he said that it made him 'vomit mentally'. Later the
same year Allingham's *Diary* records:[9]

> We spoke of William Morris (from whom I had just had a long
> letter).
> T. said, 'He's gone crazy.' I said I agreed with many of M's notions.
> Labour does not get its fair share.
> T. 'There's brain labour as well as hand labour.'
> A. 'And there are many who get money without any labour. The
> question, how to hinder money from accumulating into lumps,
> is a puzzling one.'
> T. 'You must let a man leave money to his children. I was once in
> a coffee-shop in the Westminster Road at 4 o'clock in the morn-
> ing. A man was raging "Why has So-and-So a hundred pounds,
> and I haven't a shilling?" I said to him, "If your father had left
> you £100 you wouldn't give it away to somebody else." He
> hadn't a word to answer. I knew he hadn't.'
> Lady T. came down to dinner, very pale – spoke and was spoken
> to little and went upstairs again, almost carried by Hallam. A
> dear, almost angelic woman.

In September 1883 Tennyson and Hallam joined Gladstone for a
cruise in the *Pembroke Castle*. The party included, besides Gladstone,
his wife, their daughter Mary and their son Herbert, Laura Tennant,

then a girl of about twenty, Sir Donald Currie, Sir Arthur Gordon, Gladstone's private secretary Algernon West, and others. When they embarked at Barrow-in-Furness thousands of cheering people lined the shores. Sir William Harcourt joined the ship at Ardnamurchan Point. It was he who made the ill-timed quip when Tennyson remarked that his first pipe after breakfast was the best in the day: 'Ah, the earliest pipe of half-awakened *bards*!' But Tennyson was not amused.

The ship sailed up the west coast of Scotland, round Cape Wrath to Kirkwall and then across the North Sea to Christiansund. Walking on the deck one morning with Laura Tennant, discussing various forms of greeting, Tennyson remarked that the kiss was always the most acceptable. 'You won't dare to kiss Mary's hair, next time we pass her,' said Laura. 'Won't I!' replied the old poet, in the highest spirits. 'You'll see.' When they passed Mary Gladstone, Tennyson could not bring himself to kiss her hair. 'I couldn't,' he said, 'the sun is kissing it.' So he asked Laura to kiss him instead, 'and would any day,' she wrote in her diary, 'I love him.' That evening Tennyson burnt a big hole in the breast of his coat, by putting his pipe alight into his pocket; he asked Laura to mend it, saying that her eyes had caused the burn.

When not flirting with Laura, Tennyson sat with Gladstone, discussing Homer and Dante, and talking of old friends. In the evening he would read his poems to the company: 'The Northern Cobbler', 'Rizpah', 'The Children's Hospital', 'The Two Voices', breaking down over 'The Grandmother'. After reading 'The Promise of May', he exclaimed: 'And they called that a failure: why, it's a perfect gem!' Leaning over the stern of the boat another evening, he declared that the moonlit sea was 'like a great river, rushing to the City of God'. From Christiansund they steamed past Elsinore to Copenhagen and were invited to dine with the King and Queen of Denmark. Tennyson could not face this; but the next day, when the royal party came on board for a return visit, among the other toasts, the Queen drank the great English poet's health. This time the royal party included the Czar and Czarina of Russia, the Princess of Wales, the King and Queen of Greece, and a bevy of princes, princesses, grand dukes, ministers, generals and admirals. After luncheon, the Princess of Wales asked Tennyson to read, so he settled down between her and the Czarina to read 'The Bugle Song' from *The Princess*, and 'The Grandmother'. When he had finished, the Czarina complimented him and, not being able with his short sight to see who she was, he patted her affectionately on the shoulder, which produced an awkward moment.

In June next year, Hallam married Audrey Boyle, the niece of the novelist Mary Boyle, who had come to stay at Watts's house 'The Briary', Freshwater, the year before. They were married in Henry VII's Chapel at Westminster. Emily attended the ceremony in her bath chair, robed, as one newspaper correspondent put it, in white samite, mystic, wonderful. 'The sight of the Laureate, Lord Houghton, Mr. Matthew Arnold . . . in a group together was probably witnessed for this occasion only. I confess I missed Mr. Swinburne.' Many people who had come to the Abbey simply to see the Laureate were disappointed that he did not wear his 'historical wideswake' and great cloak; instead 'here was an elderly gentleman in conventional attire devoid of a single eccentricity of genius'. Hallam's marriage did not interfere with his dedication to his father's service, which meant that, for the time being, he and Audrey continued to live at Aldworth and Farringford.

Soon after the wedding, Tennyson had to record his vote in the House of Lords for or against Gladstone's Bill for an extension of the franchise. With Lord Salisbury, he was definitely against such an extension without a proper distribution of the franchise between town and country and further education of the people, who, he felt, were too much the prey of demagogues. Freedom, he believed, should 'slowly broaden down from precedent to precedent'. In his poem 'Compromise', published in the *St James's Gazette* under the pseudonym 'John Yorke Adam' on 29 October, he advised Gladstone to be cautious.

Steersman, be not precipitate in thine act
    Of steering, for the river here, my friend,
    Parts in two channels, moving to one end –
This goes straight forward to the cataract:
    That streams about the bend;
But though the cataract seems the nearer way,
Whate'er the crowd on either bank may say,
Take thou the 'bend', 'twill save thee many a day.

Nevertheless he voted for proceeding with the Franchise Bill, in consideration of an undertaking given by the Government to bring in a Redistribution Bill. But he was in many ways suspicious of Gladstone's policy at home and loathed his foreign and imperial policy, which had resulted in the murder of General Gordon in the Sudan, as a result of his unwillingness to send an expeditionary force for the General's relief until too late. But, then, Gordon should have returned home long before, as instructed. He was appalled, too, by the assassination of Lord Frederick Cavendish, the Viceroy, in Phoenix Park, Dublin, and the mutilation of horses and cattle which

G*                     [181]

accompanied the agrarian disturbances all over Ireland, 'I love Mr Gladstone, but I hate his policy,' he said on more than one occasion. The last straw, as far as he was concerned, was the reduction in the number of our battleships. In 'The Fleet', which appeared in *The Times* on 23 April 1885, he declaimed passionately:

> You, you *if* you shall fail to understand
>   What England is, and what her all-in-all,
> On you will come the curse of all the land,
>   Should this old England fall
>   Which Nelson left so great.
>
> His isle, the mightiest Ocean-power on earth,
>   Our own fair isle, the lord of every sea –
> Her fuller franchise – what would that be worth –
>   Her ancient fame of Free –
>   Were she . . . a fallen state?
>
> Her dauntless army scattered, and so small,
>   Her island-myriads fed from alien lands –
> The fleet of England is her all-in-all;
>   Her fleet is in your hands,
>   And in her fleet her Fate.
>
> You, you, that have the ordering of her fleet,
>   *If* you should only compass her disgrace,
> When all men starve, the wild mob's million feet
>   Will kick you from your place,
>   But then too late, too late.

This poem was deeply resented by the Liberals and produced an even larger crop of parodies in the press than Tennyson's acceptance of a peerage. Of course, he was accused of rampant jingoism. But Britain now felt herself menaced at sea by both France and Russia. No one yet saw Germany as a potential threat.

When Tennyson was staying in London at this time at Queen Anne's Gate with James Knowles, who was editing the *National Review*, Gladstone asked to be invited to dinner. Tennyson at once refused to meet him and said that he would dine alone in his room on the plea of a headache. After dinner, however, Knowles suggested that Gladstone should go upstairs and persuade his old friend to come down. 'Ten minutes later the sound of shuffling feet was heard on the staircase and Tennyson and Gladstone came into the room arm in arm. Soon they were seated side by side on the sofa, discussing Greek mythology.' After Gladstone's departure, Tennyson said to Knowles: 'I'm sorry I said all those hard things about the old man.'

But next morning at breakfast, he was unusually grumpy and silent, until, at last, putting down his knife and fork, he burst out: 'I never said anything bad enough about the old rascal!'[10]

And then came a sudden, almost annihilating blow. Lionel, who had gone to India with his wife at the invitation of Tennyson's old friend Lord Dufferin, the Viceroy, died at the age of thirty-two on his passage home through the Red Sea on 20 April 1886. He had caught jungle fever shooting in Assam and lain for three months in hospital in Calcutta before embarking for home at the beginning of April. He was buried at sea. 'The thought of it tears me to pieces,' said Tennyson. 'He was so full of promise and so young.' He recorded his death in the lines to Dufferin in the *In Memoriam* stanza:

And now the Was, the Might-have-been,
  And those lone rites I have not seen,
And one drear sound I have not heard,

And dreams that scarce will let me be,
  Not there to bid my boy farewell,
  When That within the coffin fell,
Fell – and flashed into the Red Sea,

Beneath a hard Arabian moon
  And alien stars. To question, why
  The sons before the fathers die,
Not mine! and I may meet him soon;

But while my life's late eve endures,
  Nor settles into hueless gray,
  My memories of his briefer day
Will mix with love for you and yours.

The Queen wrote a letter of sympathy: 'I say from the depth of a heart which has suffered cruelly, and lost almost all it cared for and loved best, I feel for you.' But in the midst of his grief, Tennyson was asked by the Prince of Wales to write an ode to be sung at the opening of the Indian and Colonial Exhibition by the Queen on 4 May. As usual, he rose to the occasion.

Sharers of our glorious past,
Brothers, must we part at last?
Shall we not through good and ill
Cleave to one another still?
Britain's myriad voices call,
'Sons, be welded each and all,
Into one imperial whole,
One with Britain, heart and soul!

One life, one flag, one fleet, one Throne!'
Britons, hold your own!

*Ein Reich! Ein Volk! Ein Führer!* – the same sentiment has been expressed more recently elsewhere, with frightful results. The difference is that Tennyson felt passionately that such a common-wealth of English-speaking nations, with the stabilising power of the *Pax Britannica*, could only be a force for good in the world. And, indeed, in the light of the growing violence and chaos of our present century, he was not far wrong. But still, the same year produced the strident anger and bitterness of *Locksley Hall Sixty Years After*. The speaker of the original *Locksley Hall* is now eighty (Tennyson himself was seventy-seven) and looks back over his past, after a long life as squire and landlord. His cousin Amy is now dead and so is her hated husband, as well as his own wife Edith:

> Gone with whom for forty years my life in golden sequence ran,
> She with all the charm of woman, she with all the strength of man,
>
> Strong in will and rich in wisdom, Edith, yet so lowly sweet,
> Woman to her inmost heart, and woman to her tender feet,
>
> Very woman of very woman, nurse of ailing body and mind,
> She that linked again the broken chain that bound me to my kind.

It has long been accepted that in these lines Tennyson is thinking of his own wife Emily, though as usual he declared that 'there is not one touch of biography in it from beginning to end'. In fact, the poem has as many biographical touches as the original *Locksley Hall*.

> Poor old voice of eighty crying after voices that have fled!
> All I loved are vanished voices, all my steps are on the dead.

His historical reflections bring him no comfort.

> Half the marvels of my morning, triumphs over time and space,
> Staled by frequence, shrunk by usage into commonest common-
> place!
>
> 'Forward' rang the voices then, and of the many mine was one.
> Let us hush this cry of 'Forward' till ten thousand years have gone.
>
> Far among the vanished races, old Assyrian kings could flay
> Captives whom they caught in battle – iron-hearted victors they.
>
> Ages after, while in Asia, he that led the wild Moguls,
> Timur built his ghastly tower of eighty thousand human skulls,
>
> Then, and here in Edward's time, an age of noblest English names,
> Christian conquerors took and flung the conquered Christian into
> flames.

Love your enemy, bless your haters, said the Greatest of the great;
Christian love among the Churches looked the twin of heathen
hate.

From the golden alms of Blessing man had coined himself a curse:
Rome of Caesar, Rome of Peter, which was crueller? which was
worse? . . .

Are we devils? Are we men?
Sweet St. Francis of Assisi, would that he were here again,

He that in his Catholic wholeness used to call the very flowers
Sisters, brothers – and the beasts – whose pains are hardly less than
ours!

Chaos, Cosmos! Cosmos, Chaos! who can tell how all will end?
Read the wide world's annals, you, and take their wisdom for your
friend.

Hope the best, but hold the Present fatal daughter of the Past,
Shape your heart to front the hour, but dream not that the hour
will last.

Ay, if dynamite and revolver leave you courage to be wise:
When was age so crammed with menace? madness? written,
spoken lies?

And this was the serene Laureate of what seems to many today the
golden age of good Queen Victoria, that age of peace and plenty and
England's greatness! As for the condition of literature in that age:

Authors – essayist, atheist, novelist, realist, rhymester, play your
part,
Paint the mortal shame of nature with the living hues of Art.

Rip your brothers' vices open, strip your own foul passions bare;
Down with Reticence, down with Reverence – forward – naked –
let them stare.

Feed the budding rose of boyhood with the drainage of your sewer;
Send the drain into the fountain, lest the stream should issue pure.

Set the maiden fancies wallowing in the troughs of Zolaism, –
Forward, forward, ay and backward, downward too into the
abysm. . . .

Heated am I? you – you wonder – well, it scarce becomes mine
age –
Patience! let the dying actor mouth his last upon the stage. . . .

[185]

It is well that while we range with Science, glorying in the Time,
City children soak and blacken soul and sense in city slime?

There among the glooming alleys Progress halts on palsied feet,
Crime and hunger cast our maidens by the thousand on the street.

There the Master scrimps his haggard sempstress of her daily
  bread,
There a single sordid attic holds the living and the dead.

There the smouldering fire of fever creeps across the rotted floor,
And the crowded couch of incest in the warrens of the poor.

So, at the age of seventy-seven, at the pinnacle of success, the mood
of *Maud* returns upon him. And yet

Plowmen, shepherds, have I found, and more than once, and still
  could find,
Sons of God, and kings of men in utter nobleness of mind;

Truthful, trustful, looking upwards to the practised hustings liar;
So the Higher wields the Lower, while the Lower is the Higher.

One such, well known to the Tennysons, had recently died in his
ninety-second year, an old shepherd who had tended the Farringford
flock for thirty years. When Alfred and Emily were going away for
any length of time, his grandson tells us, 'the old man would always
come to dine and spend the evening'. Alfred loved the simple poetry
of his speech and would spend many an hour talking with him in his
little flint cottage close under the northern slope of the High Down.
When a visitor read him Tennyson's 'Revenge', he remarked: 'What
a head-piece he must have, and 'ee don't look it, do 'ee?' The visitor
said that most people thought he looked every inch a poet, and the
old shepherd, with his homely wisdom, rejoined: 'Well, you wouldn't
think it to hear him talk.' But a little before his death, he said to the
nurse: 'I should like to see the Master again. He is a wonderful man
for nature and life.'

*Locksley Hall Sixty Years After* raised as great a storm as *Maud*.
And it may be that much of this fury and violence had its roots in a
deep-seated sexual frustration, in emotion that, as T. S. Eliot
divined, 'attained no ultimate clear purgation'. 'When I see society
vicious and the poor starving in great cities,' Tennyson said, 'I feel
that it is a mighty wave of evil passing over the world. But there will
be some strange development which I shall not live to see. . . . You
must not be surprised at anything that comes to pass in the next
fifty years. All ages are ages of transition, but this is an awful
moment of transition. . . . I tried in my *Idylls* to teach men the need

for the ideal, but I feel sometimes as if my life had been a very useless one.' Indeed, the next fifty years brought the first Great War and its aftermath of revolution in Europe; it saw the advent of Stalin's Russia and Hitler's Germany and then a second annihilating war – two of the most appalling decades in history. Tennyson's prophetic forebodings were only too well justified, though even he could not have imagined cruelty and misery on such a scale, not Hitler's gas ovens nor the death camps of Soviet Russia.

Next year, 1887, saw the Queen's Jubilee, the fiftieth anniversary of her coronation, which Tennyson celebrated in an ode set to music by Stanford. It was first performed at Buckingham Palace for the Queen's benefit, then sung at the laying of the foundation stone of the Imperial Institute in South Kensington.

> You, the Patriot Architect,
> You that shape for Eternity,
> Raise a stately memorial,
> Make it regally gorgeous,
> Some Imperial Institute,
> Rich in symbol, ornament,
> Which may speak to the centuries,
> All the centuries after us,
> Of this great Ceremonial,
> And this year of her Jubilee.

> Fifty years of ever-broadening Commerce!
> Fifty years of ever-brightening Science!
> Fifty years of ever-widening Empire!

> You, the Mighty, the Fortunate,
> You, the lord-territorial –
> You, the lord-manufacturer,
> You, the hardy, laborious,
> Patient children of Albion,
> You, Canadian, Indian,
> Australasian, African,
> All your hearts be in harmony,
> All your voices in unison,
> Singing 'Hail to the glorious
> Golden year of her Jubilee!'

Tennyson said that he wrote a great part of his ode in the beautiful metre of Catullus' 'Collis o Heliconii'. But perhaps the most charitable comment was made by William Morris, writing to his daughter Jenny: 'I am sorry poor old Tennyson thought himself bound to write an ode on our fat Vic's Jubilee. . . . It is like Martin Tupper for all the world.' But the Imperial Institute has gone the way of many of the most solid and elaborate monuments of the Victorian age, superseded by that wilderness of glass and concrete, the Imperial College of Science, with only the 'Patriot Architect's' white, green-domed tower surviving as the landmark of a departed age.

Yet Tennyson was still writing such fine poetry as 'Vastness', which is, if anything, more pessimistic than *Locksley Hall Sixty Years After*, which it preceded by about a year.

> Spring and Summer and Autumn and Winter, and all these old
>     revolutions of earth;
> All new-old revolutions of Empire – change of the tide – what is all
>     of it worth?
>
> What the philosophies, all the sciences, poesy, varying voices of
>     prayer?
> All that is noblest, all that is basest, all that is filthy with all that
>     is fair?
>
> What is it all, if we all of us end but in being our own corpse-
>     coffins at last,
> Swallowed in Vastness, lost in Silence, drowned in the deeps of a
>     meaningless Past?
>
> What but a murmur of gnats in the gloom, or a moment's anger of
>     bees in their hive?
>
> Peace, let it be! for I loved him, and love him for ever: the dead
>     are not dead but alive.

With such a bald statement Tennyson tried to convince himself of personal survival, arguing that because of his love for Arthur Hallam, Arthur Hallam was still alive. During these last years, too, he wrote 'The Ancient Sage', a pessimistic poem composed after reading a life of the Chinese sage Lao-tse; he wrote the beautiful 'Demeter and Persephone' of 1887, which seems to have had an influence on T. S. Eliot's later poetry and is a wonderful production of Tennyson's Indian summer, demonstrating once more that his classical poems are nearly always his most beautiful.

# 13

In August 1887 Tennyson chartered Sir Allen Young's yacht *Stella* for a short cruise round the coasts of Devon and Cornwall. 'My father often gazed into the depths of the sea, searching, as he said, for some ruins of town or castle, parts of the ancient Lyonesse,' his son tells us. At Land's End innumerable mackerel boats with their brown sails made 'pretty Cuyp pictures'. From Lundy Island, they sailed to St Bride's Bay and drove to St David's, where Tennyson admired the Cathedral and the ruined Bishop's Palace, bordered by the little stream whose banks were beautiful with lady fern and yellow iris. When they left for the yacht 'the towns-people crowded round our carriage, to see my father, and shake him by the hand.' Tennyson thought Clovelly one of the most beautiful places he had ever seen. It reminded him of Enoch Arden's village. They climbed the steps to the top of the village and walked to Clovelly Court, 'the most paradisal country seat next to Wilton'. At 'dark Tintagel' he was recognised by an old woman, who rushed out of her cottage and began reciting passages from *Idylls of the King*.

On the way back they stopped at Falmouth, Fowey and Plymouth and then set sail for the Channel Islands, spending a day at St Helier, Jersey, with Frederick, who had become a fervent spiritualist and believer in table-rapping, of which Tennyson observed: 'I grant you that spiritualism must not be judged by its quacks: but I am convinced that God and the ghosts of men would choose something other then mere table-legs through which to speak to the heart of man. . . . I cannot see what grounds of proof (as yet) you have to go on. There is really too much flummery mixed up with it, supposing, as I am inclined to believe, there is something in it.' The old brothers talked much of the past, of 'the red honey gooseberry' and the 'golden apples' in the Somersby garden, and of the tilts and tourneys they held in the fields, and of the waste shore of Mablethorpe. Afterwards Frederick said that not for twenty years had he had such a happy day as that spent talking to his brother.[1] After exploring the island of Alderney, they sailed for Cherbourg, and next morning anchored in Freshwater Bay.

Next year the American actress Mary Anderson, who was then playing in *A Winter's Tale* in London, visited Aldworth. Tennyson looked upon her as 'the flower of girlhood' and in June took her to the New Forest, where they picnicked together, and she watched him as he played ducks and drakes in a stream, intoning 'Flow on cold rivulet to the sea'. Before she left she signed an agreement to produce *The Cup* in New York.

Another visitor to Aldworth that summer was Edmund Gosse who walked up from Haslemere. He wrote to his wife on 6 August:[2]

> As I approached the house at last, there was a sort of butterfly dancing about in blue velvet, which was the poet's second grandson, Michael Tennyson. . . . Lord Tennyson was pacing up and down the lawn, a queer figure, in black broadcloth, with a soft black sombrero, and black kid gloves, shuffling along without a stick, a book under his arm. I was desired to go to him, and I asked how he was. 'Grown old and ugly, old and ugly, ha! ha! ha!' he said. He said at once, 'How do you come?'; and when I said I had walked, he said I must have my tea at once. So we went into the dining-room, and there (to my surprise and pleasure) I found Aldis Wright – there was no other visitor in the house. We five sat round a small table to tea. Lord Tennyson was opposite to me; he has grown very queer and Rembrandtish, the skin like parchment, all the hair gone from the dome of the head, and scanty grey tufts over the ears, thin long grizzled goatee on the chin; he looks like a very old Yankee preacher of the conventional 'Punch' type. Otherwise just the same, only not formidable at all but very kind and genial. He startled me at tea by saying 'How's Churton Collins?' and then 'Would you like to know what I think of him?' Of course I, with a wry smile, said I should. 'Well, he's a jackass. That's what he is. But don't say I said so.'

(In 1880 and 1881, Collins had published a series of articles in the *Cornhill* tracing all the echoes and adaptions from other authors to be found in Tennyson's poems; and he had lately savagely attacked Gosse's book *From Shakespeare to Pope,* in which he had discovered and exposed many inaccuracies which had severely damaged Gosse's reputation as a scholar. Gosse was still smarting from this attack when he went to Aldworth.)

Then he said, 'How's Leicester Warren? It was at his house that

I first met *you*.' He had not heard of Lord de Tabley's [that is, Leicester Warren's] accession to the title, nor anything else lately about him. Mrs. Hallam Tennyson, who is a very charming woman, led the conversation, and they were all markedly kind and attentive to me. Then Hallam said that his mother wished to see me for a few minutes, and I was taken by Lord Tennyson into a room where Lady Tennyson, lying flat on her back, received me on her couch. She has one of the sweetest voices I ever heard, and a very bright smile, and is altogether a quite angelic old martyr sort of lady. In the dining-room is her portrait by Watts, a great beauty. It was one of Lady Tennyson's bad days, and I only stayed five minutes. Then Hallam showed me various portraits and family relics, until Lord Tennyson, now on the lawn with Aldis Wright, came and beckoned me out. It was a most exquisite afternoon, and we sat and talked for half an hour in a sort of bower at the corner of the lawn. Lord Tennyson had a cluster of books he was reading – Winwood Reade's 'Martyrdom of Man', Furness's variorum 'Merchant of Venice', and a book by John Fiske. He discussed all these; and he talked about Patmore and Woolner, very freely indeed. Apropos of Winwood Reade, I mentioned the late Lord Amberley who, I said, 'was of the same religious kidney'. Tennyson caught up the phrase and said 'that's a curious organ; where does it hang out?' and he tried to make a pun about 'the liver' and 'an evil liver', but as he said 'ah that won't quite come off.' He laughed at all this, and he kept on teasing me about the 'religious kidney'.

About 6 Tennyson suddenly said he felt chilly, and he rose. Hallam and Aldis Wright went off together, while Lord Tennyson took me round his place. He showed me how difficult it had been to settle at Aldworth – the old Lord Egremont putting every possible obstruction in the way. He said that when the house was a-building, Lord Egremont rode up to see how it was getting on; Tennyson's foreman had put up 'Tress-passers will be prosecuted'. Lord Egremont growled out, taking for granted that the master had written the notice – 'call *him* a poet? He can't even spell'.

The grounds at Aldworth are not extensive, but they are beautifully laid out in little dales and boskages. One exquisite little Arcadian lawn surrounded by conifers I said was 'like a vale in Tempe'. The poet instantly corrected me: 'Cliffs all round Tempe'. Then he took me to see his crimson Himalayan poppies, of which he is proud. The next thing was the house. I must come, he said, and see the house. Hallam offered to take me round, but Lord Tennyson said, no, he should do it himself. He walked slowly and laboriously upstairs, stopping every other step to say something in his deep Lincolnshire growl. His study is most exquisite, with an infinite view of Sussex, marble relievos life-size of the 12 Caesars, which he bought at a sale of the sculptor Munro, and myriads of books. Then he would needs climb with me to the very top of the house, to a little attic-boudoir sacred to Mrs. Hallam Tennyson, whom he disturbed lying down. This room has a tiny balcony in the angle of the roof, and Lord Tennyson stood out here with me to point out the view. One is conscious of his extreme near-sight, and he seems to infer the features of the landscape rather than to see them. As he came downstairs he said, 'You may stay to dinner and William will drive you down into Haslemere,' but I thought it best not to prolong my visit further. It was now 6.45, so I said goodbye, but Lord Tennyson and Hallam would see me on my way and walked $\frac{1}{2}$ a mile past their front gate with me over the common. Tennyson talked about Pope, quoted various lines, pressed me over and over for my opinion on this point or that, when I was as adroit as possible, of course, in evading giving one and getting his instead. He spoke of Austin Dobson very warmly, 'a good fellow and a very clever poet'. Finally, in parting, he said 'Never come up to Marley again without coming over here to see us,' and so we said goodbye, the strange old piratical figure, tall, in black, with the flapping hat and the thick-rimmed spectacles, like a sort of vision of a superannuated highwayman, benevolently waving me an adieu over the heather.

To-day (August 6) is his birthday; he enters his 80th year. The stumbling gait and the extreme grimness and withered aspect of his head make him seem a great deal more infirm than he really is. He quite thrilled me by saying, as he took me round the grounds 'but I am afraid I shall tire you – after your long walk.' It seemed so pretty of him and so quaint a supposition. I fancy, in spite of his scarecrow appearance, that he is very tough and hale, and one hopes he may shuffle around in this way for a dozen years yet. He was delightfully full of literature, evidently read incessantly and reads new things. He growled to me about the critics – they charged him with having imitated other people. He said 'There's a fellow that says two of my best lines come out of an unpublished Chinese poem of the 12th century.' I answered 'So much the better for the Chinese poem,' and he replied 'that's very good; so it is, all the better for the Chinese poem. I don't believe that there is any such Chinese poem.' He hotly maintained that every good poet has the right, the duty, to steal anything that strikes him in a bad poet and improve it. He said 'the dunces fancy it is the thought that makes poetry live; it isn't, it's the expression, the form, but we mustn't tell them so – they wouldn't know what we meant.'

The beginning of this year, 1888, had been saddened for Tennyson by the death of Edward Lear at Villa Tennyson, San Remo. Lear had been ill for some time, but on his better days he still rose at four-thirty each morning to work for ten or twelve hours on his enormous painting *Enoch Arden*, intended as a present for his old friend. He was also struggling to complete his series of one hundred and thirty landscape engravings illustrating Tennyson's poems. Thirty-six of these had been published already and the poet had, with much grumbling, signed a hundred copies of the first edition at the request of the publisher, who had made this a condition for publishing the book at all. Tennyson had also recently contributed towards the cost of buying Lear's big picture *Argos from the Citadel of Mycenae*, presented by members of the college to Trinity, Cambridge.

The year closed for Tennyson with his first serious illness, a severe attack of rheumatic gout, brought on by walking in the rain and getting drenched. He lay on the sofa near the south window of his study, often in great pain; but he said that 'looking out on the great landscape, he had wonderful thoughts about God and the universe, and felt as if looking into another world'. At night he had strange dreams of fir woods, cliffs and temples. One night he thought he had to visit all the ironclads of the Fleet. The year before he had gone to Portsmouth to see the launching of a new torpedo boat and was horrified when he saw the torpedo exploding on its target. But scientists were just as busy then as now inventing ever more destructive weapons, necessary if Britain was to hold her own in the eversharpening struggle among the nations. Another night he dreamed that he was the Pope and was weighed down by the sins and miseries of the world. When he came downstairs again, he talked of Job and asked for the *Gospel According to St John*. 'He was marvellously patient,' his son tells us, 'and his humorous view of his own helpless condition helped him through some weary hours. At the crisis of his illness he made an epigram about himself, and on the pain killing the devil that was born in him eighty years back.' In November the doctors ordered his removal in an invalid carriage to Farringford. He had lost a great deal of weight and now weighed only nine and a half stones. On 23 December he had a second relapse, and it was not till February that he could be carried downstairs to the drawing-room.

But he was scarcely able to move his limbs. It was nearly two more months before he could walk out of doors, and May before he had fully recovered. But as he lay on his couch in pain, he wrote 'The Human Cry':

> We feel we are nothing – for all is Thou and in Thee;
> We feel we are something – *that* also has come from Thee;
> We know we are nothing – but Thou wilt help us to be.
> Hallowed by Thy name – Halleluiah!

In his weakness, as he read it aloud his voice grew tremulous and he broke down and sobbed as he finished the prayer. At the height of his illness it was thought that he would never have the use of his limbs again. He was nursed by Sister Emma Durham, 'a little blue-eyed woman, alert, intelligent, with a sense of humour and a natural candour and sincerity', who seemed to understand him perfectly, and she stayed with him until he had fully recovered. When he refused to go to bed in the evening, she would come into the room with a candle and say 'Follow the Gleam', and the author of 'Merlin and the Gleam' would get up and follow her instantly. On another occasion, when she interrupted an after-dinner conversation with Montague Butler and Charles Stanford, he told her to go away and learn Latin. But she soon came back again and announced: 'Tempus fugit, my lord', and he stood up at once, 'like a ramrod', she said.[3]

Between the attacks of his illness, he wrote the lines 'By an Evolutionist', probably the 'epigram' mentioned by Hallam.

> What hast thou done for me, grim Old Age, save breaking my
>     bones on the rack?
> Would I had past in the morning that looks so bright from afar!

OLD AGE

> Done for thee? starved the wild beast that was linkt with thee
>     eighty years back.
> Less weight now for the ladder-of-heaven that hangs on a
>     star. . . .

> I have climbed to the snows of Age, and I gaze at a field in the
>     Past,
> Where I sank with the body at times in the sloughs of a low
>     desire,
> But I hear no yelp of the beast, and the Man is quiet at last
>     As he stands on the heights of his life with a glimpse of a height
>     that is higher.

Being a man, and an outstandingly fine one at that, it was natural that Tennyson should have had moments of 'low desire', but there is no evidence that he ever succumbed to them, after his youthful infatuation with Rosa Baring.

In May 1889 he went for another cruise with Hallam and Nurse Durham in Lord Brassey's yacht *Sunbeam*. As before, they sailed along the coasts of Devon and Cornwall and up the navigable rivers. The inclement weather prevented them from visiting the south coast of Ireland and Bantry Bay as originally planned. During the cruise Tennyson was in high spirits and he read his poems aloud with such passion that more than once tears ran down his cheeks and he could hardly continue. He was inspired to begin writing again, and during his time at sea wrote 'Parnassus':

> What be those two shapes high over the sacred fountain,
> Taller than all the Muses, and huger than all the mountain? . . .
> These are Astronomy and Geology, terrible Muses!

Indeed, he felt that everything now shrank into insignificance when confronted with the infinite space revealed by astronomy and the infinite time revealed by geology. These were the terrors that haunted the Victorian imagination, just as the terrors of nuclear fission haunt ours today.

After being deeply moved by Hayley's life of George Romney, some time in 1889 Tennyson wrote a Browningesque dramatic monologue, 'Romney's Remorse'. In his delirium the painter is tormented by the thought of how he had deserted his wife years ago for the sake of his art, because Sir Joshua Reynolds had told him that 'marriage spoils an artist'. He returns to her at the end of his life, ill and broken, to be nursed by

> The truest, kindliest, noblest-hearted wife
> That ever wore a Christian marriage-ring.
>   My curse upon the Master's apothegm,
> That wife and children drag an Artist down!

His fame, founded on all those flattering society portraits, now seems nothing more to him than a soap bubble:

>     The painter's fame? but mine, that grew
> Blown into glittering by the popular breath,
> May float awhile beneath the sun, may roll
> The rainbow hues of heaven about it –
>         There!
> The coloured bubble bursts above the abyss
> Of Darkness, utter Lethe.
>         Is it so?

[195]

Her sad eyes plead for my own fame with me
To make it dearer.
                    Look, the sun has risen
To flame along another dreary day.

How far did Tennyson put himself in the place of Romney, who had
sacrificed his wife to his art? How far was he aware that Emily had
sacrificed herself for him, smoothing his path, taking on the more
distasteful daily duties, so that nothing should interfere with his
poetry, until her final collapse? 'Romney's Remorse' would seem to
point to the conclusion that in his last years Tennyson had become
aware of it. But this poem is not nearly so powerful as the earlier
'Lucretius', whose wife, tormented by her husband's coldness, mixes
an aphrodisiac with his drink, rousing all his long-suppressed sexual
instincts and filling him with terror – those feelings that Tennyson
feared more than anything else, because to him they represented 'the
Beast' and all that was 'low' in man. For once, with Rosa Baring,
they had brought him bitter humiliation, and only now, fifty years
afterwards, could he forgive her for it in the charming 'Roses on the
Terrace'; that is, the terrace at Aldworth and the terrace at Harrington Hall, the scene of the ecstasy and misery of *Maud*:

Rose, on this terrace fifty years ago,
    When I was in my June, you in your May,
Two words '*My* Rose' set all your face aglow,
    And now that I am white, and you are gray,
That blush of fifty years ago, my dear,
    Blooms in the Past, but close to me today
As this red rose, which on our terrace here
    Glows in the blue of fifty miles away.

When Stephen Spring Rice visited Aldworth this September,
looking out of his bedroom window at a quarter-past eight one
morning, he was astonished to see his host *running* in the sun; and
Tennyson surprised Palgrave at this time by walking down and
climbing back up the path which leads from the house to the Weald,
a descent of four hundred feet, which is difficult to negotiate without
running. In his eightieth year Tennyson seemed once more as
vigorous as ever. Margot Tennant, afterwards Mrs Asquith, on a
visit to Aldworth about this time, describes him as:[4]

a magnificent creature to look at. He has everything: height,
figure, carriage and freedom of expression. Added to this he
had what George Meredith called 'the feminine hint to
perfection'. He greeted me by saying: 'Well, are you as clever

and spurty as your sister?' We sat down to tea and he asked me
if I wanted him to dress for dinner, adding: 'Your sister said of
me that I was both untidy and dirty.' To which I replied:
'Did you mind this?'

Tennyson: 'I wondered if it was true. Do you think I am
dirty?'

Margot: 'You are very handsome.'

Tennyson: 'I can see by that remark that you think I am.
Very well then, I will dress for dinner. Have you read Jane
Welsh Carlyle's letters?'

Margot: 'Yes, I have, and I think them excellent. It seems a
pity,' I added, with the commonplace that is apt to overcome
one in a first conversation with a man of eminence, 'that they
were ever married; with anyone but each other, they might
have been perfectly happy.'

Tennyson: 'I totally disagree with you. By any other arrange-
ment four people would have been unhappy instead of two. . . .'

The hours kept at Aldworth are peculiar; we dined early and
after dinner the poet went to bed. At ten o'clock he came
downstairs and, if asked, would read his poetry to the company
till midnight.

I dressed for dinner with great care that night and, placing
myself next to him when he came down, I asked him to read
out loud for me.

Tennyson: 'What shall I read?'

Margot: '*Maud.*'

Tennyson: 'That was the poem I was cursed for writing! When
it came out no word was bad enough for me! I was a blackguard,
a ruffian and an atheist. You will live to have as great a
contempt for literary critics as I have, my child. . . .'

While he was speaking, I found on the floor, among piles of
books, a small copy of *Maud*, a shilling volume, bound in blue
paper. I put it in his hand and, pulling the lamp nearer, he
began to read.

There is only one man – a poet also – who reads as my host
did: that is my beloved friend, Professor Gilbert Murray. When
I first heard him at Oxford, I closed my eyes and felt as if the
old poet were with me again.

Tennyson's reading had the lilt, the tenderness and the
rhythm that makes music in the soul. It was neither singing,
nor chanting, nor speaking, but a subtle mixture of the three;
and the effect upon me was one of haunting harmonies that left
me profoundly moved.

He began: 'Birds in the high Hall-garden. . .' and skipping

the next four sections, went on to 'I have led her home, my
love, my only friend', and ended with:

> There has fallen a splendid tear
> From the passion flower at the gate . . .

> She is coming, my dove, my dear,
> She is coming, my life, my fate . . .

When he had finished, he pulled me onto his knee and said:
'Many have written as well as that, but nothing that sounded
so well.' I could not speak. He then told us that he had had an
unfortunate experience with a young lady to whom he was
reading *Maud*.

'She was sitting on my knee,' he said, 'as you are doing now,
and after reading

> Birds in the high Hall-garden
> When twilight was falling –
> Maud, Maud, Maud, Maud,
> They were crying and calling,

I asked her what bird she thought I meant. She said "A
nightingale". This made me so angry that I nearly flung her to
the ground. "No, fool . . . Rook," said I.'

I got up, feeling rather sorry for the young lady, but was so
afraid he was going to stop reading that I quickly opened *The
Princess* and put it into his hands and he went on.

The morning after my arrival I was invited by our host to
go for a walk with him, which flattered me very much; but
after walking at a great pace over rough ground for two hours
I regretted my vanity. Except my brother Glenconnor I never
met such an easy mover. The most characteristic feature left on
my mind by the walk was Tennyson's appreciation of other
poets.

On his 80th birthday on 6 August 1889, among the deluge of letters
and telegrams of congratulation was a poem from Swinburne and
letters from Browning and the Queen, who had just received a visit
from her grandson, the German Emperor. Tennyson replied: 'That
the Emperor's visit has passed off so well must be a source of thank-
fulness, not only to your Majesty but to the two nations, nations
too closely allied by the subtle sympathy of kinship not to be either
true brothers or deadly foes. As brothers what might they not do for
the world?'[5]

Browning wrote: 'Let me say I associate myself with the universal
pride of our country in your glory and in its hope that for many and

many a year we may have your very self among us: secure that your poetry will be a wonder and delight to all those appointed to come after; and for my own part let me further say I have loved you dearly. May God bless you and yours.' Stroking this letter, Tennyson said to Watts-Dunton: 'How kind. How good of such a great man to write to me like that.' But next year Browning died in Venice, and Hallam took his father's place as pall-bearer at the funeral in Westminster Abbey. Another friend, William Allingham, died a few days after Browning.

Crossing the Solent one day in October, Tennyson wrote his famous 'Crossing the Bar' on the back of an envelope, and when he read the great lines, Hallam said: 'This is the crown of your life's work.' In fact, it made such an instantaneous impression that it was quoted in newspapers and periodicals and read from pulpits all over the Kingdom. In December this year, *Demeter and Other Poems* appeared.

'Went up with my Father-in-law to the library after dinner,' Audrey, Hallam's wife, notes: 'Sat on his knee and had a long talk with him. He said that this world is so vast, so tremendous that we cannot grasp it, do what we will, therefore we must bow down and strive after the highest we can imagine to ourselves. He said: it is proved to me that there is a higher Being who is all knowing: it *cannot* be that anything can have lived without being fully known and understood.'[6]

'At Farringford,' wrote Palgrave on 20 April 1890, 'he has been entertaining large 5 o'clock tea-parties for the last three or four weeks, almost daily, and has often been even able to read to them. He has walked an hour and a half or two hours before luncheon, many days, between Mr. Arthur Coleridge and Dr. Stanford, all three telling merry stories; and at luncheon and at dinner his spirits did not fail with others, though now he is beginning to be weary of many people.' Sometimes the tea-parties were so large that they had to be held in the ballroom, and poor Emily notes: 'There were so many people here that only seeing each a little time exhausts my strength – except when a stray guest comes to look in upon me. More than enough for me!' She lay in the drawing-room as usual.

But her octogenarian husband seemed tireless. Where was that 'natural morbidness of a man who shrank from society', observed by Allingham? Indeed, where had it ever been? Tennyson now lived surrounded by a crowd of admirers. Adulation was in the very air of Farringford and Aldworth.

'I am better than I was,' Emily Tennyson wrote to her sister Anne Weld on 13 May. 'My heart has been at a low ebb during the present year but after all a great many people have been worse. Once or twice I was very unwell, yet of course I must keep things to myself as much as possible. How glad I am that dear Edward's funeral is on such a lovely day. We sent a wreath with a card in Ally's handwriting.' This was Tennyson's brother, who had spent the greater part of his life in a mental home, where he died. Two days later the Laureate was recording 'The Charge of the Light Brigade' on the phonograph sent to him by Edison. 'When Nurse Durham who had not heard him recite it heard it through the tubes she gave a great shout it was so loud and so exactly like his voice,' Emily told her sister. 'Baby shouted with delight when he heard his grandfather. . . . I could not stand the tubes [presumably, head-phones]. I tried for a moment and they pierced my brain.' Tennyson also recorded the Bugle Song from *The Princess* on the same day and then, soon after, 'The Charge of the Heavy Brigade', 'As me no more', 'The Northern Farmer, New Style' and parts of *Maud*, 'Boadicea' and the Wellington Ode. One can now barely distinguish the far-away tremulous chant through the hailstorm of surface noise on the records taken from the original worn wax cylinders, though the effect is of a highly emotional but ghostly voice reaching one from the distant past.

Meanwhile Tennyson continued to take his daily walks along the downs from Watcombe Bay by the Beacon towards the promontory that towers above the Needles. 'The views of sea and cliff, the gloom and glory over the waters on either hand, were a perpetual delight to him. The birds that made their homes on the chalk ledges, the peregrine falcons, the ravens with their "iron knell", the kestrels, the carrion-crows, the different kinds of sea-bird, from the cormorants drying themselves on the pinnacles of rock in heraldic attitude to the seagull sunning himself among the tufts of samphire and of thrift, were ever a fresh interest. A special corner, that he liked above all, was a platform of cliff over Scratchell's Bay looking up to a dazzling white precipice, seen far away by the ships at sea, and which he named Taliessin, or the "splendid brow". At other times he would wander at low tide among the queer rock-pools on the shore, and curiously examine the "branching sea-weeds" and the brilliant sea-anemones!'[7]

In the evenings Tennyson would generally read novels – Scott, Jane Austen, Stevenson, Hardy, Meredith, Henry James, 'Ouida', Hall Caine, Mrs Oliphant, Miss Braddon, Marie Corelli – with an apparently omnivorous appetite. But he would say: 'I hate some of your modern novels with numberless characters thrust into the first chapter and nothing but modern society talk; and also those morbid and introspective tales, with their oceans of sham philosophy. To read these last is like wading through glue.'[8] All the same, his taste seems to have been pretty catholic.

Watts came to paint his portrait for Trinity College, Cambridge, the seventh portrait he had done of Tennyson. But, knowing his dislike of being painted, the subject was not mentioned for two or three days, until suddenly Tennyson said; 'When are you going to paint me?' In ten days Watts finished two portraits, one of the poet in his college robes and another in peer's robes, now in the Art Gallery, Adelaide. During the sittings Hallam would read aloud from Frazer's *Golden Bough*. Watts was still a young, sprightly seventy-three, 'the gray hat crowning his silver hair, a gray cloak taking pleasant folds, while he stepped like a boy, light and neat in every movement', as his young wife describes him. He was in his eighties when he made the colossal statue of the poet which now stands in the precincts of Lincoln Cathedral. 'It is one of the greatest glories of my life that I was acquainted with one of the most splendid, perhaps the most splendid examples of man as he might be,' Watts said of his friendship with Tennyson.

Watts-Dunton, staying at Aldworth in September 1891, wrote: 'Tennyson, with whom I took a long walk of three miles this morning, is in marvellous health, every faculty (at 82) is as bright as it was when his years were 40. He is busy writing poetry as fine as anything he has ever written. Really he is a miracle.'

Hubert Parry, visiting him at Farringford in 1892, records: 'The Laureate was far from mealy-mouthed in conversation. Though eloquent in condemning immorality, in deploring sensual indifference, he did not refrain from quoting dubious anecdotes from Brantôme.' He read 'The Lotus-Eaters', the subject of one of Parry's finest choral works. Parry observed that in his reading, Tennyson 'frequently ignored stops, and ran phrases into one another, with little apparent regard for the sense, but he evidently greatly enjoyed himself. The manner of reading is most strange – I should think something after the manner of the ancient professional reciters of epics and songs amongst barbarous people. . . . After 'The Lotus-Eaters' he began talking about *Maud* and then read a great deal of that too. . . . He kept talking until quite late and then went to say good-night to his wife. It is the most old-fashioned house I ever knew, with dim candle lamps in the passages, four-poster beds, hundreds of Mrs. Cameron's photographs, ugly wall papers and early Victorian furniture.

'January 3rd. After breakfast T. read me the Wellington Ode, which he appeared to want me to set. It is a grand poem, but not suitable for music as it stands. I also had to play him my version of "The Lotus-Eaters". After lunch they kindly sent me in a dog-cart to Newport, where I picked up a train.'[9]

In March 1892 *The Foresters* was produced at Daly's Theater,

New York, with great success. In April Bram Stoker came to Farringford to discuss Irving's drastic alterations to the text of *Becket*. Irving's production unfortunately did not take place during Tennyson's lifetime, but the play was widely admired when it was acted in February 1893.

Tennyson's long walks were now becoming a thing of the past, and he mostly sat in his summer house, looking out over the Sussex Weald. He was suffering from gout in the face and throat, which made it difficult to eat. He growled and complained a good deal, but his growls were half-playful, and he used to challenge visitors to get up twenty times from a low chair without using their hands, which he could still do with ease. He even waltzed occasionally in the ballroom. In June he went for another cruise with Hallam along the south and west coasts in Colonel Crozier's yacht *Assegai*. They landed at Exmouth and went by rail to Dulverton, 'a land of bubbling streams', and drove up the Haddon valley to Barlynch Abbey on the Exe. 'The ragged robin and wild garlic were profuse.' Another day they scaled Haddon Down beyond the Exe valley and above Haddon, 'drove through the Barle valley to Hawkridge, and then to the Tor steps, high up among the hills, with an ancient bridge across the river, flat stones laid on piers. Some tawny cows were cooling themselves in mid-stream: a green meadow on one side, on the other a wooded slope. "If it were only to see this," he said, "the journey is worth while." ' As they left Exmouth harbour, Tennyson was much struck by the red rocks and the deep green of the grass. They visited Corfe Castle and he said it was as 'hollow as a skull'.[10]

He was now contemplating a new poem, 'Akbar's Dream', a theme suggested by Jowett, and had taken him on his cruise many books from Balliol College Library, among them Abul-Fazl's *Akbar-Nama* and *Ain-i-Akbari*, translated by Blochmann, H. Elliot's *History of India*, vol. vi, Elphinstone's *History of India*, Lyall's *Asiatic Studies* and *The Holy Mervi* of Jerome Xavier. Of the Great Mogul, a contemporary of our Elizabeth I, Tennyson observes in a note: 'His tolerance of religions and his abhorrence of religious persecution put our Tudors to shame. He invented a new eclectic religion by which he hoped to unite all creeds, castes, and peoples; and his legislation was remarkable for vigour, justice, and humanity.'

In July he paid a visit to London to see the new Natural History Museum in the Cromwell Road, a veritable cathedral of Science built by Alfred Waterhouse and 'covered all over', as Dr Pevsner notes, 'with Waterhouse's favourite terra-cotta slabs, the least appealing of materials, of a soapy hardness,'[11] nevertheless, a construction of overwhelming boldness, such as only a Victorian could have conceived. Tennyson was fascinated by the display of birds' nests and said he wished he had seen them when he was young. But he was oppressed by the crowds and only too glad to get home.

An unexpected visitor to Aldworth at this time was an American, who had worked his way over to England on a cattle ship in order to recite *Maud* to its author. Tennyson 'suffered much' listening to the recitation and then paid his visitor's fare back to the States. Another American, Henry van Dyke, who had attacked *Maud*, also called and Tennyson, determined to demonstrate his error, read the poem to him with such 'incredible passion' that he was too tired to eat his lunch. In spite of his grumbles, van Dyke was struck by his kindness and good humour. He was much pleased by a letter from 'a Newcastle artisan' who wrote: 'Lord Tennyson, your poetry has been such a goodly gift to me. Excepting Shakespeare, I can never get away from his world, no other poet has so sustained me. My workshop intercourse is usually irksome, bound to be when one stands so much alone. I lose this ungeniality reading your verse and feel drawn closer to humanity. Sometimes horrid doubt throws its darkening veil about me, there is so much in this life formless and void of cheer, your verse sets my feet aright. *In Memoriam* has brought me better faith, clearer mental vision, higher ultimate hope! . . . May your years of influence be many. The age does so need a guiding hand.' A remarkable 'artisan'!

Many visitors called upon Tennyson in the week of 6 August, his eighty-third birthday, among them J. A. Symonds and Edward Burne-Jones. As Symonds records, they found him in his study, 'at one end of a large couch, shawls over his knees, and velvet skull cap defining the massive bones of his forehead. He welcomed me very kindly as an old friend.' Symonds reminded him 'how he had asked me at Farringford what Shakespeare's "long purples" were. "Aye, aye," said Tennyson, "I think they are jack-in-the-box," (his name for arum) "but I have used the words in my poetry to signify a hedgerow vetch with trailing flowers." Actually long purples are a kind of orchid, an *orchis mascula*, regarded as a phallic symbol. It is one of the flowers with which the drowned Ophelia had wreathed herself, to which, the Queen tells us, 'the liberal shepherds give a grosser name'. The arum lily, Tennyson's jack-in-the-box was, of course, also regarded as a phallic symbol, for obvious reasons. Tennyson went on to tell Symonds that he was going to write a poem on Giordano Bruno and asked him what he thought about Bruno's attitude to Christianity. Then Hallam told Symonds that he was reading to his father the chapter on Bruno in Symonds's *Renaissance in Italy*. Tennyson said that 'the great thing in Bruno was his perception of an infinite universe, filled with solar systems like our own, and all penetrated with the Soul of God. "That conception," he said, "must react destructively on Christianity – I mean its creed and dogma – its morality will always remain." Somebody had told him, he said, that astronomers could count 550 million solar systems. He observed that there was no reason why each should not have planets peopled with living and intelligent beings. Then he said, "See what becomes of the second person of the Deity, and the sacrifice of a God for fallen man upon this little earth!" ' – that, presumably, being the reason why Bruno was burnt by the Church of Rome.

Before leaving, Symonds went to pay his respects to Emily 'on her sofa, a pale sweet St Monica sort of face, looking just as when I saw her first more than twenty years ago.'[12] Symonds was accompanied on this visit by his handsome gondolier, Angelo, who hid in the bushes until they left.

In September, Helen Allingham found Tennyson too tired to read or even to look out of the window. She said that she hoped he would soon be better. 'Aren't we both being a little hypocritical?' he said.

# 14

Tennyson's last illness set in this September of 1892. On the 24th he came down to dinner for the last time. On the 25th Walter Leaf, the Homeric scholar, and Bram Stoker found him 'grand but broken', and clear and active in his mind, his long black hair falling down thin and straggling from under his skull cap. After lunch he was much better and began to talk about Homer with all his old fire, reciting long passages in Greek in a strong deep voice. They then talked of the Shakespeare–Bacon heresy, and Tennyson ridiculed the idea that *Romeo and Juliet* could have been written by 'a man who could say (as Bacon did in his essay on love) "Great spirits and great business do keep out this weak passion".'

*Henry VIII* had been running at the Lyceum the previous year, and Tennyson speculated on how much of the play was by Shakespeare, asserting of Wolsey's famous speech beginning 'Cromwell, I charge thee, throw away ambition' 'Shakespeare never wrote that. I know it, I know it, I know it,' banging the table with his fist. At tea he was 'full of humour and reminiscence, telling countless stories with his usual zest'. But he moaned now and then with pain.

'Gout was flying through his knees and jaws,' Bram Stoker, Irving's manager and the author of *Dracula*, wrote afterwards. 'He had on his black skull cap, but he presently took it off, as though it were irksome to him. In front of him was a little table with one wax candle lighted. . . . When the fire of pleasant memory began to flicker, he grew feeble and low in spirits. He spoke of the coming Spring and that he would not live to see it. Somehow he grew lower in spirits as the light died away and the twilight deepened, as if the whole man were tuned to nature's key.' He was worried about the newspapers prying into his state of health, for it had been found that the beggar who came to Farringford for broken meat was being paid 10s. 0d. a week by a reporter for the gossip of the kitchen. Turning to Bram Stoker, Tennyson said: 'Don't let them know how ill I am, or they'll have me buried before twenty-four hours! . . . I sometimes

H

wish I had never written a line.'[1] He often said this in his hatred of publicity and the prying press.

After that they sat in silence for some time, watching the poet's splendid head, now bent and weak with age, outlined against the fading light of the mullioned window. And when they rose to say goodbye, they knew that they would never see him again. Two days later G. L. Craik, his publisher Macmillan's manager, was with him, going through the proofs of his last collection, *The Death of Œnone, Akbar's Dream, and Other Poems,* published after his death in October. The book showed no weakening of his powers; it was affectionately dedicated to Jowett, who was to die a year later.

'My poor Ally has been very unwell,' Emily wrote to her sister Mrs Weld on 18 September. 'When Hallam came home, he telegraphed for Dr. Dabbs and I had had two other doctors before. Thank God, Ally seems better now.' On 28 September she wrote: 'The sickness and weakness and depression continue.' Dr Dabbs, whose love of literature made him very sympathetic to Tennyson, came to Aldworth from the Isle of Wight. On the 29th Sir Andrew Clarke came from London and did not think the poet's condition very serious, since the day before he had been well enough to drive through Haslemere with Hallam, pointing out his favourite walks on the way. 'I shall never walk there again,' he said. He was delighted with Clarke and they discussed Gray's *Elergy.* But his condition gradually deteriorated during the next few days.

On the morning of 3 October he asked for his Shakespeare in Steevens' edition. He opened it at *Cymbeline,* but was distressed to find that he could read only one or two lines. He talked of Irving's coming production of *Becket.* 'It will be successful on the stage with Irving,' he said. 'I suppose I shall never see it.' 'I fear not,' replied Dr Dabbs. Then 'Irving – I can trust Irving will do me justice.' He then became worried about the volumes of poetry that had been sent to him for his opinion and asked Hallam if he had written to any of the authors. 'I make a slave of you,' he said.

Telegrams of inquiry came from the Queen and Princess Louise. But Tennyson's pleasure at this kindness was spoilt by his fear of publicity, muttering to himself: 'The press will get hold of me now.' He asked to have the blinds up. 'I want to see the sky and the light,' he said, and repeated with great feeling, *'the sky and the light.'* Then, turning to Hallam with a far-away, unearthly look on his face: 'Have I not been walking in the garden with Gladstone and showing him my trees?' he asked and did not seem to believe his son's gentle denial.

In the afternoon of his last day, 5 October, he had a long talk with Dabbs about death and said that men cling to what is after all a shadow and only a small part of the world's great life. He asked repeatedly for his Shakespeare and when it was brought to him, though he could neither read it nor lift it up, he said: 'I have opened it!' The book fell open at one of his favourite passages in *Cymbeline* V. 4., where Posthumus says to Imogen, as he holds her in his arms at last: 'Hang there like fruit, my soul, till the tree die.' Soon afterwards, he murmured a blessing to Emily, who had slept on the sofa at the foot of his bed throughout his last illness, and to Hallam and Audrey.

By half-past five the sun had set and Tennyson lost consciousness. 'And then,' wrote Audrey, 'the most glorious moon rose and flooded the room with a clear, mysterious light, and suddenly lit up the whole of his face and bed and he looked grand and peaceful in the golden light. By a quarter past eleven, the whole room was lit by the splendid moon, and all was clear with a beautiful solemn light.'

Just before half-past one on the morning of 6 October, came several spasmodic gasps. Dr Dabbs could feel no more pulse and Hallam said: 'I can only say his own words "God accept him, Christ receive him." ' Both nurses, one a Jamaican, fell on their knees in prayer, and Alfred Tennyson drew a few quick fluttering breaths and passed away. A few hours later the old Vicar of Lurgashall, in the Weald below Blackdown, came to see him lying grand and peaceful in death. 'Lord Tennyson,' said the old man, 'God has taken you, who made you a Prince of men.'

At nine o'clock a telegram was sent to the Queen. The reply came from Balmoral: 'Most truly deeply grieved that the great poet and kind friend has left this world.' That day she wrote to Hallam and had her account of her last conversation with Tennyson copied for Emily. 'He was a great poet,' the Queen wrote in her journal, 'and his ideas were ever grand, noble and elevating. He was very loyal, and always very kind and sympathising to me, quite remarkably so. What beautiful lines he wrote for my darling Albert and for my children and Eddy! He died with his hand on his Shakespeare, and the moon shining full into the window over him. . . . A worthy end.' Indeed, almost too worthy, almost like a stage setting in the grand Victorian manner or the serene adagio of Elgar's First Symphony.

But the drama was not quite over. There was to be an even more impressive final scene. At six o'clock in the evening on 11 October, the coffin with the dead Laureate under a pall embroidered with white English roses, the last verse of 'Crossing the Bar' and his initials, surmounted by a baron's coronet and a wreath of laurel from Virgil's tomb, and crosses of flowers from all parts of Great Britain, was placed in a wagonette decorated with stag's horn moss, scarlet lobelia and Virginia creeper in all its autumn glory. The chief mourners, Hallam and Audrey, followed in a pony carriage, stacked high with wreaths; then a long train of servants and 'humble neighbours', led by the nurses, moved in silence along the track which leads through the wood and over Blackdown. 'In the darkness, which grew denser every moment, a single star was seen to shine over Aldworth.'

The funeral at the Abbey on 12 October was like a last parade of the eminent Victorians. Among those invited to join the procession following the coffin up the nave to the chancel were: Swinburne, Thomas Hardy, Edmund Gosse, J. M. Barrie, Conan Doyle, Alfred Austin, Meredith, Andrew Lang, William Morris, Gordon Wordsworth, Sidney Colvin, Palgrave, Holman Hunt, Burne-Jones, Grove, Sullivan, G. F. Watts, Irving, Ellen Terry, the Vice-Chancellors of Oxford and Cambridge, Huxley with three other officers of the Royal Society. But Watts was too grief-stricken to attend, and Swinburne refused. A branch of bay from Delphi was laid on the coffin by Alfred Austin. There was also a wreath from Shakespeare's garden at Stratford-on-Avon and one from Clevedon, where Arthur Hallam lay. Mr and Mrs Gladstone sent a wreath from Hawarden and the Queen sent one of laurel, one of flowers and one of metal inscribed in her hand 'A tribute of affectionate regard from his Sovereign'.

'We laid him yesterday among his kindred, the Poets,' Jowett wrote to Emily, who was too unwell to attend. 'There never was such a concourse before within the walls of the Abbey.' The Duke of Argyll said that he had seen nothing like it since the funeral of Wellington. Edmund Gosse, however, has left a somewhat jaundiced account, which does not seem to have been printed before.[2]

The funeral was at 12.30, and the invitation for 12. A bright, dry morning, with east wind. . . . At 11 I was at my office, and at 11.15 thought I would stroll down and take my place, but already a dense crowd surrounding the Abbey on all sides. Men were briskly selling in the crowd a sheet of pictures, in the Busch manner, of a lady in bed trying to catch a flea 'Buy A Busy Night – only one penny'. Dean's Yard closed to the public, except on showing the funeral invitation card. Mine was for the South Transept. I walked in with F. Greenwood, who was going to the triforium. At Dean's Yard door to the cloisters, a carriage deposited Mrs. Thackeray Ritchie, looking aged – face soft and pale, as with weeping, the solitary person from first to last who seemed genuinely moved. Only 11.30, but still a rush and push in the cloisters. Great confusion; standing at last at the door of the Abbey itself, in a thick mob, heard my name called in a plaintive treble – William Watson and Theodore

Watts had lost their way – 'was this the way to the procession, if not, where?' I directed, they scuttled off down the arcade like rabbits ['rats' crossed out]. No one seemed to know where we ought to go, – fierce persons shouted occasional questions, else simple hard pushing at the small door of entry. Entering, I was lost again but gradually found my place, and secured an outside seat by two courteous orientals, swathed in lilac and saffron silk garments, with gilt-threaded turbans on their heads, soft and swarthy persons who whispered all the time in unknown tongues. Various figures flitted by. Mrs. Humphry Ward, alone, looking plump and comely; a melancholy old phantom of W. M. Rossetti, Bancroft, Sir Edwin Arnold, very seedy and wretched, brawling, in vain, with the vergers for a more honourable position; Alma Tadema, Hamo Thornycroft in marvellous furs, with golden curls and fine rosy face; Le Gallienne, looking like a melancholy angel, who sat by me and chattered; little Haweis shaved clean for the nonce, and elbowing his way about like a devil, otherwise, here and everywhere, a crowd of perfectly callous nonentities, treating the thing as a show and rather a poor one. I could however see little; every corner of the Abbey was evidently filled, and at last the mob overflowed all the seats, and stood massed, flooding all the gangways. It was a huge but by no means an impressive scene to me, not comparable with Browning's funeral in the same place. The light was poor, but improved.

At last the babble and whispering was cut through by someone calling 'Attention'. We all stood up and music began. Then the priests and boys walked up, and I could see but little. The Archbishop of Canterbury lightly ascended the steps, – a moving mountain of flowers dragged along apparently by Lecky, by [Montague] Butler, by various other old gentlemen, and then a more vague mass of faces, concealed behind the shoulders of our particular crowd.

Hallam Tennyson says that the coffin was covered by a Union Jack at the request of the Prince of Wales and that the pall-bearers were the Duke of Argyll, Lord Dufferin, Lord Selborne, Lord Rosebery, Jowett, Lecky, Froude, Lord Salisbury, Dr Butler (Trinity College, Cambridge), the United States Minister, Sir James Paget and Lord Kelvin. The nave was lined with men of the Balaclava Light Brigade, by some of the London Rifle Volunteers, and by the boys of the Gordon Boys' Home, 'in token of their gratitude for what he had done for each and all of them. . . . Nothing could have been more simple and majestic than the funeral service; and the tributes of sympathy which we received from many countries and from all lands and classes were not only remarkable for their universality but for their depth of feeling.

'Next to Robert Browning and in front of the Chaucer monument my father was laid, and for weeks after the funeral multitudes passed by the new-made grave in a never-ceasing procession. Against the pillar near the grave has been placed the well-known bust by Woolner.'[3] Gosse continues:[4]

The procession was far too long to be distinguished, and in point of fact was rather poor, a stream of nonentities vaguely proceeding into some [illegible] or other. But when the ceremony was all over, the stream flowed back along the aisle of our South Transept and I saw it to perfection – Lord Salisbury, bowed like Atlas, looked elephantine and noble; Lecky still stiff and slanting outwards, like a lamp-post with a mild and whiskered face, impaled upon the top of it, Lord Rosebery flushed and restless, most of the people dreadfully tired-looking, except Jowett, a cheerful balloon of rotundity on little spindly legs, with his rosy globular face fringed with white curls; Lord Dufferin, aged extremely, and of a yellow pallor, looked weary enough to drop. Several friends extended more or less melancholy hands to press mine, as the procession passed, – Stanford perceptily flushed with musical interest, Jebb as solemn as an undertaker, Aldis Wright in the highest spirits and a terrific cold in the head, Alfred Austin, his eyes flashing like coals, admirable in demeanour, cordial and very decent. T. Hardy, W. Watson, Austin Dobson, W. Besant and Theodore Watts, a little literary island in the fashionable stream, walked together. As I left I saw Lewis Morris fatuously balancing his huge body, tied in a wasp-like frock-coat, on his heels, and nodding self-consciously to his friends. The whole thing was enormous, crushing, exceedingly well-done, national and prosaic. We had a little luncheon-party at the Club when it was all over – Hardy, W. Watson, Theo. Watts, Dobson and myself, and we went on talking till 4. Watts gave us anecdotes of T., nothing very new. But he says that two days ago, Swinburne, who was invited to take a prominent place, positively and obstinately refused to come, and will probably be so stiff-necked as to refuse the laureateship, which Hamo tells us, on good authority, will certainly be offered to him. We had an extremely lively lunch and after party.

During the Abbey service, 'Crossing the Bar' and 'The Silent

Voices' were sung, the first set by Professor Bridge and the second by Lady Tennyson, arranged for four voices by Bridge. There was also music by Purcell, and the service ended with the Dead March in *Saul*.

The laureateship was not offered to Swinburne. 'I have been making a careful examination of his case,' Gladstone wrote to Lord Acton on 20 October; 'I fear he is *absolutely* impossible.' William Morris was sounded as to whether he would accept the office, if it were offered to him; but, according to Halliday Sparling, he told his family that 'he could not see himself sitting down in crimson plush breeches and white silk stockings to write birthday odes in honour of all the blooming little Guelflings and Battenbergs that happen to come along'. In the event, the laureateship was offered to and accepted by the harmless Alfred Austin.

After the funeral, Lady Ritchie, who had loved Tennyson, wrote to Mrs Oliphant: 'I came home feeling out of gear, out of spirits, and I am only now shaking off the feeling of almost despair which came over me, as I looked at all that should have been of comfort and help. . . . It seemed to me like my whole generation passing away. . . . I was really touched by Ellen Terry's genuine grief, tho' I think, if I had only been alone with you, I should have felt in better harmony with that, to me, most *wrenching* scene.'[5] In December 1883 she had written to Tennyson: 'Who knows perhaps when we are all peacefully together again, (and I always think of the old days on Freshwater Down as the nearest thing to heaven I ever could imagine), you will still walk ahead and point to the sea and to the sky, and touch things and make them shine for us and flash into our hearts, as you have ever done.' As Professor Sidgwick wrote to his son: 'It is like the end of a reign – only that there is no concluding "vive le roi!". And, indeed, it is impossible that anyone should ever hold the sway he held over the minds of men of my generation; it is impossible that anyone's thoughts and words should be so entwined with our best moments of the spring and summer of our lives.'[6]

But with Tennyson's death, Emily's and Hallam's work increased immeasurably: 'there are such innumerable letters to write and public letters to be considered,' Emily wrote to her sister Anne Weld. Then there was the great *Memoir* to be compiled, an enormous monument of piety. 'Almost all my strength I have to give to the Memoir,' Emily wrote on 1 November. Indeed, she devoted her four remaining years to helping Hallam to collect and arrange the material, sorting and editing thousands of letters, revising her journals; nothing that might mar the exalted image should be allowed to remain. Nearly all her husband's letters to herself she destroyed, by his wish. 'I am not able to have anyone with me except Hallam,' she had written on 11 October. 'He and I feel that we live with Him still and that in this is our best hope of a fuller life in God. . . . I had been joyful in the hope of going with Him but my Hallam tells me that I can be of help in the work to be done and nothing I can do is too much to be done either for the Father or the devoted Son of our love.' Palgrave also helped. 'Isn't Mr. Palgrave wonderfully kind?' Emily wrote to her sister in November. 'He has looked over about twenty-three thousand letters for us and Hallam over about as many more, I believe.' Among these were the letters of sympathy which flooded in from all over the world. And then there were the books and articles that began to appear. 'We have to keep such reading as we can manage very much to what is written about Ally. Very trying reading, tho' meant to be complimentary but we have at least to glance over many volumes, my head is far from strong,' complained the poor lady, 'and my eyes so far from well that it is only now and then I can read a little myself.' It sounds like a prolonged martyrdom.

Emily Tennyson died suddenly of congestion of the lungs following an attack of influenza on 10 August 1896. Her last words were: 'I have tried to be a good wife.' At her funeral, Herbert Warren, President of Magdalen College, Oxford, spoke of how she had aided, encouraged, spared, and tended her husband, of 'the charm of her character, the saintliness of her spirit – the purer for suffering, the stronger out of weakness.' She was buried in the churchyard at Freshwater. At the service, her setting of 'The Silent Voices' was sung once more:

When the dumb Hour, clothed in black,
Brings the Dreams about my bed,
Call me not so often back,
Silent Voices of the dead,
Toward the lowland ways behind me,
And the sunlight that is gone!
Call me rather, silent voices,
Forward to the starry track
Glimmering up the heights beyond me
On, and always on!

# NOTES

## CHAPTER ONE

1 Charles Tennyson, *Alfred Tennyson*, London, 2nd edn, 1968, p. 5.
2 Ibid., p. 6.
3 Ibid., pp. 8–9.
4 Ibid., p. 10.
5 Ibid., pp. 27–8.
6 Christopher Ricks, *Tennyson*, London, 1972, p. 7.
7 Charles Tennyson, op. cit., p. 31.
8 Ricks, op. cit., pp. 7–8.
9 Ibid., p. 8.
10 Charles Tennyson, op. cit., p. 60.
11 Ricks, op. cit., p. 23.
12 Charles Tennyson, op. cit., p. 80.
13 Ricks, op. cit., p. 27.
14 *Tennyson Research Bulletin*, Nov. 1974, vol. 2, no. 3, 'Mablethorpe', pp. 121–3.
15 Charles Tennyson, op. cit., p. 35.

## CHAPTER TWO

1 James Pope-Hennessy, *Monckton-Milnes: The Years of Promise*, London, 1949.
2 A. C. Benson, *Fasti Etonenis*, London, 1899.
3 Quoted by Charles Tennyson, *Alfred Tennyson*, London, 2nd edn, 1968, p. 66.
4 Pope-Hennessy, op. cit.
5 John D. Jump, *Tennyson: The Critical Heritage*, London, 1967.
6 Christopher Ricks, *Tennyson*, London, 1972, p. 37.
7 Ibid., pp. 37–9.
8 Jerome C. Hixon, *Tennyson Research Bulletin*, Nov. 1975, vol. 2, no. 4.
9 Charles Tennyson, op. cit., p. 116.
10 Ibid., p. 117.
11 Ibid., pp. 123–4.

## CHAPTER THREE

1 Christopher Ricks, *Tennyson*, London, 1972, pp. 114–15.
2 Quoted by James Knowles, *Nineteenth Century*, XXXIII, 1893, p. 182.
3 But as Jack Kolb points out in 'Arthur Hallam and Emily Tennyson', *Review of English Studies*, vol. XXVIII, no. 109, February 1977, 'It seems doubtful if the blissful union envisioned in *In Memoriam* could ever have been realised. He' cites Arthur Hallam's last few letters to Emily from London with their rather spiteful accounts of his continuing flirtation with Charlotte Sotheby,

due possibly to his irritation with Emily's ill-health.

4 T. S. Eliot, 'In Memoriam', *Selected Essays*, London, 1932, p. 337.

5 Charles Tennyson, *Alfred Tennyson*, London, 2nd edn, 1968, p. 159.

6 R. W. Rader, *Tennyson's 'Maud': The Biographical Genesis*, Berkeley and Los Angeles, 1963.

7 Christopher Ricks (ed.), *The*

*Poems of Tennyson*, London, 1969, p. 688.

8 Ricks, *Tennyson*, p. 164.

9 Eliot, op. cit., p. 332.

10 James O. Hoge, *The Letters of Emily, Lady Tennyson*, Penn State, 1974, p. 3.

11 Evidently Tennyson was thinking of T. H. Huxley's abominable dictum 'for his successful progress man has been largely indebted to those qualities which he shares with the ape and the tiger'.

CHAPTER FOUR

1 Charles Tennyson, *Alfred Tennyson*, London, 2nd edn, 1968, pp. 177–8.

CHAPTER FIVE

1 Christopher Ricks, *Tennyson*, London, 1972, pp. 188–204.

2 Charles Tennyson, *Alfred Tennyson*, London, 2nd edn, 1968, p. 262.

3 Hugh l'Anson Fausset, *Tennyson*, London, 1929, p. 128. Fausset is repelled by the 'orgy of hospital love-making' in the section following the tournament.

4 Hallam Tennyson, *Alfred Lord Tennyson: A Memoir*, London, 2 vols, 1897; one-volume edn, London, 1906, pp. 240–1.

5 William Allingham, *A Diary*, ed. H. Allingham and E. B. Williams, London, 1911, entry 22 August 1880.

6 Ibid., pp. 297–8.

7 Hallam Tennyson, op. cit., pp. 230–2.

CHAPTER SIX

1 Quoted by Charles Tennyson, *Alfred Tennyson*, London, 2nd edn, 1968, pp. 245–6.

2 Hallam Tennyson, *Alfred Lord Tennyson: A Memoir*, one-volume edn, London, 1906, p. 250.

3 Christopher Ricks, *Tennyson*, London, 1972, p. 214.

4 Christopher Ricks (ed.) *The Poems of Tennyson*, London, 1969, p. 949, *n*.

5 Susan Chitty, *The Beast and the Monk, a Life of Charles Kingsley*, London, 1974.

6 Ricks, *The Poems of Tennyson*, p. 944, *n*.

7 Ricks, *Tennyson*, p. 216.

8 T. S. Eliot, 'In Memoriam', *Selected Essays*, London, 1932, p. 336.

9 Clyde de L. Ryals, *Theme and Symbol in Tennyson's Poetry to 1850*, Philadelphia, 1964.

CHAPTER SEVEN

1 W. Minto, *Autobiographical Notes of the Life of William Bell Scott*, London, 1892, 1, p. 300.

2 Charles Tennyson, *Alfred Tennyson*, London, 2nd edn, 1968, p. 275.

1 Charles Tennyson, *Alfred Tennyson*, London, 2nd edn, 1968, p. 227.
2 Ibid., p. 285.
3 Hallam Tennyson, *Alfred Lord Tennyson: A Memoir*, one-volume edn, London, 1906, pp. 333–5.
4 G. B.-J., *Memorials of Edward Burne-Jones*, London, 1904, I, p. 182.
5 Marie Hanson-Taylor and Horace E. Scudder, *The Life and Letters of Bayard Taylor*, London, 1884, p. 334.
6 Lewis Carroll, *Phantasmagoria*, London, 1869.

CHAPTER NINE

1 Kathleen Tillotson, 'Tennyson's Serial Poem', *Mid-Victorian Studies*, London, 1965.
2 A. C. Swinburne, *Under the Microscope*, London, 1872.
3 G. M. Young, 'The Age of Tennyson', *Critical Essays on the Poetry of Tennyson*, ed. J. Kilham, London, 1960, p. 35.
4 A. C. Swinburne, *Miscellanies*, London, 1886, p. 251.
5 Letter to Frederick Greenwood, C. L. Clive, *Letters of George Meredith*, Oxford, 1970, II, p. 97.
6 Betty Miller, 'Tennyson and the Sinful Queen', *Twentieth Century*, 158, 1955, pp. 155–63.
7 Hallam Tennyson, *Alfred Lord Tennyson: A Memoir*, one-volume edn, London, 1906, p. 525.
8 W. E. Gladstone, *Gleanings of Past Years*, vol. II, London, 1897, p. 166.
9 Gerhard Joseph, *Tennysonian Love*, Minneapolis, 1969, pp. 186ff.
10 Hallam Tennyson, op. cit., p. 403.
11 Ibid.
12 Hallam Tennyson, *Materials for a Life of A.T.*, II, London, 1895, privately printed, pp. 347–8.

CHAPTER TEN

1 Hallam Tennyson, *Alfred Lord Tennyson: A Memoir*, one-volume edn, London, 1906, p. 397.
2 Angus Davidson, *Edward Lear*, London, 1950 edn, p. 129.
3 Vivien Noakes, *Edward Lear*, London, 1968, p. 218.
4 Ibid., pp. 236–7.
5 Hallam Tennyson, *Materials for a Life of A.T.*, London, 1895, privately printed.
6 *Diary*, 11.7.65; Noakes, op. cit., p. 237.
7 *Diary*, 17.10.64; Noakes, op. cit., p. 237.
8 Herbert M. Schneller and Robert C. Peters, *The Letters of John Addington Symonds*, Detroit, 1967, vol. I, pp. 510–11.
9 Ibid., I, pp. 512–13.
10 Horatio F. Brown, *Letters and Papers of John Addington Symonds*, London, 1923, 'Miscellanies', pp. 1–8.
11 See *The Report of the Royal Jamaica Commission* (Parl. Papers. Vol. CCXXXIV, 8 June–10 August 1866). Reprisals went on for a month or more. Men and women were

condemned to 100 and 150 lashes, then hanged, after being literally torn to pieces, piano wires being twisted with the cords of the 'cat'. After beating, many prisoners were tied up in knots to increase their agony. A certain Colonel Hobbs made the rebels hang each other, though they begged to be shot. The courts martial were presided over by junior officers and ensigns, little more than boys, but one officer who behaved like a sadistic maniac was a veteran of the Charge of the Light Brigade. If 'niggers are tigers', what of Paleface? Tennyson sent a subscription to Eyre's defence fund, but the Jamaica Commission, headed by John Stuart Mill, called for his prosecution for murder.

12 'Women's' may be a pun on 'we men's', as argued by Martin Green in *The Labyrinth of Shakespeare's Sonnets*, London, 1974, p. 79 – a common Elizabethan pun, in fact.

13 Samuel Butler, *Shakespeare's Sonnets Reconsidered*, London, 1899, pp. 91–2, 159.

## CHAPTER ELEVEN

1 Angus Davidson, *Edward Lear*, London, 1938; Penguin edition, 1950, p. 141.
2 Charles Tennyson, *Alfred Tennyson*, London, 2nd edn, 1968, pp. 323–4.
3 Charles Tennyson and Hope Dyson, *The Tennysons, Background to Genius*, London, 1974, p. 175.
4 Hallam Tennyson, *Alfred Lord Tennyson: A Memoir*, one-volume edn, London, 1906,
pp. 439–40.
5 Ibid., pp. 452–3.
6 Charles Tennyson, op. cit., pp. 371–2.
7 Hallam Tennyson, op. cit., p. 456.
8 Harold Nicolson, *Tennyson: Aspects of his Life, Character and Poetry*, London, 1923, p. 230.
9 Hallam Tennyson, op. cit., p. 557.

## CHAPTER TWELVE

1 Hallam Tennyson, *Materials for a Life of A.T.*, III, London, 1895, privately printed, pp. 242–3.
2 Joanna Richardson, *The Pre-Eminent Victorian*, London, 1962, p. 211.
3 Henry James, *The Middle Years*, London, 1917, pp. 102–7.
4 Edmund Goose, 'Candid Snapshots', *Victorian Studies*, 8, 1964–5, pp. 340–3. (MS. at
Rutgers University Library, USA.)
5 Hallam Tennyson, *Alfred Lord Tennyson: A Memoir*, one-volume edn, London, 1906, pp. 799–800. Hope Dyson and Charles Tennyson, *Dear and Honoured Lady*, London, 1969, pp. 102–3.
6 Hope Dyson and Charles Tennyson, op. cit., p. 104.
7 Hallam Tennyson, *Memoir*, p. 783.

8 Ibid., p. 786.
9 William Allingham, *A Diary*, ed. H. Allingham and E. B. Williams, London, 1911, p. 334.

10 Charles Tennyson, *Alfred Tennyson*, London, 2nd edn, 1968, p. 479.

### CHAPTER THIRTEEN

1 Hallam Tennyson, *Alfred Lord Tennyson: A Memoir*, one-volume edn, London, 1906, pp. 703–5.
2 British Library, MS, Ashley 4536.
3 Charles Tennyson, *Alfred Tennyson*, London, 2nd edn, 1968, p. 511.
4 Margot Asquith, *Autobiography*, London, 1920, pp. 196–9.
5 Hallam Tennyson, op. cit., p. 794.
6 Joanna Richardson, *The Pre-Eminent Victorian*, London, 1962, p. 233.

7 Hallam Tennyson, op. cit., pp. 728–9.
8 Ibid., p. 730.
9 Richardson, op. cit., p. 259.
10 Hallam Tennyson, op. cit., pp. 743–4.
11 Nikolaus Pevsner, *The Buildings of England. London, except the Cities of London and Westminster*, Harmondsworth, 1952, p. 258.
12 Herbert M. Schneller and Robert C. Peters, *The Letters of John Addington Symonds*, Detroit, 1967, vol. III, pp. 743–4.

### CHAPTER FOURTEEN

1 Quoted by Joanna Richardson, *The Pre-Eminent Victorian*, London, 1962, p. 264.
2 British Library, MS. Ashley 4538.
3 Hallam Tennyson, *Alfred Lord Tennyson: A Memoir*, one-volume edn, London, 1906,

pp. 778–9.
4 British Library, MS. Ashley 4538.
5 Hester Ritchie, *Letters of Anne Thackeray Ritchie*, London, 1924, p. 221.
6 Quoted by Richardson, op. cit., p. 271.

# INDEX